1649 his advocacy of the anti-royalist cause was recognised by the offer of a post under the newly appointed Council of State. His bold vindication of the trial of Charles I, *The Tenure of Kings*, had appeared earlier in the same year. Milton accepted the offer, becoming Latin[1] Secretary to the Committee of Foreign Affairs. There was nothing distasteful about his duties. He drew up the despatches to foreign governments, translated state-papers, and served as interpreter to foreign envoys. Had his duties stopped here his acceptance of the post would, I think, have proved an unqualified gain. It brought him into contact with the first men in the state, gave him a practical insight into the working of national affairs and the motives of human action; in a word, furnished him with that experience of life which is essential to all poets who aspire to be something more than "the idle singers of an empty day". But unfortunately the secretaryship entailed the necessity of defending at every turn the past course of the revolution and the present policy of the Council. Milton, in fact, held a perpetual brief as advocate for his party. Hence the endless and unedifying controversies into which he drifted; controversies which wasted the most precious years of his

Printed and publish'd according to Order. London, Printed by Ruth Raworth for Humphrey Moseley, and are to be sold at the signe of the Princes Arms in Pauls Churchyard. 1645."

From the prefatory Address to the Reader it is clear that the collection was due to the initiative of the publisher. Milton's own feeling is expressed by the motto, where the words "*vati futuro*" show that, as he judged, his great achievement was yet to come. The volume was divided into two parts, the first containing the English, the second the Latin poems. *Comus* was printed at the close of the former, with a separate title-page to mark its importance. The prominence given to the name of Henry Lawes reflects Milton's friendship.

[1] A Latin Secretary was required because the Council scorned, as Edward Phillips says, "to carry on their affairs in the wheedling, lisping jargon of the cringing French". Milton's salary was £288, in modern money about £900.

life, warped, as some critics think, his nature, and eventually cost him his eyesight.

Between 1649 and 1660 Milton produced no less than eleven pamphlets. Several of these arose out of the publication of the famous *Eikon Basilike*. The book was printed in 1649 and created so extraordinary a sensation that Milton was asked to reply to it; and did so with *Eikonoklastes*. Controversy of this barren type has the inherent disadvantage that once started it may never end. The Royalists commissioned the Leyden professor, Salmasius, to prepare a counterblast, the *Defensio Regia*, and this in turn was met by Milton's *Pro Populo Anglicano Defensio*, 1651, over the preparation of which he lost what little power of eyesight remained.[1] Salmasius retorted, and died before his second *farrago* of scurrilities was issued: Milton was bound to answer, and the *Defensio Secunda* appeared in 1654. Neither of the combatants gained anything by the dispute; while the subsequent development of the controversy in which Milton crushed the Amsterdam pastor and professor, Morus, goes far to prove the contention of Mr Mark Pattison, that it was an evil day when

---

[1] Perhaps this was the saddest part of the episode. Milton tells us in the *Defensio Secunda* that his eyesight was injured by excessive study in boyhood: "from twelve years of age I hardly ever left my studies or went to bed before midnight". Continual reading and writing increased the infirmity, and by 1650 the sight of the left eye had gone. He was warned that he must not use the other for book-work. Unfortunately this was just the time when the Commonwealth stood most in need of his services. If Milton had not written the first *Defence* he might have retained his partial vision, at least for a time. The choice lay between private good and public duty. He repeated in 1650 the sacrifice of 1639. All this is brought out in his *Second Defence*. By the spring of 1652 Milton was quite blind. He was then in his forty-fourth year. Probably the disease from which he suffered was amaurosis. See the *Appendix* on *P. L.* III. 22–26. Throughout *P. L.* and *Samson Agonistes* there are frequent references to his affliction.

The composition of *Lycidas* may be assigned to the year 1637. In the spring of the next year Milton started for Italy. It was natural that he should seek inspiration in the land where many English poets, from Chaucer to Shelley, have found it. Milton remained abroad some fifteen months. Originally he had intended to include Sicily and Greece in his travels, but news of the troubles in England hastened his return. He was brought face to face with the question whether or not he should bear his part in the coming struggle; whether without self-reproach he could lead any longer this life of learning and indifference to the public weal. He decided as we might have expected that he would decide, though some good critics see cause to regret the decision. Milton puts his position very clearly in his *Defensio Secunda*: " I thought it base to be travelling for amusement abroad, while my fellow-citizens were fighting for liberty at home." And later: " I determined to relinquish the other pursuits in which I was engaged, and to transfer the whole force of my talents and my industry to this one important object" (i.e. the vindication of liberty).

The summer of 1639 (July) found Milton back in England. Immediately after his return he wrote the *Epitaphium Damonis*, the beautiful elegy in which he lamented the death of his school friend, Diodati. *Lycidas* was the last of the English lyrics: the *Epitaphium*, which should be studied in close connection with *Lycidas*, the last of the long Latin poems. Thenceforth, for a long spell, the rest was silence, so far as concerned poetry. The period which for all men represents the strength and maturity of manhood, which in the cases of other poets produces the best and most characteristic work, is with Milton a blank. In twenty years he composed no more than a bare handful of Sonnets, and even some of these are infected by the taint of political *animus*. Other interests claimed him—the question of Church-reform, education, marriage, and, above all, politics.

Milton's first treatise upon the government of the Church (*Of Reformation in England*) appeared in 1641. Others followed in quick succession. The abolition of Episcopacy was the watchword of the enemies of the Anglican Church—the *delenda est Carthago* cry of Puritanism, and no one enforced the point with greater eloquence than Milton. During 1641 and 1642 he wrote five pamphlets on the subject. Meanwhile he was studying the principles of education. On his return from Italy he had undertaken the training of his nephews. This led to consideration of the best educational methods; and in the *Tractate of Education*, 1644, Milton assumed the part of educational theorist. In the previous year, May, 1643, he married.[1] The marriage proved unfortunate. Its immediate outcome was the pamphlets on divorce. Clearly he had little leisure for literature proper.

The finest of Milton's prose works, *Areopagitica*, a plea for the free expression of opinion, was published in 1644. In 1645[2] appeared the first collection of his poems. In

---

[1] His wife (who was only seventeen) was Mary Powell, eldest daughter of Richard Powell, of Forest Hill, a village some little distance from Oxford. She went to stay with her father in July, 1643, and refused to return to Milton; why, it is not certain. She was reconciled to her husband in 1645, bore him four children, and died in 1652, in her twenty-seventh year. No doubt, the scene in *P. L.* x. 909–36, in which Eve begs forgiveness of Adam, reproduced the poet's personal experience, while many passages in *Samson Agonistes* must have been inspired by the same cause.

[2] I.e. old style. The volume was entered on the registers of the Stationers' Company under the date of October 6th, 1645. It was published on Jan. 2, 1645–46, with the following title-page:

"*Poems of Mr. John Milton, both English and Latin, Compos'd at several times. Printed by his true Copies. The Songs were set in Musick by Mr. Henry Lawes Gentleman of the Kings Chappel, and one of His Majesties Private Musick.*

'————*Baccare frontem*
Cingite, ne vati noceat mala lingua futuro.' VIRGIL, *Eclog.* 7.

repeated expression in his prose; it is the guiding-star that shines clear and steadfast even through the mists of politics. He has a mission to fulfil, a purpose to accomplish, no less than the most fanatic of religious enthusiasts; and the means whereby this end is to be attained are devotion to religion, devotion to learning, and ascetic purity of life.

This period of self-centred isolation lasted from 1632 to 1638. Gibbon tells us among the many wise things contained in that most wise book the *Autobiography*, that every man has two educations: that which he receives from his teachers and that which he owes to himself; the latter being infinitely the more important. During these five years Milton completed his second education; ranging the whole world of classical[1] antiquity and absorbing the classical genius so thoroughly that the ancients were to him what they afterwards became to Landor, what they have never become to any other English poet in the same degree, even as the very breath of his being; pursuing, too, other interests, such as music, astronomy[2] and the study of Italian literature; and combining these vast and diverse influences into a splendid equipment of hard-won, well-ordered culture. The world has known many greater scholars in the technical, limited sense than Milton, but few men, if any,

[1] He was closely familiar too with post-classical writers like Philo and the neo-Platonists; nor must we forget the mediæval element in his learning, due often to Rabbinical teaching.

[2] Science—"natural philosophy", as he terms it—is one of the branches of study advocated in his treatise *On Education*. Of his early interest in astronomy there is a reminiscence in *Paradise Lost*, II. 708–11; where "Milton is not referring to an imaginary comet, but to one which actually did appear when he was a boy of 10 (1618), in the constellation called Ophiuchus. It was of enormous size, the tail being recorded as longer even than that of 1858. It was held responsible by educated and learned men of the day for disasters. Evelyn says in his diary, 'The effects of that comet, 1618, still working in the prodigious revolutions now beginning in Europe, especially in Germany'" (Professor Ray Lankester).

who have mastered more things worth mastering in art, letters and scholarship.[1] It says much for the poet that he was sustained through this period of study, pursued *ohne Hast, ohne Rast*, by the full consciousness that all would be crowned by a masterpiece which should add one more testimony to the belief in that God who ordains the fates of men. It says also a very great deal for the father who suffered his son to follow in this manner the path of learning.

True, Milton gave more than one earnest of his future fame. The dates of the early pieces—*L'Allegro, Il Penseroso, Arcades, Comus* and *Lycidas*—are not all certain; but probably each was composed at Horton before 1638. Four of them have great autobiographic value as an indirect commentary, written from Milton's coign of seclusion, upon the moral crisis through which English life and thought were passing, the clash between the careless hedonism of the Cavalier world and the deepening austerity of Puritanism. In *L'Allegro* the poet holds the balance almost equal between the two opposing tendencies. In *Il Penseroso* it becomes clear to which side his sympathies are leaning. *Comus* is a covert prophecy of the downfall of the Court-party, while *Lycidas* openly "foretells the ruine" of the Established Church. The latter poem is the final utterance of Milton's lyric genius. Here he reaches, in Mr Mark Pattison's words, the high-water mark of English verse; and then—the pity of it—he resigns that place among the *lyrici vates* of which the Roman singer was ambitious, and for nearly twenty years suffers his lyre to hang mute and rusty in the temple of the Muses.

[1] Milton's poems with their undercurrent of perpetual allusion are the best proof of the width of his reading; but interesting supplementary evidence is afforded by the Common-place Book discovered in 1874, and printed by the *Camden Society*, 1876. It contains extracts from about 80 different authors whose works Milton had studied. The entries seem to have been made in the period 1637–46.

his school-days; but we are told that he had written much verse, English and Latin. And his early training had done that which was all-important: it had laid the foundation of the far-ranging knowledge which makes *Paradise Lost* unique for diversity of suggestion and interest.

Milton went to Christ's College, Cambridge, in the Easter term of 1625, took his B.A. degree in 1629, proceeded M.A. in 1632, and in the latter year left Cambridge. The popular view of Milton's connection with the University will be coloured for all time by Johnson's unfortunate story that for some unknown offence he "suffered the public indignity of corporal correction". For various reasons this story is now discredited by the best judges. It is certain, however, that early in 1626 Milton did have some serious difficulty with his tutor, which led to his removal from Cambridge for a few weeks and his transference to another tutor on his return later in the term. He spoke of the incident bitterly at the time in one of his Latin poems, and he spoke of Cambridge bitterly in after years. On the other hand he voluntarily passed seven years at the University, and resented strongly the imputations brought against him in the "Smectymnuus" controversy that he had been in ill-favour with the authorities of his college. Writing in 1642, he takes the opportunity "to acknowledge publicly with all grateful mind, that more than ordinary favour and respect, which I found above any of my equals at the hands of those courteous and learned men, the fellows of that college wherein I spent some years: who at my parting, after I had taken two degrees, as the manner is, signified many ways how much better it would content them that I would stay; as by many letters full of kindness and loving respect, both before that time, and long after, I was assured of their singular good affection towards me".[1]

---

[1] *An Apology for Smectymnuus*, P. W. III. 111. Perhaps Cambridge would have been more congenial to Milton had he been sent to Emmanuel College, long a centre of Puritanism. Dr John Preston, then Master of the college, was a noted leader of the Puritan party.

And if we look into those uncomplimentary allusions to
Cambridge which date from the controversial period of his
life we see that the feeling they represent is hardly more than
a phase of his theological bias. He detested ecclesiasticism,
and for him the two Universities (there is a fine impartiality
in his diatribes) are the strongholds of what he detested:
"nurseries of superstition"—"not yet well recovered from
the scholastic grossness of barbarous ages"—given up to
"monkish and miserable sophistry", and unprogressive in
their educational methods. But it may fairly be assumed
that Milton the scholar and poet, who chose to spend seven
years at Cambridge, owed to her more than Milton the
fierce controversialist admitted or knew. A poet he had
proved himself before leaving the University in 1632. The
short but exquisite ode *At a Solemn Music* and the *Nativity
Hymn* (1629) were already written.

Milton's father had settled at Horton in Buckinghamshire. Thither the son retired in July, 1632. He had gone
to Cambridge with the intention of qualifying for some
profession, perhaps the Church.[1] This purpose was soon
given up, and when Milton returned to his father's house
he seems to have made up his mind that there was no
profession which he cared to enter. He would choose the
better part of studying and preparing himself, by rigorous
self-discipline and application, for the far-off divine event
to which his whole life moved.

It was Milton's constant resolve to achieve something
that should vindicate the ways of God to men, something
great that should justify his own possession of unique
powers—powers of which, with no trace of egotism, he
proclaims himself proudly conscious. The feeling finds

---

[1] Cf. Milton's own words: "the church, to whose service, by
the intentions of my parents and friends, I was destined of a
child, and in my own resolutions" (*The Reason of Church
Government*, *P.W.* II. 482). What kept him from taking orders
was primarily his objection to Church discipline and government: he spoke of himself as "Church-outed by the prelates".

INTRODUCTION

LIFE OF MILTON

MILTON's life falls into three clearly defined divisions. The first period ends with the poet's return from Italy in 1639; the second at the Restoration in 1660, when release from the fetters of politics enabled him to remind the world that he was a great poet; the third is brought to a close with his death in 1674. *Paradise Lost* belongs to the last of these periods; but we propose to summarise the main events of all three.

John Milton was born on December 9, 1608, in London. He came, in his own words, *ex genere honesto*. A family of Miltons had been settled in Oxfordshire since the reign of Elizabeth. The poet's father had been educated at an Oxford school, possibly as a chorister in one of the College choir-schools, and imbibing Anglican sympathies had conformed to the Established Church. For this he was disinherited by his Roman Catholic father. He settled in London, following the profession of scrivener. A scrivener combined the occupations of lawyer and law-stationer. It appears to have been a lucrative calling; certainly John Milton (the poet was named after the father) attained to easy circumstances. He married about 1600, and had six children, of whom several died young. The third child was the poet.

The elder Milton was evidently a man of considerable culture, in particular an accomplished musician, and a composer whose madrigals were deemed worthy of being printed side by side with those of Byrd, Orlando Gibbons and other leading musicians of the time. To him, no doubt, the poet owed the love of music of which we see frequent indications in the poems.[1] Realising, too, that in his son

---

[1] Milton was very fond of the organ; see *Il Penseroso*, 161, note. During his residence at Horton Milton made occasional

lay the promise and possibility of future greatness, John
Milton took the utmost pains to have the boy adequately
educated; and the lines *Ad Patrem* show that the ties of
affection between father and child were of more than
ordinary closeness.

Milton was sent to St Paul's School about the year 1620.
Here two influences, apart from those of ordinary school-
life, may have affected him particularly. The headmaster
was a good English scholar; he published a grammar containing many extracts from English poets, notably Spenser;
it is reasonable to assume that he had not a little to do with
the encouragement and guidance of Milton's early taste for
English poetry.[1] Also, the founder of St Paul's School,
Colet, had prescribed as part of the school-course the study
of certain early Christian writers, whose influence is said to
be directly traceable in Milton's poems and may in some
cases have suggested his choice of sacred themes.[1] While
at St Paul's, Milton also had a tutor at home, Thomas
Young, a Scotchman, afterwards an eminent Puritan
divine—the inspirer, doubtless, of much of his pupil's
Puritan sympathies. And Milton enjoyed the signal
advantage of growing up in the stimulating atmosphere of
cultured home-life. Most men do not realise that the word
'culture' signifies anything very definite or desirable before
they pass to the University; for Milton, however, home-
life meant, from the first, not only broad interests and
refinement, but active encouragement towards literature
and study. In 1625 he left St Paul's. Of his extant English
poems[2] only one, *On the Death of a Fair Infant*, dates from

journeys to London to hear, and obtain instruction (probably
from Henry Lawes) in, music. It was an age of great musical
development. See "Milton's Knowledge of Music" by Mr
W. H. Hadow, in *Milton Memorial Lectures* (1908).

[1] See the paper "Milton as Schoolboy and Schoolmaster" by
Mr A. F. Leach, read before the British Academy, Dec. 10, 1908.

[2] His paraphrases of *Psalms* cxiv, cxxxvi scarcely come under
this heading. Aubrey says in his quaint *Life* of Milton: "Anno
Domini 1619 he was ten yeares old, as by his picture [the
portrait by Cornelius Jansen]: and was then a poet."

NOTE

MANY of the Scriptural and classical quotations and references given in the *Notes* have been pointed out by previous editors.

This volume completes the edition of *Paradise Lost*.

A. W. V.

JOHN MILTON

PARADISE LOST

BOOKS IX AND X

EDITED BY

A. W. VERITY

CAMBRIDGE
AT THE UNIVERSITY PRESS
1965

PUBLISHED BY
THE SYNDICS OF THE CAMBRIDGE UNIVERSITY PRESS

Bentley House, 200 Euston Road, London, N.W. 1
American Branch: 32 East 57th Street, New York, N.Y. 10022
West African Office: P.M.B. 5181, Ibadan, Nigeria

First Edition 1896
Reprinted 1913
1918
1935
1937
1952
1956
1962
1964
Reset 1965

Printed in Great Britain at the University Printing House, Cambridge
(Brooke Crutchley, University Printer)

CONTENTS

(v)

MILTON'S PARADISE LOST

BOOKS IX AND X

the poet left his study at Horton to do battle for the Commonwealth amid the vulgar brawls of the market-place:

> "Not here, O Apollo,
> Were haunts meet for thee."

Fortunately this poetic interregnum in Milton's life was not destined to last much longer. The Restoration came, a blessing in disguise, and in 1660[1] the ruin of Milton's political party and of his personal hopes, the absolute over-throw of the cause for which he had fought for twenty years, left him free. The author of *Lycidas* could once more become a poet.

Much has been written upon this second period, 1639–60. We saw what parting of the ways confronted Milton on his return from Italy. Did he choose aright? Should he have continued upon the path of learned leisure? There are writers who argue that Milton made a mistake. A poet, they say, should keep clear of political strife: fierce controversy can benefit no man: who touches pitch must expect to be, certainly will be, defiled: Milton sacrificed twenty of the best years of his life, doing work which an underling could have done and which was not worth doing: another *Comus* might have been written, a loftier *Lycidas*: that literature should be the poorer by the absence of these possible masterpieces, that the second greatest genius which England has produced should in a way be the "inheritor of unfulfilled renown", is and must be a thing entirely and terribly deplorable. This is the view of the purely literary critic.

There remains the other side of the question. It may fairly be contended that had Milton elected in 1639 to live the scholar's life apart from "the action of men", *Paradise*

---

[1] Milton probably began *Paradise Lost* in 1658; but it was not till the Restoration in 1660 that he definitely resigned all his political hopes, and became quite free to realise his poetical ambition.

XX   LIFE OF MILTON

Lost, as we have it, or *Samson Agonistes* could never have been written. Knowledge of life and human nature, insight into the problems of men's motives and emotions, grasp of the broader issues of the human tragedy, all these were essential to the author of an epic poem; they could only be obtained through commerce with the world; they would have remained beyond the reach of a recluse. Dryden complained that Milton saw nature through the spectacles of books: we might have had to complain that he saw men through the same medium. Fortunately it is not so: and it is not so because at the age of thirty-two he threw in his fortunes with those of his country; like the diver in Schiller's ballad he took the plunge which was to cost him so dear. The mere man of letters will never move the world. Æschylus fought at Marathon: Shakespeare was practical to the tips of his fingers; a better business man than Goethe there was not within a radius of a hundred miles of Weimar.

This aspect of the question is emphasised by Milton himself. The man, he says, "who would not be frustrate of his hope to write well hereafter in laudable things, ought himself to be a true poem, that is, a composition and pattern of the best and honourablest things; not presuming to sing high praises of heroic men, or famous cities, unless he have in himself the experience and the practice of all that which is praiseworthy".[1] Again, in estimating the qualifications which the writer of an epic such as he contemplated should possess, he is careful to include "insight into all seemly and generous arts and affairs".[2]

Truth usually lies half-way between extremes: perhaps it does so here. No doubt, Milton did gain very greatly by breathing awhile the larger air of public life, even though that air was often tainted by much impurity. No doubt, too, twenty years of contention must have left their mark

[1] *An Apology for Smectymnuus, P. W.* III. 118.
[2] *The Reason of Church Government, P. W.* II. 481.

even on Milton. In one of the very few places where he
"abides our question", Shakespeare writes (*Sonnet* CXI):

> "O! for my sake do you with Fortune chide,
>   The guilty goddess of my harmful deeds,
>   That did not better for my life provide,
>   Than public means, which public manners breeds:
>   Thence comes it that my name receives a brand;
>   And almost thence my nature is subdued
>   To what it works in, like the dyer's hand."

Milton's genius was subdued in this way. If we compare
him, the Milton of the great epics and of *Samson Agonistes*,
with Homer or Shakespeare—and none but the greatest
can be his parallel—we find in him a certain want of
humanity, a touch of narrowness. He lacks the large-
heartedness, the genial, generous breadth of Shakespeare;
the sympathy and sense of the *lacrimæ rerum* that even in
Troilus and Cressida or *Timon of Athens* are there for those
who have eyes wherewith to see them. Milton reflects in
some degree the less gracious aspects of Puritanism, its
intolerance, want of humour, one-sided intensity; and it
seems natural to assume that this narrowness was to a great
extent the price he paid for twenty years of ceaseless special
pleading and dispute. The real misfortune of his life lay in
the fact that he fell on evil, angry days when there was no
place for moderate men. He had to be one of two things:
either a controversialist or a student: there was no *via
media*. Probably he chose aright; but we could wish that
the conditions under which he chose had been different.
And he is so great, so majestic in the nobleness of his life,
in the purity of his motives, in the self-sacrifice of his
indomitable devotion to his ideals, that we could wish not
even to seem to pronounce judgment at all.

The last part of Milton's life, 1660–74, passed quietly.
At the age of fifty-two he was thrown back upon poetry,
and could at length discharge his self-imposed obligation.
The early poems he had never regarded as a fulfilment of
the debt due to his Creator. Even when the fire of political

strife burned at its hottest, Milton did not forget the purpose which he had conceived in his boyhood. Of that purpose *Paradise Lost* was the attainment. Begun about 1658, it was finished in 1663, the year of Milton's third[1] marriage; revised from 1663 to 1665; and eventually issued in 1667. Before its publication Milton had commenced (in the autumn of 1665) its sequel *Paradise Regained*, which in turn was closely followed by *Samson Agonistes*. The completion of *Paradise Regained* may be assigned to the year 1666—that of *Samson Agonistes* to 1667. Some time was spent in their revision; and in January, 1671, they were published together, in a single volume.

In 1673 Milton brought out a reprint of the 1645 edition of his *Poems*, adding most of the sonnets[2] written in the

[1] Milton's second marriage took place in the autumn of 1656, i.e. after he had become blind. His wife died in February, 1658. Cf. the *Sonnet*, "Methought I saw my late espoused saint", the pathos of which is heightened by the fact that he had never seen her.

[2] The number of Milton's sonnets is twenty-three (if we exclude the piece "On the New Forcers of Conscience"), five of which were written in Italian, probably during the time of his travels in Italy, 1638, 1639. Ten sonnets were printed in the edition of 1645, the last of them being that entitled (from the *Cambridge* MS.) "To the Lady Margaret Ley". The remaining thirteen were composed between 1645 and 1658. The concluding sonnet, therefore (to the memory of Milton's second wife), immediately preceded his commencement of *Paradise Lost*. Four of these poems (XV, XVI, XVII, XXII) could not, on account of their political tone, be included in the edition of 1673. They were published by Edward Phillips together with his memoir of Milton, 1694 (*Sonnet* XVII having previously appeared in a *Life* of Vane). The sonnet on the "Massacre in Piedmont" is usually considered the finest of the collection, of which Mr Mark Pattison edited a well-known edition, 1883. The sonnet inscribed with a diamond on a window pane in the cottage at Chalfont where the poet stayed in 1665 is (in the judgment of a good critic) Miltonic, if not Milton's (Garnett, *Life of Milton*, p. 175).

interval.[1] The last four years of his life were devoted to prose works of no particular interest.[2] He continued to live in London. His third marriage had proved happy, and he enjoyed something of the renown which was rightly his. Various well-known men used to visit him—notably Dryden,[3] who on one of his visits asked and received permission to dramatise[4] *Paradise Lost*.

Milton died in 1674, November 8th. He was buried in St Giles' Church, Cripplegate. When we think of him we have to think of a man who lived a life of very singular purity and devotion to duty; who for what he conceived to be his country's good sacrificed—and no one can well estimate the sacrifice—during twenty years the aim that

[1] The 1673 edition also gave the juvenile piece *On the Death of a Fair Infant* and *At a Vacation Exercise*, which for some reason had been omitted from the 1645 edition.

[2] The treatise on *Christian Doctrine* (unpublished during Milton's lifetime and dating, it is thought, mainly from the period of his theological treatises) is valuable as throwing much light on the theological views expressed in the two epic poems and *Samson Agonistes*. See *Milton Memorial Lectures* (1908), pp. 109–42. The discovery of the MS. of this treatise in 1823 gave Macaulay an opportunity of writing his famous essay on Milton, which has been happily described as a Whig counterblast to Johnson's Tory depreciation of the poet.

Milton's *History of Britain*, though not published till 1670, had been written many years earlier; four of the six books, we know, were composed between 1646 and 1649.

[3] The lines by Dryden which were printed beneath the portrait of Milton in Tonson's folio edition of *Paradise Lost* published in 1688 are too familiar to need quotation; but it is worth noting that the younger poet had in Milton's lifetime described the great epic as "one of the most noble, and most sublime poems which either this age or nation has produced" (prefatory essay to *The State of Innocence*, 1674). Further, tradition assigned to Dryden (a Roman Catholic and a Royalist) the remark, "this fellow (Milton) cuts us all out and the ancients too".

[4] See Marvell's "Commendatory Verses", 17–30, and the *Notes*, pp. 72, 73.

was nearest to his heart and best suited to his genius; who, however, eventually realised his desire of writing a great work *in gloriam Dei*.

PARADISE LOST

We have seen that the dominating idea of Milton's life was his resolve to write a great poem—great in theme, in style, in attainment. To this purpose was he dedicated as a boy: as Hannibal was dedicated, at the altar of patriotism, to the cause of his country's revenge, or Pitt to a life of political ambition. Milton's works—particularly his letters and prose pamphlets—enable us to trace the growth of the idea which was shaping his intellectual destinies; and as every poet is best interpreted by his own words, Milton shall speak for himself.

Two of the earliest indications of his cherished plan are the *Vacation Exercise* and the second *Sonnet*. The *Exercise* commences with an invocation (not without significance, as we shall see) to his "native language", to assist him in giving utterance to the teeming thoughts that knock at the portal of his lips, fain to find an issue thence. The bent of these thoughts is towards the loftiest themes. Might he choose for himself, he would select some "grave subject":

> "Such where the deep transported mind may soar
> Above the wheeling poles, and at Heaven's door
> Look in, and see each blissful deity.
>
> . . . .
>
> Then sing of secret things that came to pass
> When beldam Nature in her cradle was."

But recognising soon that such matters are inappropriate to the occasion—a College festivity—he arrests the flight of his muse with a grave *descende cælo*, and declines on a lower range of subject, more fitting to the social scene and the audience. This *Exercise* was composed in 1628, in Milton's twentieth year, or, according to his method of dating, *anno ætatis* XIX. It is important as revealing—

firstly, the poet's consciousness of the divine impulse within, for which poetry is the natural outlet; secondly, the elevation of theme with which that poetry must deal. A boy in years, he would like to handle the highest 'arguments', challenging thereby comparison with the *sacri vates* of inspired verse, the elect few whose poetic appeal is to the whole world. A vision of Heaven itself must be unrolled before his steadfast eagle-gaze: he will win a knowledge of the causes of things such as even Virgil, his master, modestly disclaimed. Little wonder, therefore, that, filled with these ambitions, Milton did not shrink, only two years later (1629–30), from attempting to sound the deepest mysteries of Christianity—the Nativity and the Passion of Christ; howbeit, sensible of his immaturity, he left his poem on the latter subject unfinished.[1]

The *Sonnet* to which reference has been made deserves quotation at length:

"How soon hath Time, the subtle thief of youth,
    Stolen on his wing my three-and-twentieth year!
    My hasting days fly on with full career,
    But my late spring no bud or blossom shew'th.
Perhaps my semblance might deceive the truth,
    That I to manhood am arrived so near;
    And inward ripeness doth much less appear,
    That some more timely-happy spirits endu'th.
Yet be it less or more, or soon or slow,
    It shall be still in strictest measure even
    To that same lot, however mean or high,
Toward which Time leads me, and the will of Heaven;
    All is, if I have grace to use it so,
    As ever in my great Task-Master's eye."

[1] A passage in the sixth *Elegy* shows that the *Nativity Ode* (a prelude in some respects to *Paradise Lost*) was begun on Christmas morning, 1629. *The Passion* may have been composed for the following Easter; it breaks off with the notice—"This Subject the Author finding to be above the years he had when he wrote it, and nothing satisfied with what was begun, left it unfinished." Evidently Milton was minded to recur to both subjects; see later.

Mr Mark Pattison justly calls these lines "an inseparable part of Milton's biography": they bring out so clearly the poet's solemn devotion to his self-selected task, and his determination not to essay the execution of that task until the time of complete "inward ripeness" has arrived. The *Sonnet* was one of the last poems composed by Milton during his residence at Cambridge. The date is 1631. From 1632 to 1638 was a period of almost unbroken self-preparation, such as the *Sonnet* foreshadows. Of the intensity of his application to literature a letter written in 1637 (the exact day being Sept. 7, 1637) enables us to judge.

"It is my way", he says to Carlo Diodati, in excuse for remissness as a correspondent, "to suffer no impediment, no love of ease, no avocation whatever, to chill the ardour, to break the continuity, or divert the completion of my literary pursuits. From this and no other reasons it often happens that I do not readily employ my pen in any gratuitous exertions."[1] But these exertions were not sufficient: the probation must last longer. In the same month, on the 23rd, he writes to the same friend, who had made enquiry as to his occupations and plans: "I am sure that you wish me to gratify your curiosity, and to let you know what I have been doing, or am meditating to do. Hear me, my Diodati, and suffer me for a moment to speak without blushing in a more lofty strain. Do you ask what I am meditating? By the help of Heaven, an immortality of fame. But what am I doing? πτεροφυῶ, I am letting my wings grow and preparing to fly; but my Pegasus has not yet feathers enough to soar aloft in the fields of air."[2] Four years later we find a similar admission—"I have neither yet completed to my mind the full circle of my private studies. . . ."[3]

---

[1] *P. W.* III. 492.
[2] *P. W.* III. 495.
[3] *P. W.* II. 476.

This last sentence was written in 1640 (or 1641). Meanwhile his resolution had been confirmed by the friendly
and flattering encouragement of Italian *savants*—a
stimulus which he records in an oft-cited passage:[1]

"In the private academies[2] of Italy, whither I was
favoured to resort, perceiving that some trifles[3] which I
had in memory, composed at under twenty or thereabout,
(for the manner is, that every one must give some proof of
his wit and reading there,) met with acceptance above
what was looked for; and other things,[4] which I had
shifted in scarcity of books and conveniences to patch up
amongst them, were received with written encomiums,
which the Italian is not forward to bestow on men of this
side the Alps; I began thus far to assent both to them and
divers of my friends here at home, and not less to an inward prompting which now grew daily upon me, that by
labour and intense study (which I take to be my portion in
this life), joined with the strong propensity of nature, I
might perhaps leave something so written to aftertimes, as
they should not willingly let it die."

It was during this Italian journey (1638–39) that Milton
first gave a hint of the particular direction in which this
ambition was setting: at least we are vouchsafed a glimpse
of the possible subject-matter of the contemplated poem,

[1] *The Reason of Church Government*, P. W. II. 477, 478; a few
lines have been quoted in the *Life* of Milton. A passage similar
to the concluding sentence might be quoted from the pamphlet
Animadversions, published the same year (1641) as the *Church
Government*; see P. W. III. 72.

[2] He refers to literary societies or clubs, of which there were
several at Florence, e.g. the Della Crusca, the Svogliati, etc.

[3] I.e. Latin pieces; the *Elegies*, as well as some of the poems
included in his *Sylvæ*, were written before he was twenty-one.

[4] Among the Latin poems which date from his Italian
journey are the lines *Ad Salsillum*, a few of the *Epigrams*, and
Mansus. Perhaps, too, the "other things" comprehended those
essays in Italian verse which he had the courage to read before
a Florentine audience, and they the indulgence to praise.

and there is that on which may be built conjecture as to its style. He had enjoyed at Naples the hospitality of the then famous writer Giovanni Battista Manso, whose courteous reception the young English traveller, *ut ne ingratum se ostenderet*, acknowledged in the piece of Latin hexameters afterwards printed in his *Sylvæ* under the title *Mansus*. In the course of the poem Milton definitely speaks of the remote legends of British history—more especially, the Arthurian legend—as the theme which he might some day treat. "May I", he says, "find such a friend[1] as Manso",

> "*Siquando[2] indigenas revocabo in carmina reges,*
> *Arturumque etiam sub terris bella moventem,*
> *Aut dicam invictæ sociali fœdere mensæ*
> *Magnanimos heroas, et (O modo spiritus adsit)*
> *Frangam Saxonicas Britonum sub Marte phalanges!*"

This was in 1638. In the next year, after his return to England, he recurs to the project in the *Epitaphium Damonis* (162–71), his account being far more detailed:

> "*Ipse[3] ego Dardanias Rutupina per æquora puppes*
> *Dicam, et Pandrasidos regnum vetus Inogeniæ.*
> *Brennumque Arviragumque duces, priscumque Belinum,*
> *Et tandem Armoricos Britonum sub lege colonos;*

[1] I.e., a friend who would pay honour to him as Manso had paid honour to the poet Marini. Manso had helped in the erection of a monument to Marini at Naples; and Milton alludes to this at the beginning of the poem. From Manso he would hear about Tasso.

[2] "If ever I shall revive in verse our native kings, and Arthur levying war in the world below; or tell of the heroic company of the resistless Table Round, and—be the inspiration mine!—break the Saxon bands neath the might of British chivalry" (*Mansus*, 80–4). His Common-place Book has a quaint reference to "Arturs round table".

[3] "I will tell of the Trojan fleet sailing our southern seas, and the ancient realm of Imogen, Pandrasus' daughter, and of Brennus, Arviragus, and Belinus old, and the Armoric settlers subject to British laws. Then will I sing of Iogerne, fatally

Tum gravidam Arturo fatali fraude Iögernen;
Mendaces vultus, assumptaque Gorlöis arma,
Merlini dolus. O, mihi tum si vita supersit,
Tu procul annosa pendebis, fistula, pinu,
Multum oblita mihi, aut patriis mutata Camœnis
Brittonicum strides!"

Here, as before, he first glances at the stories which date from the very dawn of British myth and romance, and then passes to the most fascinating of the later cycles of national legend—the grey traditions that cluster round the hero of the *Idylls of the King*, the son of mythic Uther. And this passage, albeit the subject which it indicates was after-wards rejected by Milton, possesses a twofold value for those who would follow, step by step, the development of the idea which had as its final issue the composition of *Paradise Lost*. For, first, the concluding verses show that whatever the theme of the poem, whatever the style, the instrument of expression would be English. Just as Dante had weighed the merits of the vernacular and Latin and chosen the former, though the choice imposed on him the creation of an ideal, transfigured Italian out of the baser elements of many competing dialects, so Milton—more fortunate than Dante in that he found an instrument ready to use—will use that "native language" whose help he had petitioned in the *Vacation Exercise*. An illustration of his feeling on this point is furnished by the treatise on *Church Government*. He says there that his work must make for "the honour and instruction" of his country: "I applied

pregnant with Arthur—how Uther feigned the features and assumed the armour of Gorlois, through Merlin's craft. And you, my pastoral pipe, an life be lent me, shall hang on some sere pine, forgotten of me; or changed to native notes shall shrill forth British strains." In the first lines he alludes to the legend of Brutus and the Trojans landing in England. *Rutu-pina* = Kentish. The story of Arthur's birth at which he glances is referred to in the *Idylls of the King*. The general drift of the last verses is that he will give up Latin for English verse; *strides* is a future, from *strido* (cf. *Æneid* IV. 689).

myself to that resolution which Ariosto followed...to fix
all the industry and art I could unite to the adorning of my
native tongue; not to make verbal curiosities the end (that
were a toilsome vanity), but to be an interpreter and relater
of the best and sagest things among mine own citizens
throughout this island in the mother dialect. That what the
greatest and choicest wits of Athens, Rome, or modern
Italy, and those Hebrews of old did for their country, I, in
my proportion, with this over and above, of being a
Christian, might do for mine;[1] not caring to be once
named abroad, though perhaps I could attain to that, but
content with these British islands as my world." Here is
a clear announcement of his ambition to take rank as a
great national poet. The note struck is patriotism. He will
produce that which shall set English on a level with the
more favoured Italian, and give his countrymen cause to be
proud of their

> "dear dear land,
> Dear for her reputation through the world".[2]

To us indeed it may appear strange that Milton should
have thought it worth while to emphasise what would now
be considered a self-evident necessity: what modern poet,
with a serious conception of his office and duty, would
dream of employing any other language than his own? But
we must remember that in those days the empire of the
classics was unquestioned: scholarship was accorded a
higher dignity than now: the composition of long poems

---

[1] *P. W.* II. 478. Reference has been made so frequently to
this pamphlet on *The Reason of Church Government urged against
Prelaty* (1641), that it may be well to explain that the introduction to the second book is entirely autobiographical. Milton
shows why he embarked on such controversies, how much it
cost him to do so, what hopes he had of returning to poetry,
what was his view of the poet's mission and of his own capacity
to discharge that mission. His prose works contain nothing
more valuable than these ten pages of self-criticism.

[2] *Richard II*, II. i. 57, 58.

in Latin was still a custom honoured in the observance: and whoso sought to appeal to the "laureate fraternity" of scholars and men of letters, independently of race and country, would naturally turn to the *lingua franca* of the learned. At any rate, the use of English—less known than either Italian or French—placed a poet at a great disadvantage, so far as concerned acceptance in foreign lands; and when Milton determined to rely on his *patriæ Camœnæ*, he foresaw that this would circumscribe his audience, and that he might have to rest content with the applause of his own countrymen.

Again, these lines in the *Epitaphium* give us some grounds of surmise as to the proposed form of his poem. The historic events—or traditions—epitomised in the passage were too far separated in point of time, and too devoid of internal coherence and connection, to admit of dramatic treatment. Milton evidently contemplated a narrative poem, and for one who had drunk so deep of the classical spirit a narrative could scarce have meant aught else than an epic. Indeed thus much is implied by some sentences in *The Reason of Church Government*, which represent him as considering whether to attempt "that epic form whereof the two poems of Homer, and those other two of Virgil and Tasso, are a diffuse, and the book of Job a brief model...or whether those dramatic constitutions, wherein Sophocles and Euripides reign, shall be found more doctrinal and exemplary to a nation".[1]

But 'dramatic' introduces a fresh phase; and as the first period of the history of *Paradise Lost*, or rather of the idea which finally took shape in that poem, closes with the *Epitaphium* (1639), it may not be amiss to summarise the impressions deduced up to this point from the various passages which we have quoted from Milton. We have seen, then, Milton's early resolve; its ambitious scope; his self-preparation; the encouragement he received in Italy

[1] *P. W.* ii. 478, 479.

and from friends at home; his announcement in 1638, repeated in 1639, that he has discovered a suitable subject in British fable—more especially, in the legend of the Coming and Passing of Arthur; his formal farewell to Latin verse, in favour of his native tongue; his desire to win recognition as a great national *vates*; and his selection of the epic style.

In respect of chronology we have reached the year 1639–40. The second period extends from 1640 to 1642. We shall see that some verses of *Paradise Lost* were written about 1642: after 1642, up till 1658, we hear no more of the poem—proof that the idea has been temporarily abandoned under stress of politics. Therefore 1642 may be regarded as the ulterior limit of this second period. And it is not, I think, fanciful to consider that *Paradise Lost* entered on a fresh stage about 1640, because between that year and 1642 Milton's plans underwent a twofold change by which the character of the poem was entirely altered.

First, the subject for which he had shown so decided a bias is discarded: after 1639 no mention is made of King Arthur. We have no hint of the cause which led Milton to drop the subject; but it may well have lain in his increasing republicanism. He could not have treated the theme from an unfavourable standpoint. The hero of the poem must have been for him, as for the Milton of our own age, a type of all kingly grandeur and worth; and it would have gone sore against the grain with the future apologist for regicide to exercise his powers in creating a royal figure that would shed lustre on monarchy, and in a measure plead for the institution which Milton detested so heartily. Only a Royalist could have retold the story, making it illustrate "the divine right of kings", and embodying in the character of the blameless monarch the Cavalier conception of Charles I. Perhaps too he was influenced by discovering, after fuller research, the mythical character of the legend. So much is rather implied by some remarks in his *History of Britain*. Milton with his intense earnestness was not the

poet to build a long work on what he had found to be mainly fiction. Be this as it may, Milton rejected the subject, and it finds no place in a list of one hundred possible subjects of his poem.

Secondly, from this period, 1640–2, dates an alteration in the design of the contemplated work. Hitherto his tendency has been towards the epic form: now (1640 or 1641) we find him preferring the dramatic. Shall he imitate Sophocles and Euripides? Shall he transplant to English soil the art of the "lofty grave tragedians" of Greece? The question is answered in a decided affirmative. Had Milton continued the poem of which the opening lines were written in 1642 we should have had—not an epic but—a drama, or possibly a trilogy of dramas, cast in a particular manner, as will be observed presently. This transference of his inclinations from the epic to the dramatic style appears to date from 1641. It is manifested in the Milton MS. at Trinity College.

When the present library of Trinity College, the erection of which was begun during the Mastership of Isaac Barrow, was completed, one of its earliest benefactors was a former member of Trinity, Sir Henry Newton Puckering. Among his gifts was "a thin folio MS. of less than thirty leaves", which had served Milton as a note-book. How it came into the possession of Sir Henry Puckering is not known. He was contemporary with, though junior to, Milton, and may possibly have been one of the admirers who visited the poet in the closing years of his life; or perhaps there was some family connection by means of which the MS. passed into his hands. But if the history of the note-book be obscure, its value is not; for it contains the original drafts of several of his early poems: notably of *Arcades*, *Lycidas* and *Comus*, together with fourteen of the Sonnets, and memoranda relating to his great work. And the bulk of the MS. (forty out of forty-seven written pages) is in Milton's autograph.

It is known that the little volume was rebound in 1736, by which date some of the leaves had got loose, and there

is some uncertainty as to the correctness of the order of just the last few pages. But as regards pages 1–42, there seems no reason to doubt that the MS. exists exactly as Milton used it and that we have in all essentials the order in which its contents were entered by him. They cover a long period (1633–58), from *Arcades*, with which the MS. begins, to the last of his Sonnets—"Methought I saw". It is rather more than half way through the MS. that we light on the entries which have so direct a bearing on the history of *Paradise Lost*.

These are notes, written by Milton himself (probably in 1641), and occupying seven pages of the manuscript, on subjects which seemed to him suitable, in varying degrees of appropriateness, for his poem. Some of the entries are very brief—concise jottings down, in two or three words, of any theme that struck him. Others are more detailed: the salient features of some episode in history are selected, and a sketch of the best method of treating them added. In a few instances these sketches are filled in with much minuteness and care: the 'economy' or arrangement of the poem is marked out—the action traced from point to point. But, *Paradise Lost* apart, this has been done in only a few cases—a half dozen, at most. As a rule, the source whence the material of the work might be drawn is indicated. The subjects themselves, numbering just one hundred, fall, in a rough classification, under two headings— Scriptural and British: and by 'British' are meant those which Milton drew from the chronicles of British history prior to the Norman Conquest. The former are the more numerous class: sixty-two being derived from the Bible, of which the Old Testament claims fifty-four. Their character will be best illustrated by quotation of a few typical examples:

> Abram in Ægypt.
> Josuah in Gibeon.   Josu. 10.
> Jonathan rescu'd   Sam. 1. 14.
> Saul in Gilboa   1 Sam. 28. 31.

Gideon Idoloclastes   Jud. 6. 7.
Abimelech the usurper.   Jud. 9.
Samaria liberata[1]   2 Reg. 7.
Asa or Æthiopes.   2 chron. 14. with
the deposing his mother, and burning her Idol.

These are some of the subjects drawn from the New Testament:

Christ bound
Christ crucifi'd
Christ risen.
Lazarus   Joan. 11.
Christus patiens

The Scene in yᵉ garden beginning frō yᵉ comming thither till Judas betraies & yᵉ officers lead him away yᵉ rest by message & chorus. his agony may receav noble expressions

Of British subjects[2] there are thirty-three. The last page is assigned to "Scotch stories or rather brittish of the north parts". Among these *Macbeth* is conspicuous. Practically they may be grouped with the thirty-three, and the combined list is remarkable—first, because it does not include the Arthurian legend, which had once exercised so powerful a fascination on Milton; secondly, because in its brevity, as compared with the list of Scriptural subjects, it suggests his preference for a sacred poem.

Of the Scriptural subjects the story of the Creation and Fall assumes the most prominent place. Any friend of

---

[1] The title is an obvious allusion to Tasso's *Gerusalemme Liberata*.

[2] Milton's attitude towards them is illustrated indirectly by his *History of Britain*. In his paper on "Milton as an Historian" read before the British Academy recently (Nov. 25, 1908) Professor Firth says: "It was not only by his treatment of the mythical period of English history that Milton's interest in the legendary and anecdotic side of history was revealed. It appeared in the later books as well as the earlier, and the introduction of certain episodes, or the space devoted to them, might often be explained by their inclusion in the list of suggested subjects for his 'British Tragedies'."

Milton glancing through these papers in 1641 could have conjectured, with tolerable certainty, where the poet's final choice would fall. For no less than four of the entries refer to *Paradise Lost*. Three of these stand at the head of the list of sacred themes. In two at least his intention to treat the subject in dramatic form is patent. The two first—mere enumerations of possible *dramatis personæ*—run thus;[1] it will be seen that the longer list is simply an expansion of the other:

the Persons	the Persons
Michael	Moses[2]
Heavenly Love	Justice.[3] Mercie Wisdome
Chorus of Angels	Heavenly Love
Lucifer	Hesperus the Evening Starre
Adam ⎫ with the serpent	Chorus of Angels
Eve ⎭	Lucifer
Conscience	Adam
Death	Eve
Labour ⎫	Conscience[4]
Sicknesse ⎪	Labour ⎫
Discontent ⎬ mutes	Sicknesse ⎪
Ignorance ⎪	Discontent ⎬ mutes
with others ⎭	Ignorance ⎭
Faith	Feare
Hope	Death
Charity	Faith
	Hope
	Charity

These lists are crossed out; and underneath stands a much fuller sketch, in which the action of the tragedy is

[1] Neither is introduced with any title.

[2] Milton first wrote "Michael", as in the other list, but subsituted "Moses".

[3] The epithet *Divine*, qualifying *Justice*, was inserted and then crossed out again. "Wisdome" was added.

[4] After *Conscience* Milton added *Death*, as in the first list; then deleted it, and placed Death among the 'mutes' (*mutæ personæ*, characters who appeared without speaking).

shown, and the division into acts observed. Here, too, we first meet with the title *Paradise Lost*. The scheme is as follows:

Paradise Lost   The Persons

Moses προλογίζει recounting how he assum'd his true bodie, that it corrupts not because of his with god in the mount declares the like of Enoch and Eliah, besides the purity of yᵉ pl   ¹ that certaine pure winds, dues, and clouds præserve it from corruption whence   horts¹ to the sight of god, tells they² cannot se Adam in the state of innocence by reason of thire sin³

Justice   ⎫
Mercie   ⎬ debating what should become of man if he fall
Wisdome ⎭

Chorus of Angels sing a hymne of yᵉ creation⁴

Act 2

Heavenly Love
Evening starre
chorus sing the mariage song⁵ and describe Paradice

Act 3

Lucifer contriving Adams ruine
Chorus feares for Adam and relates Lucifers rebellion and fall⁶

Act 4

Adam ⎫
Eve   ⎬ fallen
Conscience cites them to Gods examination⁷
Chorus bewails and tells the good Adā hath lost

¹ The margin of the MS. is frayed here.
² *they*, i.e. the imaginary audience to whom the prologue is addressed. Cf. the commencement of *Comus*.
³ After this the first act begins.
⁴ Cf. VII. 253–60, note.
⁵ Cf. IV. 711.
⁶ Cf. bks. V–VI.
⁷ Cf. X. 97 *et seq.*

Act 5

Adam and Eve, driven out of Paradice
         præsented by an angel with[1]

Labour ⎫
greife ⎪
hatred ⎪
Envie ⎪
warre ⎪
famine ⎬ mutes to whome he gives thire names
Pestilence ⎬ likewise winter, heat Tempest[2] &c
sicknesse ⎪
discontent ⎪
Ignorance ⎪
Feare ⎪
Death enterd ⎪
into ye world ⎭
Faith ⎫
Hope ⎬ comfort him and ĩstruct him
Charity ⎭
Chorus breifly concludes

This draft of the tragedy, which occurs on page 35 of the
MS., is not deleted; but Milton was still dissatisfied, and
later on, page 40, we come to a fourth, and concluding,
scheme—which reads thus:

Adam unparadiz'd[3]

The angel Gabriel, either descending or entering,[4] shewing
since this globe was created, his frequency as much on earth, as
in heavn, describes Paradise. next the Chorus shewing the
reason of his[5] comming to keep his watch in Paradise after
Lucifers rebellion by command from god, & withall expressing
his desire to see, & know more concerning this excellent new
creature man. the angel Gabriel as by his name signifying a

---

[1] Cf. bks. XI–XII.   [2] See X. 651, note.
[3] Underneath was written, and crossed out, an alternative
title—*Adams Banishment.*
[4] Cf. *Comus,* "The Attendant Spirit descends or enters"
(*ad init.*).
[5] *his,* i.e. the chorus's; he makes the chorus now a singular,
now a plural, noun.

prince of power tracing[1] paradise with a more free office passes
by the station of ye chorus & desired by them relates what he
knew of man as the creation of Eve with thire love, & mariage.
after this Lucifer appeares after his overthrow, bemoans himself,
seeks revenge on man the Chorus prepare resistance at his first
approach at last after discourse of enmity on either side he
departs wherat the chorus sings of the battell, & victorie in
heavn against him & his accomplices, as before after the first
act[2] was sung a hymn of the creation. heer[3] again may appear
Lucifer relating, & insulting in what he had don to the destruction of man. man next & Eve having by this time bin seduc't
by the serpent appeares confusedly cover'd with leaves conscience in a shape accuses him, Justice cites him to the place
whither Jehova call'd for him in the mean while the chorus
entertains[4] the stage, & his [sic] inform'd by some angel the
manner of his fall heer[3] the chorus bewailes Adams fall. Adam
then & Eve returne accuse one another but especially Adam
layes the blame to his wife, is stubborn in his offence Justice
appeares reason[5] with him convinces him the[3] chorus admonisheth
Adam, & bids him beware by Lucifers example of impenitence
the Angel is sent to banish them out of paradise but before
causes to passe before his eyes in shapes a mask of all the evills[6]
of this life & world he is humbl'd relents, dispaires. at last
appeares Mercy comforts him promises the Messiah, then calls
in faith, hope, & charity, instructs him he repents gives god the
glory, submitts to his penalty the chorus breifly concludes.
compare this with the former draught.

"It appears plain", says Todd, "that Milton intended to
have marked the division of the Acts in this sketch, as well
as in the preceding. Peck has divided them; and closes the
first Act with Adam and Eve's love." The other Acts may
be supposed to conclude at the following points: Act 2 at
"sung a hymn of the creation"; Act 3 at "inform'd...the

---

[1] passing through; cf. *Comus*, 423.
[2] I.e. in the third draft.
[3] Each of these sentences was an after-thought, added below
or in the margin.
[4] occupies.
[5] I.e. reasons; or '*to* reason'.
[6] See XI. 477–93, note.

manner of his fall"; Act 4 at "bids him beware...
impenitence"; Act 5 at "the chorus breifly concludes".

It is in regard to the first Act that this fourth draft, which
Milton bids us "compare with the former", marks a
distinct advance. Milton made Moses the speaker of the
prologue in the third draft because so much of the subject-
matter of *Paradise Lost* is drawn from the Mosaic books of
the Old Testament. But the appearance of a descendant of
Adam, even in a prologue, where much latitude is allowed
by convention, seems an awkward prelude to scenes
coincident with Adam's own creation. It is far more
natural that, before the subject of man's fall is touched
upon at all, we should be told who man is, and that this
first mention of him should come from the supernatural
beings who had, or might have, witnessed the actual
creation of the universe and its inhabitants. The explanation, too, why Moses is able to assume his natural body is
very forced. And altogether this fourth draft exhibits more
of drama, less of spectacle, than its predecessor.

With regard to the subject, therefore, thus much is clear:
as early as 1641–2 Milton has manifested an unmistakeable
preference for the story of the lost Paradise, and the
evidence of the Trinity MSS. coincides with the testimony
of Aubrey and Phillips, who say that the poet did, about
1642, commence the composition of a drama on this theme
—of which drama the opening verses of *Paradise Lost*,
book IV (Satan's address to the sun), formed the exordium.
It is, I think, by no means improbable that some other
portions of the epic are really fragments of this unfinished
work. Milton may have written two or three hundred lines,
have kept them in his desk, and then, years afterward,
when the project was resumed, have made use of them
where opportunity offered. Had the poem, however, been
completed in accordance with his original conception we
should have had a tragedy, not an epic.

Of this there is abundant proof. The third and fourth
sketches, as has been observed, are dramatic. On the first

page of these entries, besides those lists of *dramatis personæ* which we have treated as the first and second sketches, stand the words "*other* Tragedies", followed by the enumeration of several feasible subjects. The list of British subjects is prefaced with the heading—"British Trag." (i.e. tragedies). Wherever Milton has outlined the treatment of any of the Scriptural themes a tragedy is clearly indicated. Twice, indeed, another form is mentioned—the pastoral, and probably a dramatic pastoral was intended.[1] These, however, are exceptions, serving to emphasise his leaning towards tragedy.

But what sort of tragedy? I think we may fairly conclude that, if carried out on the lines laid down in the fourth sketch, *Adam unparadiz'd* would have borne a very marked resemblance to *Samson Agonistes*: it would have conformed, in the main, to the same type—that, namely, of the ancient Greek drama. With the romantic stage of the Elizabethans Milton appears to have felt little sympathy:[2] else he would scarce have written *Il Penseroso*, 101, 102. Nor do I believe that his youthful enthusiasm for Shakespeare remained unmodified:[3] certainly, the condemnation of one important aspect of Shakespearian tragedy in the preface to *Samson Agonistes* is too plain to be misinterpreted. So had Milton been minded to dramatise the story of Macbeth—we have marked its presence in the list of Scottish subjects—his *Macbeth* would have differed *toto cælo* from Shakespeare's. In the same way, his tragedy of *Paradise Lost* would have been wholly un-Shakespearian,

[1] These are the two entries in the MS.: "Theristria. a Pastoral out of Ruth"; and—"the sheepshearers in Carmel a Pastoral. 1 Sam. 25". There is but one glance at the epical style; in the list of "British Trag." after mentioning an episode in the life of King Alfred appropriate to dramatic handling, he adds—"A Heroicall Poem may be founded somwhere in Alfreds reigne. especially at his issuing out of Edelingsey on the Danes. whose actions are wel like those of Ulysses".

[2] See *Appendix* to *Samson Agonistes*.

[3] See note on *L'Allegro*, 133, 134.

wholly un-Elizabethan. Nor would it have had any affinity to the drama of Milton's contemporaries,[1] those belated Elizabethans bungling with exhausted materials and forms that had lost all vitality. Tragedy for Milton could mean but one thing—the tragic stage of the Greeks, the "dramatic constitutions" of Sophocles and Euripides: and when we examine these sketches of *Paradise Lost* we find in them the familiar features of Athenian drama— certain signs eloquent of the source on which the poet has drawn.

Let us, for example, glance at the draft of *Adam un- paradiz'd*. Milton has kept the 'unities' of place and time. The scene does not change; it is set in some part of Eden, and everything represented before the eyes of the audience occurs at the same spot. But whoso regards the unity of place must suffer a portion of the action to happen off the stage—not enacted in the presence of the audience (as in a modern play where the scene changes), but reported. In *Samson Agonistes* Milton employs the traditional device of the Greek tragedians—he relates the catastrophe by the mouth of a messenger. So here: the temptation by the serpent is not represented on the scene: it is described— partly by Lucifer, "relating, and insulting in what he had don to the destruction of man"; partly by an angel who informs the Chorus of the manner of the fall. Again, the unity of time is observed. The time over which the action of a tragedy might extend, according to the usual practice of the Greek dramatists, was twenty-four hours. In *Samson Agonistes* the action begins at sunrise and ends at noon, thus occupying seven or eight hours. In *Adam unparadiz'd* the action would certainly not exceed the customary twenty-four hours. Again a Chorus is intro- duced (sure sign of classical influence), and not only introduced, but handled exactly as Milton, following his

[1] In the treatise *On Education*, 1644, he speaks of "our com- mon rhymers and play-writers" as "despicable creatures", *P. W.* III. 474.

Greek models, has handled it in *Samson Agonistes*: that is to say, closely identified with the action of the tragedy, even as Aristotle recommends that it should be. Further, in the fourth scheme the division into acts is carefully avoided—an advance this on the third scheme. Similarly, in *Samson Agonistes* Milton avoids splitting up the play into scenes and acts, calling attention to the fact in his preface. Proofs[1] of Milton's classical bias might be multiplied from these Milton MSS.; and personally I have no doubt that when he began the tragedy of which Aubrey and Phillips speak, he meant to revive in English the methods and style of his favourite Greek poets. But the scheme soon had to be abandoned; and not till a quarter of a century later was it executed in *Samson Agonistes*.[2] With Milton as with Dante the greatest came last—after long delay: the life's work of each marked the life's close: and, the work done, release soon came to each, though to Dante sooner.[3]

[1] Thus, apart from *P. L.*, the Scriptural themes whereof the fullest sketches are given, are three tragedies severally entitled "Abram from Morea, or Isack redeemed—Baptistes" (i.e. on the subject of John the Baptist and Herod)—and "Sodom Burning". In each two unities (time and place) are kept, and a Chorus used. In "Isack redeemed" the incident of the sacrifice is reported, and the description of the character of the hero Abraham as Milton meant to depict him is simply a paraphrase on Aristotle's definition of the ideal tragic hero. Most of the other subjects have a title such as the Greek tragedians employed —e.g. "Elias Polemistes", "Elisæus Hydrochóos", "Zedechiah νεοτερίζων.".

[2] The point is important because it disposes of the notion that Milton borrowed the idea of writing a tragedy on the classical model from the play of *Samson* by the Dutch poet Vondel.

[3] "There is at once similarity and difference in the causes which made each postpone the execution of his undertaking till a comparatively late period in his life; and a curious parallel may be observed in the length of time between the first conception and the completion of their monumental works, as well as in the period that elapsed between the end of their labours and their death." (Courthope.)

The third period in the genesis of *Paradise Lost* dates from 1658. In that year, according to Aubrey, Milton began the poem as we know it. By then he had gone back to the epic style. He was still Secretary, but his duties were very light, and allowed him to devote himself to poetry. At the Restoration he was in danger, for some time, of his life, and was imprisoned for a few months. But in spite of this interruption, and of his blindness,[1] the epic was finished about 1663. The history of each of his longer poems shows that he was exceedingly careful in revising his works—loth to let them go forth to the world till all that was possible had been done to achieve perfection.[2] It is Aubrey's statement that *Paradise Lost* was completed in 1663; while Milton's friend Thomas Ellwood, the Quaker, describes in a famous passage of his *Autobiography*, how in 1665 the poet placed a manuscript in his hands—"bidding me take it home with me and read it at my leisure, and, when I had so done, return it to him with my judgment thereupon. When I came home, and had set myself to read it, I found

---

[1] According to Edward Phillips, Milton dictated the poem to any one who chanced to be present and was willing to act as amanuensis; afterwards Phillips would go over the MS., correcting errors, under his uncle's direction. The original transcript submitted to the Licenser is extant, and is one of the many literary treasures that have gone to America. It "passed from the possession of the first printer of the poem, Samuel Simmons, to Jacob Tonson [the publisher], and thence to his collateral descendants, remaining in the same family... until 1904", when it was bought by an American collector. (From an article in *The Athenæum* on "*Miltoniana* in America".)

[2] "When we look at his earlier manuscripts, with all their erasures and corrections, we may well wonder what the *Paradise Lost* would have been if he had been able to give it the final touches of a faultless and fastidious hand. When we think of it composed in darkness, preserved in memory, dictated in fragments, it may well seem to us the most astonishing of all the products of high genius guided by unconquerable will" (J. W. Mackail).

it was that excellent poem which he intituled *Paradise
Lost*." Ellwood's account may be reconciled with Aubrey's
on the reasonable supposition that the interval between
1663 and 1665 was spent in revision. Still, some delay in
publishing the poem ensued. On the outbreak of the
Plague in 1665 Milton had left London, retiring to Chalfont
in Buckinghamshire, where Ellwood had rented a cottage
for him. He returned in the next year, 1666; but again
there was delay—this time through the great Fire of
London which disorganised business. Not till 1667 did
Paradise Lost appear in print. The agreement (now in the
possession of the British Museum) drawn up between
Milton and his publisher—by which he received an immediate payment of £5, and retained certain rights over
the future sale of the book—is dated April 27, 1667. The
date on which *Paradise Lost* was entered in the Stationers'
Register is August 20, 1667. No doubt, copies were in
circulation in the autumn of this year.

The system of licensing publications, against which
Milton had protested so vehemently in his *Areopagitica*,
had been revived by the Press Act of 1662 and was now
strongly enforced. "By that act", says Dr Masson, "the
duty of licensing books of general literature had been
assigned to the Secretaries of State, the Archbishop of
Canterbury, and the Bishop of London; but it was ex-
ceptional for any of those dignitaries to perform the duty
in person. It was chiefly performed for them by a staff of
under-licencers, paid by fees." Five or six of his chaplains
acted so for the Archbishop; and according to tradition one
of them, to whom *Paradise Lost* was submitted, hesitated to
give his *imprimatur* on account of the lines in the first book
about eclipses perplexing monarchs with fear of change
(I. 594–9). Milton must have remembered grimly the
bitter gibes in his pamphlets, e.g. in the *Animadversions*
(1641) against "monkish prohibitions, and expurgatorious
indexes", and "proud Imprimaturs not to be obtained
without the shallow surview, but not shallow hand of some

mercenary, narrow-souled, and illiterate chaplain". The wheel had come full circle with a vengeance.

This first edition of *Paradise Lost* raises curious points[1] of bibliography into which there is no need to enter here; but we must note three things. The poem was divided into —not twelve books but—ten. In the earlier copies issued to the public there were no prose *Arguments*; these (written, we may suppose, by Milton himself) were printed all together and inserted at the commencement of each of the later volumes of this first edition—an awkward arrangement changed in the second edition. Milton prefixed to the later copies the brief prefatory note on *The Verse*, explaining why he had used blank verse; and it was preceded by the address of *The Printer to the Reader*. It seems that the number of copies printed in the first edition was 1500; and the statement of another payment made by the publisher to Milton on account of the sale of the book shows that by April 26, 1669, i.e. a year and a half after the date of publication, 1300 copies had been disposed of.

In 1674 the second edition was issued—with several changes. First, the epic (said to be 670 lines longer than the *Æneid*) was divided into twelve books, a more Vergilian number, by the subdivision of books VII and X. Secondly, the prose *Arguments* were transferred from the beginning and prefixed to their respective books. Thirdly, a few changes were introduced into the text—few of any great

---

[1] For example, no less than nine distinct title-pages of this edition have been traced. This means that, though the whole edition was printed in 1667, only a limited number of copies were bound up and issued in that year. The rest would be kept in stock, unbound, and published in instalments, as required. Hence new matter could be inserted (such as the prose *Arguments*), and in each instalment it would be just as easy to bind up a new title-page as to use the old one. Often the date had to be changed: and we find that two of these pages bear the year 1667; four, 1668; and three, 1669. Seven have Milton's name in full; two, only his initials. Mr Leigh Sotheby collated them carefully in his book on Milton's autograph, pp. 81–84.

significance. It was to the second edition that the commendatory verses by Samuel Barrow and Andrew Marvell were prefixed. Four years later, 1678, came the third edition, and in 1688 the fourth. This last was the well-known folio published by Tonson; *Paradise Regained* and *Samson Agonistes* were bound up with some copies of it, so that Milton's three great works were obtainable in a single volume. The first annotated edition of *Paradise Lost* was that edited by Patrick Hume in 1695, being the sixth reprint. And during the 18th century editions[1] were numerous. "Milton scholarship",[2] it has been justly said, "was active throughout the whole period."

There is, indeed, little (if any) ground for the view which one so frequently comes across—that *Paradise Lost* met with scant appreciation, and that Milton was neglected by his contemporaries, and without honour in his lifetime. To the general public epic poetry will never appeal, more especially if it be steeped in the classical feeling that pervades *Paradise Lost*; but there must have been a goodly number of scholars and lettered readers to welcome the work—else why these successive editions, appearing at no very lengthy intervals? One thing, doubtless, which prejudiced its popularity was the personal resentment of the Royalist classes at Milton's political actions. They could not forget his long identification with republicanism; and there was much in the poem itself—covert sneers and gibes—which would repel many who were loyal to the Church and the Court. Further, the style of *Paradise Lost* was something very different from the prevailing tone of

[1] Pre-eminent among them is Bishop Newton's edition (1749). He was the first editor who took pains to secure accuracy of text, doing, on a smaller scale, for Milton what Theobald did for Shakespeare. His services too in the elucidation of certain aspects (notably the Scriptural) of Milton's learning have never been surpassed.

[2] See Professor Dowden's Tercentenary paper "Milton in the Eighteenth Century (1701–1750)".

the literature then current and popular. Milton was the last of the Elizabethans, a lonely survival lingering on into days when French influence was beginning to dominate English taste. Even the metre of his poem must have sounded strange to ears familiarised to the crisp clearness and epigrammatic ring of the rhymed couplet.[1] Yet, in spite of these obstacles, many whose praise was worth the having were proud of Milton: they felt that he had done honour to his country. He was accorded that which he had sought so earnestly—acceptance as a great national poet; and it is pleasant to read how men of letters and social distinction would pay visits of respect to him, and how the white-winged Fame bore his name and reputation abroad, so that foreigners came to England for the especial purpose of seeing him. And their visits were the prelude of that foreign renown and influence from which he seemed to have cut himself off when he made his native tongue the medium of his great work. "Milton was the first English poet to inspire respect and win fame for our literature on the Continent, and to his poetry was due, to an extent that has not yet been fully recognised, the change which came over European ideas in the eighteenth century with regard to the nature and scope of the epic. *Paradise Lost* was the mainstay of those critics who dared to vindicate, in the face of French classicism, the rights of the imagination over the reason in poetry."[2]

[1] Cf. Marvell's "Commendatory Verses", 45–54.

[2] Professor J. G. Robertson, "Milton's Fame on the Continent", a paper read before the British Academy, Dec. 10, 1908.

Perhaps the strangest and most delightful evidence of Milton's acceptance among foreigners was Mr Maurice Baring's discovery of the popularity of *Paradise Lost*, in a prose translation, amongst the Russian peasantry and private soldiers:

"The schoolmaster said that after all his experience the taste of the peasants in literature baffled him. 'They will not read modern stories', he said. 'When I ask them why they like *Paradise Lost* they point to their heart and say, "It is near to the heart; it speaks; you read, and a sweetness comes to you"'."

There has been much discussion about the 'sources' of *Paradise Lost*, and writers well nigh as countless as Vallombrosa's autumn leaves have been thrust forth from their obscurity to claim the honour of having 'inspired' (as the phrase is) the great epic. Most of these unconscious claimants were, like enough, unknown to Milton; but some of them do seem to stand in a relation which demands recognition.

I should place first the Latin tragedy *Adamus Exul* (1601), written in his youth by the great jurist Hugo Grotius after the model of Seneca. Apart from the question of actual resemblances to *Paradise Lost*, it might fairly be conjectured, if not assumed, that Milton read this tragedy. He knew Grotius personally and knew his works. Describing, in the *Second Defence*, his Italian tour in 1638, Milton mentions his stay in Paris and friendly reception by the English ambassador, and adds: "His lordship gave me a card of introduction to the learned Hugo Grotius, at that time ambassador from the Queen of Sweden to the French court; whose acquaintance I anxiously desired."[1] He quotes the opinions of Grotius with high respect in his treatise on divorce.[2] The alternative titles of the fourth draft of Milton's own contemplated tragedy, viz. *Adam unparadiz'd* and *Adams Banishment*, certainly recall the title *Adamus Exul*; and it may be noted that this draft was sketched in that period (about 1641) of Milton's life to which his meeting with Grotius belongs. Of the likeness between *Paradise Lost* and the *Adamus Exul*, and other works dealing with the same theme, it is impossible to say how much, if not all, is due to identity of subject and (what is no less important) identity of convention as to the machinery proper for its treatment. But I do not think that community of subject accounts entirely for the resemblances between *Paradise Lost* and Grotius's tragedy. The conception of Satan's character and motives unfolded

[1] *P. W.* i. 255.
[2] See chapters XVII, XVIII of *The Doctrine and Discipline*.

in his long introductory speech in the *Adamus*, the general
idea of his escaping from Hell and surveying Eden, his
invocation of the powers of evil (amongst them Chaos and
Night)—these things and some others, such as the Angel's
narrative to Adam of the Creation, seem like far-off
embryonic dawnings of the splendours of the epic. It
should be added that Grotius's other religious plays were
known in England. A free rendering of his *Christus Patiens*
into rhymed heroics was published in London in 1640
under the title *Christ's Passion*; while his tragedy *Sophom-
paneas, or Joseph*, appeared in an English version in 1650.
And a sidelight may be thrown not merely on the contemporary estimate of Grotius by the exceptionally
eulogistic mention of his works in the *Theatrum Poetarum*
(1675) of Milton's nephew Edward Phillips. The *Theatrum*
is commonly supposed to reflect in some degree Milton's
own views[1] and it is significant therefore to find Grotius
described as one "whose equal in fame for Wit & Learning,
Christendom of late Ages hath rarely produc'd, particularly
of so happy a Genius in Poetry, that had his Annals, his
Book *De Veritate Christianæ Religionis*...and other his
extolled works in Prose, never come to Light, his extant
and universally approved Latin Poems, had been sufficient
to gain him a Living Name".

It is an easy transition from the *Adamus Exul* to the
Adamo of the Italian poet Giovanni Battista Andreini
(1578–1652), a Florentine, which is said to owe something
to Grotius's tragedy. Voltaire, in his *Essai sur la Poésie
Epique* written in 1727, related that Milton during his

[1] See v. 177, 673, notes. Other touches in the *Theatrum* of
Miltonic interest are the accounts of Spenser and Sylvester,
and the praise of Henry Lawes in the notice of Waller. One
may conjecture, too, that the obscure Erycus Puteanus would
not have had his niche but for *Comus*. The *Theatrum* includes
also Andreini—but not Vondel. Phillips's account of Milton
himself is admirably discreet: and he expressly terms *Paradise
Lost* and *Paradise Regained* "Heroic Poems". The relations
between uncle and nephew were more than ordinarily close.

residence at Florence saw "a comedy called *Adamo*.[1] ...
The subject of the play was the Fall of Man: the actors,
the Devils, the Angels, Adam, Eve, the Serpent, Death,
and the Seven Mortal Sins. ... Milton pierced through the
absurdity of that performance to the hidden majesty of the
subject; which, being altogether unfit for the stage, yet
might be, for the genius of Milton, and his only, the
foundation of an epick poem." What authority he had for
this legend Voltaire does not say. It is not alluded to by
any of Milton's contemporary biographers. It may have
been a mere invention by some ill-wisher of the poet, a
piece of malicious gossip circulated out of political spite
against the great champion of republicanism. But the
authenticity of the story is not perhaps very important, for
independently there seems to be evidence in the *Adamo*
itself that Milton was acquainted with it even before his
visit to Italy. One cannot read the scene of the *Adamo*
(v. 5) in which the World, personified, tempts Eve with
all its pomps and vanities, without being reminded of the
scene in *Comus* of the temptation of the Lady. And, as
with the *Adamus Exul*, some of the coincidences of incident
and treatment between the *Adamo* and *Paradise Lost*, or
Milton's early dramatic sketches of the action, seem to
constitute a residuum of resemblance after full allowance
has been made for the influence of practical identity of
theme. Thus the list of characters in the *Adamo* has
abstractions like the World, Famine, Labour, Despair,
Death: and the appearance of these and kindred evils of
life to Adam and Eve (Act IV, scenes 6 and 7) recalls the

---

[1] It had been printed in 1613 (Milan), and again in 1617. The
title-page of the first edition describes the work as "L'Adamo,
Sacra Rapresentatione". It is more "a hybrid between a
miracle play and an opera" (Courthope) than a "comedy". A
translation by Cowper and Hayley was printed in their edition
of Milton; and it is in this translation that the work is known to
me. The fact that Cowper took the *Adamo* theory seriously is
significant.

early drafts of the scheme of *Paradise Lost* and also the vision shown to Adam in the eleventh (477–99) book of the poem. Andreini makes Michael drive Adam and Eve out of Paradise and depicts a final struggle between Michael and Lucifer. Andreini's representation of the Serpent's temptation of Eve has been thought to have left some impression on the parallel scene in *Paradise Lost*. After the Fall Lucifer summons the spirits of air and fire, earth and water—a counterpart to *Paradise Regained*, II. 115 *et seq.* And occasionally a verbal similarity arrests—as where Lucifer says (IV. 2, end):

> "Let us remain in hell!
> Since there is more content
> To live in liberty, tho' all condemn'd,
> Than, as his vassals, blest"[1]
>   ("*Poi, ch' è maggior contento
>   viver in libertà tutti damnati,
>   che sudditi beati*");

and inveighs (IV. 2):

>   "*Ahi luce, ahi luce odiata!*"

or where the Angels describe Man (II. 1):

> "For contemplation of his Maker form'd"
> ("*Per contemplar del suo gran Fabro il merto*").

Leaving the matter for a moment we will pass to the third claimant, the Dutch poet, Joost van den Vondel. He

---

[1] See I. 263, note; but of course the idea was not peculiar to any writer. So tradition, literary or theological, may explain the following similarity, which is at least an interesting illustration of *P. L.* v. 688, 699. Andreini makes Lucifer (I. 3) address his followers:

> "I am that Spirit, I, who for your sake
> Collecting dauntless courage, to the north
> Led you far distant from the senseless will
> Of him who boasts to have created heav'n."

The reference occurs again in the *Adamo*, III. 8.

Tradition also may account for another feature common to the *Adamo*, the *Adamus* and *Paradise Lost*, viz. the long description of the convulsions and deterioration in the physical universe after the Fall of Man.

was contemporary with Milton, and the author of a great
number of works. Among them were several dramas on
Scriptural subjects. With three of them Milton is supposed
by some writers to have been acquainted. These are
Lucifer (1654), a drama on the revolt of the angels and their
fall from heaven; *John the Messenger* (1662), and *Adam in
Banishment* (1664). In a work published a few years since
it was contended that Milton borrowed a good deal from
these three poems.

That Milton had heard of Vondel may be conceded.
Vondel enjoyed a great reputation; beside which, there was
in the 17th century much intercourse between England and
Holland, and Milton from his position as Secretary, no less
than from his controversies with Salmasius and Morus,
must have had his thoughts constantly directed towards
the Netherlands. Also, we learn that he had some knowledge of the Dutch language. But it will be observed that
the earliest of the poems with which he is thought to have
been too conversant, namely *Lucifer*, was not published till
after his blindness, while by the time that the last of them,
Adam in Banishment, appeared, *Paradise Lost* was almost
completed. It is impossible that Milton read a line of the
works himself; if he knew them at all, it must have been
through the assistance of some reader or translator; and
considering how many details concerning the last years of
Milton's life have survived, it is exceeding curious that
this reader or translator should have escaped mention, and
that the Vondelian theory should not have been heard of
till a century after the poet's death. For there were plenty
of people ready to do him an ill-turn and damage his repute;
and plagiarism from his Dutch contemporary would have
been an excellent cry to raise. As it is, Milton's biographers
—and contemporaries—Phillips, Aubrey, Toland, Antony
à Wood, are absolutely silent on the subject. Phillips indeed and Toland expressly mention the languages in which
Milton used to have works read to him. The list is exten-
sive: it includes Hebrew, Syriac, Greek, Latin, Italian,

Spanish and French: and it does *not* include Dutch. I think that this fact tells heavily against the hypothesis of Milton's indebtedness to Vondel. Still, it must be admitted that critics of eminence accept it.

There remains the so-called Cædmon *Paraphrase*. In the Bodleian is the manuscript of an Old English metrical *Paraphrase* of parts[1] of the Old Testament. This work was long attributed to the Northumbrian religious writer Cædmon, of whom Bede speaks. Cædmon lived in the seventh century. He is supposed to have died about 670. There is no reason for thinking that he was not the author of sacred poems, as Bede represents him to have been; but there is also no possibility of believing that the *Paraphrase*, as we have it, was written by him. It is a composite work in which several hands may be traced, and the different styles belong to a date long subsequent to Cædmon.[2] The MS. was once in the possession of Archbishop Ussher. He presented it in 1651 to his secretary, the Teutonic scholar, Francis Dujon, commonly called Franciscus Junius. Junius published the MS. at Amsterdam in 1655. Milton never saw the *Paraphrase* in print, for the same reason that he never saw Vondel's *Lucifer*. But inasmuch as Junius had been settled in England since 1620, it is quite likely that he knew Milton;[3] if so, he may have mentioned the *Paraphrase*, and even translated[4] parts of it.

---

[1] Namely *Genesis*, *Exodus* and *Daniel*. It is the paraphrase of *Genesis* that would have concerned Milton most.

[2] See the article by Mr Henry Bradley in the *Dictionary of National Biography*. There is also a good discussion of the authorship of the work in the Appendix to Professor Ten Brink's *Early English Literature*.

[3] This was first pointed out by Sharon Turner; see also Masson, *Life*, VI. 557.

[4] In a very ingenious paper in *Anglia*, IV. pp. 401–5, Professor Wuelcker argues that Milton had not much knowledge of Anglo-Saxon. In his *History of Britain* he habitually quotes Latin Chronicles, and in one place virtually admits that an Old English chronicle was not intelligible to him.

Here, however, as in the previous cases of Andreini and Vondel, we cannot get beyond conjecture, since there is no actual record or external evidence of Milton's acquaintance with the *Paraphrase* or its translator.

These then are the four possible 'sources' of *Paradise Lost* seemingly most deserving of mention; and of them the *Adamus Exul* and the *Adamo* strike me as unquestionably the most important, for various reasons. Milton's acquaintance with them may be referred to the early period when the influence on him of other writers would be greatest. The *Adamus* and the *Adamo* both present some points of resemblance to the early drafts of *Paradise Lost*. With the *Adamus* there is the special consideration of Milton's personal knowledge and admiration of its author. With the *Adamo*, apart from the possibility that Voltaire's story had some basis, there is the consideration of Milton's special devotion to Italian literature. With neither is there, at least not in the same degree as in the case of Vondel's works and the Cædmon *Paraphrase*, the difficulty involved by the poet's blindness. That he knew the *Adamus*[1] and the *Adamo* appears to me, now, hardly an open question. In these and similar works disinterred by the industry of Milton's editors lay the general conception, the theological machinery, the cosmic and supra-cosmic scene of a poem on the Fall of Man. So much is simply a matter of history; and to claim for Milton or any other writer who chose this theme the merit of absolute originality is simply to ignore history. The composition of religious poetry was the great literary activity of the earlier part of the 17th century, and Milton did on the grand scale what others did on the lower. The work of these lesser writers could not be without its influence on him, since no poet can detach himself from the conditions of his age or the associations of

[1] As regards the *Adamus Exul* William Lauder had *some* case, but spoilt it by his forgeries; for a sample of his libellous malevolence see I. 261–3, note. Todd (II. 585–9) has an Appendix on "Lauder's Interpolations".

a subject that has become common property and passed
into a convention. But that the qualities which have made
Paradise Lost immortal were due, in the faintest degree, to
any other genius than that of Milton himself: this is a fond
delusion, vainly imagined, without warranty, and altogether
to be cast out.

We must indeed recognise in *Paradise Lost*, the meeting-
point of Renaissance and Reformation, the impress of
four great influences: the Bible, the classics, the Italian
poets, and English literature. Of the Bible Milton possessed a knowledge such as few have had. There are
hundreds of allusions to it: the words of Scripture underlie
some part of the text of every page of *Paradise Lost*; and
apart from verbal reminiscences there is much of the spirit
that pervades that noblest achievement of the English
tongue. Scarcely less powerful was the influence of the
classics. Milton's allusiveness extends over the whole
empire of classical humanity and letters, and to the
scholar his work is full of the exquisite charm of endless
reference to the noblest things that the ancients have
thought and said. That he was deeply versed in Italian
poetry the labours of his early editors have abundantly
proved; and their comparative studies are confirmed by
the frequent mention of Dante,[1] Petrarch, Tasso, Ariosto

---

[1] See Dr Paget Toynbee's *Dante in English Literature*, I. 2,
120, 486, II. 587. Among the points noted are these: Dante
resemblances occur in Milton's early poems before his visit to
Italy; in his Commonplace Book Milton illustrates his views
several times by references to Dante; his rendering of three
lines of the *Inferno* in his treatise *Of Reformation* (see *P. L.* III.
444–97, note) is the first instance of the use of blank verse as a
medium for the translation of Dante and may have suggested
the use of that metre to Cary; Milton was one of the first
English poets to use Dante's *terza rima*—see his translation of
Psalm ii. headed "Done August 8, 1653. Terzetti". Dr
Toynbee also states that Milton's copy (the 3rd ed., Venice,
1529) of the *Convivio* is extant: "Milton has written his name
in the book and the date, 1629. The volume belonged to Heber

and others in his prose works and correspondence. In English literature I imagine that he had read everything worth reading. Without doubt, he was most affected by " our admired Spenser ".[1] He was, says Dryden, " the poetical son of Spenser. Milton has acknowledged to me that Spenser was his original." And there was a Spenserian school of poets, mostly Cambridge men, and some of them contemporary with Milton at the University, with whose works he evidently had a considerable acquaintance. Among these the two Fletchers were conspicuous—Giles Fletcher, author of the sacred poems *Christ's Victorie on Earth* and *Christ's Triumph in Heaven*; and Phineas Fletcher, author of *The Purple Island.* The influence of the Fletchers is manifest in Milton's early poems,[2] and it is traceable in *Paradise Lost.* Finally, we must not forget Sylvester. Joshua Sylvester (of whom little is known beyond that he was born in 1563, died in 1618, and diversified the profession of merchant with the making of much rhyme) translated into exceedingly Spenserian verse *The Divine Weeks and Works* of the French poet, Du Bartas.[3] The subject of this very lengthy work is the story of Creation, with the early history of the Jews. The

[the book-collector, half-brother of the bishop], and was sold at his sale in 1834." It contained also the *Sonnets* (1563) of the Italian poet Casa and the marginal markings, if made by Milton, show that he had " read the Sonnets with great attention ".

[1] *Animadversions, P. W.* III. 84. On Milton's feeling for Spenser see the note to *Il Penseroso,* 116–20.

[2] See the *Introductions* to *Comus* and *Lycidas.* Phineas Fletcher's *Apollyonists* might also be mentioned (see II. 650, 746, notes). Besides the Fletchers, there was Henry More, the famous " Cambridge Platonist ". Milton must have known him at Christ's College.

[3] Sylvester translated a good deal from Du Bartas beside *The Divine Weeks*; and rhymed on his own account. The first collected edition of his translation of *The Divine Weeks* was published in 1605–6, instalments having appeared between 1592 and 1599. Dr Grosart collected Sylvester's works into two bulky volumes.

translation was amazingly popular. Dryden confessed that
he had once preferred Sylvester to Spenser.[1] There is no
doubt that Milton studied *The Divine Weeks* in his youth.
"That Poem hath ever had many great admirers among
us" is the suggestive comment of his nephew Edward
Phillips. It is certainly one of the works[2] whereof account
must be taken in any attempt to estimate the literary
influences that moulded Milton's style.

But a writer may be influenced by others, and not
'plagiarise'; and it is well to remember that from Virgil
downwards the great poets have exercised their royal right
of adapting the words of their forerunners and infusing
into them a fresh charm and suggestion, since in allusion
lies one of the chief delights of literature. It is well, also,
to realise wherein lies the greatness of *Paradise Lost*, and
to understand that all the borrowing in the world could not
contribute a jot to the qualities which have rendered the
epic "a possession for ever". What has made the poem
live is not the story, nobly though that illustrates the eternal
antagonism of righteousness and wrong, and the over-
throw of evil; not the construction, though this is sufficiently
architectonic; nor the learning, though this is vast; nor the
characterisation, for which there is little scope: not these
things, though all are factors in the greatness of the poem,

---

[1] Spenser himself admired Du Bartas greatly; see the *Envoy*
addressed to the French poet Bellay at the end of *The Ruines of
Rome*.

In a paper read before the British Academy on some MS.
notes, "dealing mainly with the place of astronomy in poetry",
by Spenser's Cambridge friend Gabriel Harvey, Professor
Gollancz gave the following extract referring to Du Bartas and
Spenser:

"Mr Digges hath the whole Aquarius of Palingenius by
heart, and takes much delight to repeat it often. Mr Spenser
conceives the like pleasure in the fourth day of the first Week
of Bartas which he esteems as the proper profession of Urania."

[2] See some remarks and illustrations in Professor Mackail's
The Springs of Helicon (1909), pp. 195, 196.

and in all Milton rises to the height of his argument—but the incomparable elevation of the style, "the shaping spirit of Imagination", and the mere majesty of the music.

THE STORY OF THE POEM

A sketch of the action of the whole poem, following the sequence of the twelve books, may be useful to those who are acquainted only with parts of *Paradise Lost*:—

I. The scene Hell—the time nine days after the expulsion of Satan and his followers from Heaven. They lie on the burning lake, stupefied. Satan first recovers, rouses Beëlzebub, discusses with him their position, and then makes his way from the lake to a "dreary plain" of dry land. Beëlzebub follows; Satan calls to his comrades to do likewise. Rising on the wing they reach the same firm land. Their numbers and names described. They range themselves in battle-array before Satan, who addresses them. They may still (he says) regain Heaven; or there may be other worlds to win—in particular, a new world, inhabited by new-created beings, of which report had spoken: let these matters be duly conferred of. Straightway, a vast palace—Pandemonium—is made, to serve as council-chamber. Here a council is held; only the great Angels are present.

II. The scene—at first—Pandemonium; the debate begins. Satan invites their counsel—"who can advise may speak". Moloch, Belial and Mammon speak—their several counsels: last Beëlzebub, who reverts to Satan's hint of the new world. Why not ruin it? or make it their own? or win its inhabitants to their side? What better revenge against the Almighty? The plan approved—but who will discover this world? None volunteer: and then Satan offers to undertake the journey. His offer accepted; the council leaving Pandemonium breaks up; the result announced to the rest of the Angels. How they pass the time till his return—some exploring Hell (now more closely described). Meanwhile he reaches Hell-gates, is suffered to pass by

Sin and Death, voyages through Chaos (described), and at last comes within sight of the Universe hung in space (i.e. Chaos). We leave him directing his course towards the World.

III. The scene—at first—Heaven. The Almighty perceives Satan, points him out to the Son, tells what his design is, and its destined success; tells also that Man will be saved ultimately—if he can find a Redeemer. "The Son of God freely offers himself a ransom for Man"; is accepted by the Father, and praised by the Angelic host. Meanwhile —the scene changing—Satan, having reached the outer surface (described) of the Universe, wanders through various regions (described), until, coming to the single opening in the surface, he descends into the inside of the Universe. He arrives at the sphere of the Sun; disguising himself as a young Angel from Heaven, enquires from Uriel, the Sun-spirit, the way to Earth—pretending "desire to behold the new Creation"; is directed by Uriel, descends again, and alights on Mt Niphates.

IV. There, pausing awhile, he gives way to regret that he has rebelled, and rage at his outcast state; passion distorts his face, so that Uriel, watching, now knows him for an evil spirit. Thence, recovering self-control, Satan journeys on towards Eden, the main scene (described); sees Adam and Eve (famous description of them); overhears what they say concerning the Tree of Knowledge, and perceives at once the means whereby to compass their fall. At nightfall he essays to tempt Eve in a dream; is discovered by Gabriel, who, warned by Uriel, has descended to Eden to defend Man. A battle between Satan and Gabriel imminent, but averted. Satan flies.

V. The scene still Eden. A further picture of Adam and Eve—their worship and work. Raphael (the scene having changed for a brief space to Heaven) comes to warn them of their danger, at the bidding of the Almighty—so that Man, if he falls, may fall knowingly, by his own fault. Raphael received and entertained; admonishes Adam;

explains who his enemy is, and why: which leads to an account of the rebellion in Heaven—its beginning described.

VI. The scene of the events narrated by Raphael Heaven. He describes the three days' war in Heaven, at the end of which Satan and his followers were cast into Hell. The warning to Adam repeated.

VII. The scene Eden. Raphael describes the Creation of the World, which is accomplished by the Son of God.

VIII. The scene the same. Adam enquires concerning the stars and Heavenly bodies; Raphael answers doubt-fully. Adam recounts his own first experience of Eden—how the Almighty forbade him to touch the Tree of Knowledge, under pain of what penalty; how he first saw Eve. The day declines, and Raphael departs—once more warning Adam.

IX. The scene the same. "Adam and Eve...go forth to their labours, which Eve proposes to divide in several places, each labouring apart." Adam dissuades; she persisting, he yields. So Satan (in the form of a serpent) finds her alone and tempts her. She eats of the fruit and induces Adam to do so. Their sense of sin and shame.

X. The Son of God descends to Eden, and pronounces doom on Adam and Eve and the Serpent. Meanwhile Satan, returning to Pandemonium, announces the result of his journey, and lo! on a sudden he and his followers are changed to reptiles. Sin and Death now ascend from Hell to Eden, to claim the World as theirs; but the Almighty foretells their ultimate overthrow by the Son, and com-mands the Angels to make changes in the elements and stars, whereby the Earth becomes less fair. The repentance of Adam and Eve, who seek comfort in supplication of the Deity. The scene has changed often.

XI. The Son interceding, the Father sends Michael to Eden (henceforth the scene) to reveal the future to Adam—above all, his hope of redemption. After announcing to Adam his approaching banishment from Eden, Michael

takes him to a high mountain and unrolls before him a vision of the World's history till the Flood.

XII. Then he traces the history of Israel after the Flood, till the coming of Christ, with the subsequent progress of Christianity: ending with renewed promise of redemption. The fiery Cherubim now descend. Michael leads Adam and Eve to the gates of Eden; and they go forth, sad yet consoled with the hope of salvation at the last.

MILTON'S PREFACE ON "THE VERSE" OF *PARADISE LOST*

Milton's attitude towards rhyme reminds us of the condemnations showered on it by Elizabethan critics. Ascham in the *Schoolmaster* (1570) sneers at "our rude beggerly ryming, brought first into Italie by *Gothes* and *Hunnes*, whan all good verses and all good learning to, were destroyed by them... and at last receyued into England by men of excellent wit indeede, but of small learning, and lesse judgement in that behalfe." "Barbarous" is his darling epithet for rhymed verse. Puttenham is of a like mind, waving aside "the rhyming poesie of the barbarians", and Webbe in his *Discourse of English Poetry* (1586) takes up the tale, ridiculing it as "tinkerly verse"—"brutish poesie"—"a great decay of the good order of versifying". Why Milton should have adopted the same position as these Elizabethan critics who approached the question in a spirit of the merest pedantry, and based their objections to rhyme solely on the fact that, as a metrical principle, it was not employed by the ancients, it is not easy to say. He uses rhyme occasionally in *Samson Agonistes*, in spite of his denunciation of it here; and his own early poems are sufficient refutation of the heresy that therein lies "no true musical delight". Moreover, though he appeals to the example of some European poets "of prime note" in support of his view, yet he must have foreseen the obvious and just retort that the weight of "custom" was against

him, and that, in particular, the Italian exponents of *versi scioltī* whom he could cite on his side made a poor showing beside those great masters of rhyme—Dante, Ariosto, Tasso[1]—to whom he himself owed so much. His contemptuous dismissal of what "in every country of modern Europe had been adopted as the basis of metrical composition"[2] was a characteristic touch of his resentment of criticism and defiance of authority.

There is a polemical tone in his remarks, as though he were replying to some unnamed antagonist; and I cannot help thinking that this preface was meant to be his contribution to the controversy then raging over the comparative advantages of rhymed and unrhymed metres on the stage. In fact, significant in itself, Milton's opinion becomes doubly so if regarded from the standpoint of his contemporaries. Hardly could they fail to see in it a retort to what Dryden had written in the behalf of rhyme—notably in his *Essay of Dramatic Poesy* (1665), in which the rhymed couplet had been set forth as the best vehicle of dramatic expression. In play after play Dryden had put his theory into practice: others had followed his example: to rhyme or not to rhyme—that had become the great question; and here was Milton brushing the matter on one side as of no moment, with the autocratic dictum that rhyme was a vain and fond thing with which a "sage and serious" poet need have no commerce. His readers must have detected the contemporary application of his words—just as later on they must have interpreted his preface to *Samson Agonistes*, with its pointed eulogy of the Greek stage and its depreciation of Restoration tragedy (and "other common interludes"), as a counterblast to the comparison which Dryden had drawn between the modern and the classical drama, in the interests of the former. There is force too in the suggestion that the association of rhyme with the

[1] See, however, p. 67.
[2] Courthope.

amatory Caroline poets (*Lycidas*, 67–9) would not make Milton more favourable to it.

Curiously enough, *Paradise Lost* and *Paradise Regained* both contain a good deal of rhyme. We may compare it with the rare rhymed verse, accidental or designed ("leonine"), in the Latin poets. Cowper noted some instances in his fragment of a commentary on *Paradise Lost*. "Rhyme", he said, "is apt to come uncalled, and to writers of blank verse is often extremely troublesome."[1] Indeed complete absence of rhyme argues some artificiality. To quote Mr Robert Bridges: "Rhyme occurs in *Paradise Lost* (see I. 146, 8, 51; II. 220, 1; IV. 24–7), but only as a natural richness among the varieties of speech; and it would seem that it cannot be forbidden in a long poem but by the scrupulosity which betrays art." Possibly, however, the amount of rhyme in the two epics exceeds what Milton would have desired. It illustrates, I think, the terrible difficulty of revision imposed by his blindness. Yet such is the spell of the rhythm of his verse that one may be unconscious of the rhyme till its presence is pointed out. Of consecutive rhymed lines, some being actual rhymed couplets, the following passages are examples. *Paradise Lost*, II. 220, 221; IV. 956, 957; VI. 709, 710; IX. 105, 106, 477, 478; XI. 230, 231, 597, 598, 671, 672; *Paradise Regained*, III. 214, 215; IV. 591, 592. In II. 893, 894, a slight difference of pronunciation, indicated by Milton's spelling, may account for what appears to the eye as a couplet. In V. 167, 168, 274, 275, IX. 191, 192, the assonance has the effect of rhyme. Of course, the most frequent rhyme is that which comes with an interval of one or two intervening lines, as in two out of the three passages remarked by Mr Bridges. Other examples[2] are: *Paradise Lost*, I. 274, 276, 711, 713 764, 767; II. 390, 393,

[1] "The blank verse Italians have often done this [i.e. rhymed]: in fact, it is excessively difficult to prevent in Italian" (Saintsbury).

[2] The list is illustrative, not exhaustive.

942, 944; III. 140, 142, 168, 170; IV. 222, 224, 288, 290, 678, 680; V. 160, 162, 383, 385, 857, 859; VI. 14, 16, 161, 163, 174, 176; VIII. 1, 3, 171, 173, 229, 231; IX. 590, 591, 606, 608; XI. 201, 204, 206, 637, 639, 740, 741; XII. 353, 355, 366, 368; *Paradise Regained*, II. 206, 208, 245, 247, 250; IV. 25, 27, 145, 147, 222, 224. As remarked before, I cannot help thinking that a portion of this rhyme represents Milton's inability to focus the full measure of his fastidious taste[1] on the revision of his work.

Superfluous as it may seem to us that he should justify his adoption of blank verse—wherein his surpassing skill is the best of all justifications—we have cause to be grateful to the "stumblings" of the unlettered which led him to write this preface, since it happily defines the qualities for which the metre of *Paradise Lost* is remarkable.

The distinguishing characteristic of Milton's blank verse is his use of what Mr Saintsbury calls the verse-paragraph. Blank verse is exposed to two dangers: it may be formal and stiff by being circumscribed in single lines or couplets; or diffuse and formless through the sense and rhythm being carried on beyond the couplet. In its earlier stages, exemplified by works like *Gorboduc*, the metre suffered from the former tendency. It either closed with a strong pause at the end of every line, or just struggled to the climax of the couplet. Further it never extended until Marlowe took the "drumming decasyllabon" into his hands, broke up the fetters of the couplet-form, and by the process of overflow carried on the rhythm from verse to verse according as the sense required. It is in his plays that we first get verse in which variety of cadence and pause and beat takes the place of rhyme. Milton entered on the heritage that Marlowe and Shakespeare bequeathed, and brought blank verse to its highest pitch of perfection as an instrument of narration.

[1] It would have resented surely the substitution of *Chersonese* in most modern texts for the *Chersoness* of the original editions in *Paradise Regained*, IV. 74. See the termination of the previous line.

Briefly, that perfection lies herein: if we examine a page of *Paradise Lost* we find that what the poet has to say is, for the most part, conveyed, not in single lines, nor in rigid couplets—but in flexible combinations of verses, which wait upon his meaning, not twisting or constraining the sense, but suffering it to be "variously drawn out", so that the thought is merged in its expression.

These combinations, or paragraphs, are informed by a perfect internal concent and rhythm[1]—held together by a chain of harmony. With a writer less sensitive to sound this free method of versifying would result in mere chaos. But Milton's ear is so delicate, that he steers unfaltering through the long, involved passages, distributing the pauses and rests and alliterative balance with a cunning which knits the paragraph into a coherent, regulated whole. He combines, in fact, the two essential qualities of blank verse— freedom and form: the freedom that admits variety of effect, without which a long narrative becomes intolerably monotonous; and the form which saves an unrhymed measure from drifting into that which is nearer to bad prose than to good verse. And restoration of form was precisely what the metre needed. With the later Jacobean and Caroline dramatists metrical freedom had turned to "licence and slipshodness...then comes Milton,...takes non-dramatic blank verse in hand once for all, and introduces into it the order, proportion, and finish which dramatic blank verse had then lost".[2] Milton in fact was the re-creator of blank verse, "the first to establish this peculiarly English form of metre in non-dramatic poetry".[2] Nor was he unconscious of the character of his achievement. Here, in the last lines of his preface, he congratulates himself upon "an example set"; and many years

[1] Cf. Professor Mackail's fine metaphor for it—"the planetary wheeling of the long period"—"that continuous planetary movement" (Lecture II on Milton in *The Springs of Helicon*, pp. 156, 196).

[2] Saintsbury, *History of English Prosody*, II. 208, 224.

before, in the grand passage apostrophising the Divine
Goodness at the end of the treatise *Of Reformation*, he had
written, with obvious reference to the great design that
ruled his whole life: "Then, amidst the hymns and hal-
lelujahs of saints, some one may perhaps be heard offering
at high strains in new and lofty measure to sing and
celebrate thy divine mercies and marvellous judgments in
this land throughout all ages."[1] It were hard to frame an
apter summary of the metre of *Paradise Lost* than "new
and lofty".

As he lays such stress upon the internal economy and
balance of his verse-paragraphs, much must depend on the
pause or rest which in English prosody answers, to some
extent, to the classical *cæsura*. Dr Masson notes that
Milton's favourite pause is at the end of the third foot.
These are typical specimens:

> " I, at first, with two fair gifts
> Created him endowed | —with happiness
> And immortality; | that fondly lost,
> This other served but to eternize woe,
> Till I provided death: | so death becomes
> His final remedy" | (XI. 57–62).

Next in frequency comes the pause after the second
foot; cf.
> "ere fallen
> From innocence" | (XI. 29, 30).

"Made one with me, | as I with thee am one" (XI. 44).

Scarcely need we say that in this, as in everything else,
Milton never forgets that variety of effect is essential.

It remains to note two other remarks made by Milton.
One of the elements, he says, of "true musical delight" is
"fit quantity of syllables". By this, I think, he meant that
every word should bear its natural accent, i.e. that a word
should not be forced by the exigence of the metre to bear
an accent alien to it. Rather, a poet should be careful to

---

[1] *P. W.* II. 418.

"span words with just note and accent",[1] so that each
stress should fall naturally, and the "fit quantity" of the
component parts of a line not be violated. Considering the
length of *Paradise Lost*, it is marvellous how he maintains
an unfaltering appropriateness of accent. But another
interpretation of his words is possible, namely that by "fit
quantity of syllables" he meant "that blank verse might be
extended beyond the usual number of ten syllables when
its sense and feeling so required".[2] Taken in this way,
"quantity" would have reference to the trisyllabic element
in his verse by which the number of syllables in a line is
increased, and perhaps more obviously to the hypermetrical
element.

One peculiarity of the metre of *Paradise Lost*, pointed
out by Coleridge, is the rarity of verses with an extra
syllable (or two extra syllables) at the close. Shakespeare,
of course, uses them freely—especially in his later plays,
and the percentage of them in *Comus* and *Samson
Agonistes* is high. But in *Paradise Lost* Milton avoids
them. There are several varieties of this extra-syllable
verse—e.g. lines (i) where the supernumerary syllable
comes at the close; (ii) where it comes in the course of the
line, particularly after the second foot; (iii) where there
are two extra syllables at the end, as in the line, "Like one |
that means | his pro|per harm, | in má*nacles*" (*Coriolanus*,
I. 9. 57); and (iv) where there are two extra syllables in the
middle, as in *Coriolanus*, I. I. 230, "Our must|y super-
flu*ity*|. See our | best elders". In *Comus* there are
examples of all four varieties: in *Paradise Lost* of only
two[3]—(i) and (iii). This paucity is an illustration of what

[1] *Sonnet* to Henry Lawes.

[2] Courthope, *History of English Poetry*, III. 428. Personally I
think that in a specifically metrical context "quantity" conveys
the notion "long" or "short", i.e. with or without accent
(stress).

[3] In most of the cases of *one* extra syllable it is a present
participle that is affected. I believe that the cases with *two* such

must be recognised as the great metrical feature of the epic—that its metre is mainly iambic, and consequently decasyllabic in character. Such verse has a slower, statelier movement, and is therefore appropriate to a narrative poem that deals with the loftiest themes in an elevated, solemn style. Verse, on the other hand, that admits the supernumerary syllable at the close of the line tends towards a conversational rapidity of rhythm which makes it suitable for the purposes of the dramatist. It is typical of Milton's "inevitable", almost infallible, art that he should vary his style so precisely to fit the several characteristics and requirements of the drama and of epic narration. Such variation illustrates "a quality for which he seldom or never gets the full credit due to him, a dramatic sense of extreme delicacy. With him, as with Sophocles, this quality is so fine that it may easily elude observation."[1]

Again, another element of the pleasure offered by poetry lies in "apt numbers". Here Milton referred to that adaptation of expression to subject whereby the sound becomes an echo to the sense. This adaptation is shown in its simplest form by the suggestion of specific effects such as movement or sound.[2] But it dominates the whole relation of the manner to the matter. No one has understood the art of blending the thought with its expression better than Milton. "What other poets effect," says Dr

---

syllables are—in Milton—confined to words like *society*; cf. *P.R.* I. 302, "Such solitude before choicest soci*ety*". So in *P. L.* VIII. 216. Of course in these cases an "Alexandrine" solves the difficulty.

[1] *The Springs of Helicon*, p. 175 (see also p. 178).

[2] Cf. e.g. I. 742–6, 768, II. 947–50, 1021, 1022, VII. 495 (note), X. 521–8 (note). So in II. 641 we get the sense of vast space; in II. 879–83 of combined movement and jarring noise; in II. 890–906 of confusion; in IV. 181 (note) of scornful laughter; in VII. 480 of length. A very elaborate example (admirably analysed in Mayor's *Modern English Metre*, pp. 99–106) is the description of the march of the fallen angels in I. 549–62.

Guest,[1] "as it were by chance, Milton achieved by the aid of science and art; he studied the aptness of his numbers, and diligently tutored an ear which nature had gifted with the most delicate sensibility. In the flow of his rhythm, in the quality of his letter sounds, in the disposition of his pauses, his verse almost ever fits the subject, and so insensibly does poetry blend with this—the last beauty of exquisite versification—that the reader may sometimes doubt whether it be the thought itself, or merely the happiness of its expression, which is the source of a gratification so deeply felt."

We have seen that Milton may have had in view the scansion of his verse when he referred to the "fit quantity of syllables". That scansion has as its basic principle the "pure iambic"—*carmen iambicum*—so much canvassed by Elizabethan metricists. This stately, self-contained line of five feet in rising rhythm—"O Prince, O chief of many throned powers—" lies at the centre of the prosody of *Paradise Lost*. So much is patent; nor are the main means by which it is varied obscure. By letting the lines run on so that the rhythm of the unit of five feet passes into the richer harmony of groups of units Milton gives us the "verse-paragraph". And by substituting each of the possible variations of the disyllabic foot—namely, the trochee (or inversion of rhythm), the spondee and the pyrrhic—he tempers the monotony of a single-foot measure to "stops of various quills". But these foot-modifications had become part of the machinery of blank verse as developed since the pioneer days. There is nothing specifically Miltonic about the use of them in *Paradise Lost*, except possibly as regards the spondee. Cowper was inclined to think that "the grand secret to which his [Milton's] verse is principally indebted for its stately movement" is the frequent employment of spondaic feet: "the more long syllables there are in a verse, the more the line of it is pro-

---

[1] *English Rhythms*, p. 530.

tracted, and consequently the pace, with which it moves, is the more majestic". That Milton's use of the trochee (or rare double trochee) was due to the partiality of the Italians for this foot seems a needless assumption, the trochee having been firmly established by Marlowe. And "pyrrhic" is merely a rather pedantic-sounding term for a quite ordinary feature of blank verse—namely, the occurrence of a foot with a weak stress. Dr Abbott estimates that of Shakespeare's lines "rather less than one of three has the full number of five emphatic accents". I doubt whether the instances are so frequent in Milton; but they are sufficiently common to make it desirable to remember that five stresses are not indispensable—rather that for variety's sake it is necessary that one or more should occasionally be remitted. Taken as a whole, the obviously disyllabic element of Milton's poetry does not present much difficulty: the crux lies in the less obviously trisyllabic strata.

This is a subject on which irreconcilable opinions are held; the Miltonic blank verse described by Dr Masson is simply a different thing from the Miltonic blank verse described by Mr Bridges; and the essential truth seems to me to lie very much nearer to the views of the latter critic. I think that Milton himself would have been astonished at the elaborate trisyllabic apparatus—bacchics and amphibrachs and cretics rare—with which the verse of *Paradise Lost* has been credited. The base-principle of the slow-moving, majestic iambic decasyllable is lost in the mazes of so complex a system. On the other hand, to attempt to ban the trisyllabic foot altogether from his metre involves impossible twistings and distortions. We shall not be far astray if we steer a middle course and admit the anapæst ("the foot-of-all-work of English prosody") and (to a much less important share) the dactyl and the tribrach.[1] These may be taken to represent collectively "the trisyl-

[1] See Saintsbury, *A History of English Prosody*, I. 403, II. 259, 260.

labic foot, which was inherent in the nature of the [English] language, and had been recognised by long poetical usage".[1] It reproduces "the swift triple rhythm"[1] of Old English poetry, while the iambic element corresponds with the typical movement of the Greek senarius. And in the verse of *Paradise Lost* it is the iambic movement that prevails, especially perhaps in the first six books, which are cast more in the typically grand Miltonic manner than the second half of the poem, where the less impressive and less coherent interest of the subject is reflected in the style. But the measure of this iambic predominance depends on the degree to which the principle of elision of vowels applies.

"Elision" comprehends not merely the case where a vowel must be dropped altogether in pronunciation, but those more numerous cases where the metre indicates, or seems to indicate, that a vowel has *something* less than its normal quantitative value, so that it is either slurred or made almost to coalesce with a preceding or succeeding sound. Such elision resolves itself practically into cases of the open vowel and the vowel (or double vowel) followed by a liquid. Elision of the former type belongs to poetic usage, of the latter to the currency of everyday speech; and each is permissive, not obligatory. Moreover, elision is a matter of scansion, not necessarily of pronunciation and reading. It is, I think, perfectly true to say that "Milton came to scan his verses one way, and read them another". But is it not true of all poetic elision? Who knows what precisely happened to the elided vowels of Greek and Latin verse? Metrically their suppression

---

[1] Courthope. Compare also Mayor (*Modern English Metre*, p. 15): "Anapaestic rhythm was familiar to the Elizabethan poets, not merely from its use by older writers, such as the author of *Piers Ploughman*, but from the later 'tumbling verse' as used by Skelton and Udall." And again (p. 44): "Trisyllabic rhythm is a marked feature of the Old English alliterative verse, and of the 'tumbling measure' which followed it."

may have been absolute, as it is (I am told) in Greek MSS.:
but in actual declamation? Similarly, though I cannot
doubt that Milton scanned "th' Aonian mount" and
"th' oblivious pool", yet I should not like to say that he
read the words so. Nor should I like to have to determine
whether in scansion he extended this principle of the
elision of the open vowel beyond monosyllables like *the* and
to and the terminal *y* which slides so easily into a vowel at
the beginning of the next word. Thus it satisfies my "gross
unpurged ear" to scan "Who highly thus t' entitle me
vouchsaf'st" (x. 170); but to wrest an iambus out of the
second foot of the line "Virtue in her shape how lovely;
saw and pined" (IV. 848) by eliding the double vowel *ue*
("Virt*ue* in | her shape") seems a needless violence, when
the easy access of the anapæst ("Virtue | in her shape")
solves all. And so with many another line.

Some light is thrown on this difficult question of Milton's
elisions by the Cambridge autographs of his earlier poems.
The evidence, indeed, is not conclusive because the MSS.
are not consistent in giving always an elided form where
the metre requires one as an alternative to a trisyllabic
scansion. But one cannot help drawing some inference
from elisions like "Temper'd to th' oaten flute", and elided
forms such as *watrie—westring—batning—wandring—
toured*, and the many contractions of the inflections of
verbs, such as *honour'st—tun'st—forc't—nur'st—stoopt—
stolne—dan'ct*.[1] With some of these examples before us, it
is not hard to conjecture how Milton would have scanned,
say, *Paradise Lost*, XI. 779, "Wandering that watery desert;
I had hope". Similarly when we come across lines of the
epic in which *Heaven* appears to be equivalent to a mono-
syllable, it is apposite to remember that his autograph has
heavn in the prose draft of *Adam unparadiz'd* (line 2).
And *faln* in the prose draft of *Isaac redeemd* serves as a

---

[1] Cf. *Lycidas*, 4, 12, 23, 29, 31, 33; *Arcades*, 21; *Comus*, 39;
Sonnets II and XIII.

metrical gloss on 1. 84, "If thou beest he—but Oh how fallen! how changed!" The drift of such elisions and contractions is obviously to diminish the trisyllabic element, and maintain that iambic rhythm which was ever present[1] to Milton's ear and ever wafting the proud full sail of his verse.

[1] Two groups of exceptions to the general movement of his lines have been remarked, viz. passages where he indulges his taste for sonorous proper names, and passages "where he follows the Authorised Version of the Bible—especially where the speaker is the Deity".

PARADISE LOST

BOOK IX

THE ARGUMENT

SATAN, having compassed the Earth, with meditated guile returns as a mist by night into Paradise; enters into the Serpent sleeping. Adam and Eve in the morning go forth to their labours, which Eve proposes to divide in several places, each labouring apart: Adam consents not, alleging the danger, lest that enemy, of whom they were forewarned, should attempt her found alone. Eve, loth to be thought not circumspect or firm enough, urges her going apart, the rather desirous to make trial of her strength; Adam at last yields. The Serpent finds her alone: his subtle approach, first gazing, then speaking, with much flattery extolling Eve above all other creatures. Eve, wondering to hear the Serpent speak, asks how he attained to human speech and such understanding, not till now; the Serpent answers, that by tasting of a certain tree in the garden he attained both to speech and reason, till then void of both. Eve requires him to bring her to that tree, and finds it to be the Tree of Knowledge forbidden. The Serpent, now grown bolder, with many wiles and arguments induces her at length to eat; she, pleased with the taste, deliberates a while whether to impart thereof to Adam or not; at last brings him of the fruit; relates what persuaded her to eat thereof. Adam, at first amazed, but perceiving her lost, resolves through vehemence of love to perish with her; and, extenuating the trespass, eats also of the fruit. The effects thereof in them both; they seek to cover their nakedness; then fall to variance and accusation of one another.

PARADISE LOST

BOOK IX

No more of talk where God or Angel-guest
With Man, as with his friend, familiar used
To sit indulgent, and with him partake
Rural repast, permitting him the while
Venial discourse unblamed. I now must change
Those notes to tragic; foul distrust and breach
Disloyal on the part of man, revolt
And disobedience; on the part of Heaven,
Now alienated, distance and distaste,
Anger and just rebuke, and judgment given,   10
That brought into this World a world of woe,
Sin and her shadow Death, and Misery,
Death's harbinger. Sad task! yet argument
Not less but more heroic than the wrath
Of stern Achilles on his foe pursued
Thrice fugitive about Troy wall; or rage
Of Turnus for Lavinia disespoused;
Or Neptune's ire, or Juno's, that so long
Perplexed the Greek, and Cytherea's son:
If answerable style I can obtain   20
Of my celestial patroness, who deigns
Her nightly visitation unimplored,
And dictates to me slumbering, or inspires
Easy my unpremeditated verse,
Since first this subject for heroic song
Pleased me, long choosing and beginning late,
Not sedulous by nature to indite
Wars, hitherto the only argument
Heroic deemed, chief mastery to dissect
With long and tedious havoc fabled knights   30

In battles feigned (the better fortitude
Of patience and heroic martyrdom
Unsung), or to describe races and games,
Or tilting furniture, imblazoned shields,
Impresses quaint, caparisons and steeds,
Bases and tinsel trappings, gorgeous knights
At joust and tournament; then marshalled feast
Served up in hall with sewers and seneschals:
The skill of artifice or office mean;
Not that which justly gives heroic name
To person or to poem. Me, of these
Nor skilled nor studious, higher argument
Remains, sufficient of itself to raise
That name, unless an age too late, or cold
Climate, or years, damp my intended wing
Depressed; and much they may, if all be mine,
Not hers who brings it nightly to my ear.

   The sun was sunk, and after him the star
Of Hesperus, whose office is to bring
Twilight upon the Earth, short arbiter
'Twixt day and night, and now from end to end
Night's hemisphere had veiled the horizon round;
When Satan, who late fled before the threats
Of Gabriel out of Eden, now improved
In meditated fraud and malice, bent
On Man's destruction, maugre what might hap
Of heavier on himself, fearless returned.
By night he fled, and at midnight returned
From compassing the Earth; cautious of day,
Since Uriel, regent of the sun, descried
His entrance, and forewarned the Cherubim
That kept their watch. Thence, full of anguish, driven,
The space of seven continued nights he rode
With darkness; thrice the equinoctial line
He circled, four times crossed the car of Night

From pole to pole, traversing each colure;
On the eighth returned, and on the coast averse
From entrance or cherubic watch by stealth
Found unsuspected way. There was a place
(Now not, though sin, not time, first wrought the change) 70
Where Tigris, at the foot of Paradise,
Into a gulf shot under ground, till part
Rose up a fountain by the Tree of Life.
In with the river sunk, and with it rose,
Satan, involved in rising mist; then sought
Where to lie hid. Sea he had searched and land
From Eden over Pontus, and the pool
Mæotis, up beyond the river Ob;
Downward as far antarctic; and in length
West from Orontes to the ocean barred   80
At Darien, thence to the land where flows
Ganges and Indus. Thus the orb he roamed
With narrow search, and with inspection deep
Considered every creature, which of all
Most opportune might serve his wiles, and found
The serpent subtlest beast of all the field.
Him, after long debate, irresolute
Of thoughts revolved, his final sentence chose
Fit vessel, fittest imp of fraud, in whom
To enter, and his dark suggestions hide   90
From sharpest sight; for in the wily snake
Whatever sleights none would suspicious mark,
As from his wit and native subtlety
Proceeding, which, in other beasts observed,
Doubt might beget of diabolic power
Active within beyond the sense of brute.
Thus he resolved, but first from inward grief
His bursting passion into plaints thus poured:
    "O Earth, how like to Heaven, if not preferred
More justly, seat worthier of Gods, as built   100

With second thoughts, reforming what was old!
For what God, after better, worse would build?
Terrestrial Heaven, danced round by other Heavens
That shine, yet bear their bright officious lamps,
Light above light, for thee alone, as seems,
In thee concentring all their precious beams
Of sacred influence! As God in Heaven
Is centre, yet extends to all, so thou
Centring receiv'st from all those orbs; in thee,
Not in themselves, all their known virtue appears   11
Productive in herb, plant, and nobler birth
Of creatures animate with gradual life
Of growth, sense, reason, all summed up in Man.
With what delight could I have walked thee round,
If I could joy in aught, sweet interchange
Of hill and valley, rivers, woods, and plains,
Now land, now sea, and shores with forest crowned,
Rocks, dens, and caves! but I in none of these
Find place or refuge; and the more I see
Pleasures about me, so much more I feel   12
Torment within me, as from the hateful siége
Of contraries; all good to me becomes
Bane, and in Heaven much worse would be my state.
But neither here seek I, no, nor in Heaven
To dwell, unless by mastering Heaven's Supreme;
Nor hope to be myself less miserable
By what I seek, but others to make such
As I, though thereby worse to me redound:
For only in destroying I find ease
To my relentless thoughts; and, him destroyed,   1
Or won to what may work his utter loss,
For whom all this was made, all this will soon
Follow, as to him linked in weal or woe;
In woe then, that destruction wide may range!
To me shall be the glory sole among

The infernal Powers, in one day to have marred
What he, Almighty styled, six nights and days
Continued making, and who knows how long
Before had been contriving? though perhaps
Not longer than since I in one night freed   140
From servitude inglorious well nigh half
The Angelic name, and thinner left the throng
Of his adorers. He, to be avenged,
And to repair his numbers thus impaired—
Whether such virtue spent of old now failed
More Angels to create, if they at least
Are his created, or to spite us more—
Determined to advance into our room
A creature formed of earth, and him endow,
Exalted from so base original,   150
With Heavenly spoils, our spoils. What he decreed
He effected; Man he made, and for him built
Magnificent this World, and Earth his seat,
Him lord pronounced, and, O indignity!
Subjected to his service Angel-wings,
And flaming ministers to watch and tend
Their earthy charge. Of these the vigilance
I dread, and, to elude, thus wrapt in mist
Of midnight vapour glide obscure, and pry
In every bush and brake, where hap may find   160
The serpent sleeping, in whose mazy folds
To hide me, and the dark intent I bring.
O foul descent! that I, who erst contended
With Gods to sit the highest, am now constrained
Into a beast, and, mixed with bestial slime,
This essence to incarnate and imbrute,
That to the highth of deity aspired!
But what will not ambition and revenge
Descend to? Who aspires must down as low
As high he soared, obnoxious first or last   170

To basest things. Revenge, at first though sweet,
Bitter ere long back on itself recoils.
Let it; I reck not, so it light well aimed
(Since higher I fall short) on him who next
Provokes my envy, this new favourite
Of Heaven, this man of clay, son of despite,
Whom, us the more to spite, his Maker raised
From dust: spite then with spite is best repaid."
   So saying, through each thicket, dank or dry,
Like a black mist low-creeping, he held on   18(
His midnight search, where soonest he might find
The serpent. Him fast sleeping soon he found,
In labyrinth of many a round self-rolled,
His head the midst, well stored with subtle wiles:
Not yet in horrid shade or dismal den,
Nor nocent yet, but on the grassy herb,
Fearless, unfeared, he slept. In at his mouth
The Devil entered, and his brutal sense,
In heart or head, possessing soon inspired
With act intelligential; but his sleep   19(
Disturbed not, waiting close the approach of morn.
   Now, whenas sacred light began to dawn
In Eden on the humid flowers, that breathed
Their morning incense, when all things that breathe
From the Earth's great altar send up silent praise
To the Creator, and his nostrils fill
With grateful smell, forth came the human pair,
And joined their vocal worship to the quire
Of creatures wanting voice; that done, partake
The season, prime for sweetest scents and airs;   20(
Then commune how that day they best may ply
Their growing work; for much their work outgrew
The hands' dispatch of two, gardening so wide:
And Eve first to her husband thus began:
   "Adam, well may we labour still to dress

This garden, still to tend plant, herb, and flower,
Our pleasant task enjoined; but, till more hands
Aid us, the work under our labour grows,
Luxurious by restraint: what we by day
Lop overgrown, or prune, or prop, or bind,   210
One night or two with wanton growth derides,
Tending to wild. Thou therefore now advise,
Or hear what to my mind first thoughts present:
Let us divide our labours—thou where choice
Leads thee, or where most needs, whether to wind
The woodbine round this arbour, or direct
The clasping ivy where to climb; while I,
In yonder spring of roses intermixed
With myrtle, find what to redress till noon.
For, while so near each other thus all day   220
Our task we choose, what wonder if so near
Looks intervene and smiles, or object new
Casual discourse draw on, which intermits
Our day's work, brought to little, though begun
Early, and the hour of supper comes unearned!"
  To whom mild answer Adam thus returned:
"Sole Eve, associate sole, to me beyond
Compare above all living creatures dear!
Well hast thou motioned, well thy thoughts employed
How we might best fulfil the work which here   230
God hath assigned us, nor of me shalt pass
Unpraised; for nothing lovelier can be found
In woman than to study household good,
And good works in her husband to promote.
Yet not so strictly hath our Lord imposed
Labour, as to debar us when we need
Refreshment, whether food, or talk between
Food of the mind, or this sweet intercourse
Of looks and smiles; for smiles from reason flow,
To brute denied, and are of love the food—   240

Love, not the lowest end of human life.
For not to irksome toil, but to delight,
He made us, and delight to reason joined.
These paths and bowers doubt not but our joint hands
Will keep from wilderness with ease, as wide
As we need walk, till younger hands ere long
Assist us. But if much converse perhaps
Thee satiate, to short absence I could yield;
For solitude sometimes is best society,
And short retirement urges sweet return.   25
But other doubt possesses me, lest harm
Befall thee severed from me; for thou know'st
What hath been warned us, what malicious foe,
Envying our happiness, and of his own
Despairing, seeks to work us woe and shame
By sly assault; and somewhere nigh at hand
Watches, no doubt, with greedy hope to find
His wish and best advantage, us asunder,
Hopeless to circumvent us joined, where each
To other speedy aid might lend at need.   26
Whether his first design be to withdraw
Our feälty from God, or to disturb
Conjugal love, than which perhaps no bliss
Enjoyed by us excites his envy more;
Or this, or worse, leave not the faithful side
That gave thee being, still shades thee and protects.
The wife, where danger or dishonour lurks,
Safest and seemliest by her husband stays,
Who guards her, or with her the worst endures."

     To whom the virgin majesty of Eve,   27
As one who loves, and some unkindness meets,
With sweet austere composure thus replied:
     "Offspring of Heaven and Earth, and all Earth's lord!
That such an enemy we have, who seeks
Our ruin, both by thee informed I learn,

And from the parting Angel overheard,
As in a shady nook I stood behind,
Just then returned at shut of evening flowers.
But that thou shouldst my firmness therefore doubt
To God or thee, because we have a foe   280
May tempt it, I expected not to hear.
His violence thou fear'st not, being such
As we, not capable of death or pain,
Can either not receive, or can repel.
His fraud is then thy fear; which plain infers
Thy equal fear that my firm faith and love
Can by his fraud be shaken or seduced;
Thoughts, which how found they harbour in thy breast,
Adam! misthought of her to thee so dear?"

    To whom with healing words Adam replied: 290
"Daughter of God and Man, immortal Eve!
For such thou art, from sin and blame entire;
Not diffident of thee do I dissuade
Thy absence from my sight, but to avoid
The attempt itself, intended by our foe.
For he who tempts, though in vain, at least asperses
The tempted with dishonour foul, supposed
Not incorruptible of faith, not proof
Against temptation. Thou thyself with scorn
And anger wouldst resent the offered wrong,   300
Though ineffectual found; misdeem not then,
If such affront I labour to avert
From thee alone, which on us both at once
The enemy, though bold, will hardly dare,
Or daring, first on me the assault shall light.
Nor thou his malice and false guile contemn—
Subtle he needs must be, who could seduce
Angels—nor think superfluous others' aid.
I from the influence of thy looks receive
Access in every virtue; in thy sight   310

More wise, more watchful, stronger, if need were
Of outward strength; while shame, thou looking on,
Shame to be overcome or overreached,
Would utmost vigour raise, and raised unite.
Why shouldst not thou like sense within thee feel
When I am present, and thy trial choose
With me, best witness of thy virtue tried?"
    So spake domestic Adam in his care
And matrimonial love; but Eve, who thought
Less attributed to her faith sincere,   320
Thus her reply with accent sweet renewed:
    "If this be our condition thus to dwell
In narrow circuit straitened by a foe,
Subtle or violent, we not endued
Single with like defence wherever met,
How are we happy, still in fear of harm?
But harm precedes not sin: only our foe
Tempting affronts us with his foul esteem
Of our integrity; his foul esteem
Sticks no dishonour on our front, but turns   330
Foul on himself; then wherefore shunned or feared
By us? who rather double honour gain
From his surmise proved false, find peace within,
Favour from Heaven, our witness, from the event.
And what is faith, love, virtue, unassayed
Alone, without exterior help sustained?
Let us not then suspect our happy state
Left so imperfect by the Maker wise,
As not secure to single or combined.
Frail is our happiness, if this be so,   340
And Eden were no Eden, thus exposed."
    To whom thus Adam fervently replied:
"O Woman, best are all things as the will
Of God ordained them; his creating hand
Nothing imperfect or deficient left

Of all that he created, much less Man,
Or aught that might his happy state secure,
Secure from outward force: within himself
The danger lies, yet lies within his power;
Against his will he can receive no harm.   350
But God left free the will; for what obeys
Reason is free, and Reason he made right,
But bid her well be ware, and still erect,
Lest, by some fair appearing good surprised,
She dictate false, and misinform the will
To do what God expressly hath forbid.
Not then mistrust, but tender love, enjoins
That I should mind thee oft, and mind thou me.
Firm we subsist, yet possible to swerve,
Since Reason not impossibly may meet   360
Some specious object by the foe suborned,
And fall into deception unaware,
Not keeping strictest watch, as she was warned.
Seek not temptation then, which to avoid
Were better, and most likely if from me
Thou sever not: trial will come unsought.
Wouldst thou approve thy constancy, approve
First thy obedience; the other who can know,
Not seeing thee attempted, who attest?
But if thou think trial unsought may find   370
Us both securer than thus warned thou seem'st,
Go; for thy stay, not free, absents thee more;
Go in thy native innocence, rely
On what thou hast of virtue, summon all;
For God towards thee hath done his part; do thine."
     So spake the patriarch of mankind; but Eve
Persisted; yet submiss, though last, replied:
     "With thy permission then, and thus forewarned,
Chiefly by what thine own last reasoning words
Touched only, that our trial, when least sought,   380

May find us both perhaps far less prepared,
The willinger I go, nor much expect
A foe so proud will first the weaker seek;
So bent, the more shall shame him his repulse."
    Thus saying, from her husband's hand her hand
Soft she withdrew, and like a wood-nymph light,
Oread or Dryad, or of Delia's train,
Betook her to the groves, but Delia's self
In gait surpassed and goddess-like deport,
Though not as she with bow and quiver armed,   390
But with such gardening tools as art, yet rude,
Guiltless of fire, had formed, or Angels brought.
To Pales, or Pomona, thus adorned,
Likest she seemed—Pomona when she fled
Vertumnus—or to Ceres in her prime,
Yet virgin of Proserpina from Jove.
Her long with ardent look his eye pursued
Delighted, but desiring more her stay.
Oft he to her his charge of quick return
Repeated; she to him as oft engaged   400
To be returned by noon amid the bower,
And all things in best order to invite
Noontide repast, or afternoon's repose.
O much deceived, much failing, hapless Eve,
Of thy presumed return! event perverse!
Thou never from that hour in Paradise
Found'st either sweet repast or sound repose;
Such ambush, hid among sweet flowers and shades,
Waited with hellish rancour imminent
To intercept thy way, or send thee back   410
Despoiled of innocence, of faith, of bliss.
    For now, and since first break of dawn, the Fiend,
Mere serpent in appearance, forth was come,
And on his quest, where likeliest he might find
The only two of mankind, but in them

The whole included race, his purposed prey.
In bower and field he sought, where any tuft
Of grove or garden-plot more pleasant lay,
Their tendance or plantation for delight;
By fountain or by shady rivulet   420
He sought them both, but wished his hap might find
Eve separate; he wished, but not with hope
Of what so seldom chanced; when to his wish,
Beyond his hope, Eve separate he spies,
Veiled in a cloud of fragrance, where she stood,
Half-spied, so thick the roses bushing round
About her glowed, oft stooping to support
Each flower of tender stalk, whose head, though gay
Carnation, purple, azure, or specked with gold,
Hung drooping unsustained: them she upstays   430
Gently with myrtle band, mindless the while
Herself, though fairest unsupported flower,
From her best prop so far, and storm so nigh.
Nearer he drew, and many a walk traversed
Of stateliest covert, cedar, pine, or palm;
Then voluble and bold, now hid, now seen,
Among thick-woven arborets, and flowers
Imbordered on each bank, the hand of Eve:
Spot more delicious than those gardens feigned
Or of revived Adonis, or renowned   440
Alcinous, host of old Laertes' son,
Or that, not mystic, where the sapient king
Held dalliance with his fair Egyptian spouse.
Much he the place admired, the person more.
As one who, long in populous city pent,
Where houses thick and sewers annoy the air,
Forth issuing on a summer's morn to breathe
Among the pleasant villages and farms
Adjoined, from each thing met conceives delight—
The smell of grain, or tedded grass, or kine,   450

Or dairy, each rural sight, each rural sound;
If chance with nymph-like step fair virgin pass,
What pleasing seemed, for her now pleases more,
She most, and in her look sums all delight:
Such pleasure took the Serpent to behold
This flowery plat, the sweet recess of Eve
Thus early, thus alone. Her heavenly form
Angelic, but more soft and feminine,
Her graceful innocence, her every air
Of gesture or least action, overawed   46
His malice, and with rapine sweet bereaved
His fierceness of the fierce intent it brought:
That space the Evil One abstracted stood
From his own evil, and for the time remained
Stupidly good, of enmity disarmed,
Of guile, of hate, of envy, of revenge.
But the hot hell that always in him burns,
Though in mid Heaven, soon ended his delight,
And tortures him now more, the more he sees
Of pleasure not for him ordained; then soon   47
Fierce hate he recollects, and all his thoughts
Of mischief, gratulating, thus excites:
    "Thoughts, whither have ye led me? with what sweet
Compulsion thus transported to forget
What hither brought us? hate, not love, nor hope
Of Paradise for Hell, hope here to taste
Of pleasure, but all pleasure to destroy,
Save what is in destroying; other joy
To me is lost. Then let me not let pass
Occasion which now smiles: behold alone   48
The woman, opportune to all attempts,
Her husband, for I view far round, not nigh,
Whose higher intellectual more I shun,
And strength, of courage haughty, and of limb
Heroic built, though of terrestrial mould;

Foe not informidable, exempt from wound,
I not; so much hath Hell debased, and pain
Enfeebled me, to what I was in Heaven.
She fair, divinely fair, fit love for Gods,
Not terrible, though terror be in love   490
And beauty, not approached by stronger hate,
Hate stronger under show of love well feigned—
The way which to her ruin now I tend."
　So spake the Enemy of mankind, enclosed
In serpent, inmate bad, and toward Eve
Addressed his way—not with indented wave,
Prone on the ground, as since, but on his rear,
Circular base of rising folds, that towered
Fold above fold, a surging maze; his head
Crested aloft, and carbuncle his eyes;   500
With burnished neck of verdant gold, erect
Amidst his circling spires, that on the grass
Floated redundant. Pleasing was his shape
And lovely; never since of serpent kind
Lovelier; not those that in Illyria changed
Hermione and Cadmus, or the god
In Epidaurus; nor to which transformed
Ammonian Jove, or Capitoline, was seen,
He with Olympias, this with her who bore
Scipio, the highth of Rome. With tract oblique   510
At first, as one who sought access but feared
To interrupt, sidelong he works his way.
As when a ship by skilful steersman wrought
Nigh river's mouth or foreland, where the wind
Veers oft, as oft so steers, and shifts her sail:
So varied he, and of his tortuous train
Curled many a wanton wreath in sight of Eve,
To lure her eye; she, busied, heard the sound
Of rustling leaves, but minded not, as used
To such disport before her through the field,   520

From every beast, more duteous at her call,
Than at Circean call the herd disguised.
He, bolder now, uncalled before her stood,
But as in gaze admiring. Oft he bowed
His turret crest, and sleek enamelled neck,
Fawning, and licked the ground whereon she trod.
His gentle dumb expression turned at length
The eye of Eve to mark his play; he, glad
Of her attention gained, with serpent-tongue
Organic, or impulse of vocal air,   53
His fraudulent temptation thus began:
    "Wonder not, sovran mistress, if perhaps
Thou canst who art sole wonder; much less arm
Thy looks, the heaven of mildness, with disdain,
Displeased that I approach thee thus, and gaze
Insatiate, I thus single, nor have feared
Thy awful brow, more awful thus retired.
Fairest resemblance of thy Maker fair,
Thee all things living gaze on, all things thine
By gift, and thy celestial beauty adore,   54
With ravishment beheld—there best beheld
Where universally admired; but here
In this enclosure wild, these beasts among,
Beholders rude, and shallow to discern
Half what in thee is fair, one man except,
Who sees thee? (and what is one?) who shouldst be seen
A Goddess among Gods, adored and served
By Angels numberless, thy daily train."
    So glozed the Tempter, and his proem tuned;
Into the heart of Eve his words made way,   55
Though at the voice much marvelling; at length,
Not unamazed, she thus in answer spake:
    "What may this mean? Language of Man pronounced
By tongue of brute, and human sense expressed!
The first at least of these I thought denied

To beasts, whom God on their creation-day
Created mute to all articulate sound;
The latter I demur, for in their looks
Much reason, and in their actions, oft appears.
Thee, Serpent, subtlest beast of all the field   560
I knew, but not with human voice endued;
Redouble then this miracle, and say,
How cam'st thou speakable of mute, and how
To me so friendly grown above the rest
Of brutal kind, that daily are in sight:
Say, for such wonder claims attention due."
    To whom the guileful Tempter thus replied:
"Empress of this fair World, resplendent Eve!
Easy to me it is to tell thee all
What thou command'st, and right thou shouldst be
        obey'd.   570
I was at first as other beasts that graze
The trodden herb, of abject thoughts and low,
As was my food, nor aught but food discerned
Or sex, and apprehended nothing high:
Till on a day, roving the field, I chanced
A goodly tree far distant to behold,
Loaden with fruit of fairest colours mixed,
Ruddy and gold. I nearer drew to gaze;
When from the boughs a savoury odour blown,
Grateful to appetite, more pleased my sense   580
Than smell of sweetest fennel, or the teats
Of ewe or goat dropping with milk at even,
Unsucked of lamb or kid, that tend their play.
To satisfy the sharp desire I had
Of tasting those fair apples, I resolved
Not to defer; hunger and thirst at once,
Powerful persuaders, quickened at the scent
Of that alluring fruit, urged me so keen.
About the mossy trunk I wound me soon;

For, high from ground, the branches would require   59
Thy utmost reach or Adam's: round the tree
All other beasts that saw, with like desire
Longing and envying stood, but could not reach.
Amid the tree now got, where plenty hung
Tempting so nigh, to pluck and eat my fill
I spared not; for such pleasure till that hour
At feed or fountain never had I found.
Sated at length, ere long I might perceive
Strange alteration in me, to degree
Of reason in my inward powers, and speech   60
Wanted not long, though to this shape retained.
Thenceforth to speculations high or deep
I turned my thoughts, and with capacious mind
Considered all things visible in Heaven,
Or Earth, or middle, all things fair and good:
But all that fair and good in thy divine
Semblance, and in thy beauty's heavenly ray,
United I beheld; no fair to thine
Equivalent or second, which compelled
Me thus, though importune perhaps, to come   61
And gaze, and worship thee of right declared
Sovran of creatures, universal Dame!"
   So talked the spirited sly Snake; and Eve,
Yet more amazed, unwary thus replied:
   "Serpent, thy overpraising leaves in doubt
The virtue of that fruit, in thee first proved.
But say, where grows the tree? from hence how far?
For many are the trees of God that grow
In Paradise, and various, yet unknown
To us; in such abundance lies our choice,   62
As leaves a greater store of fruit untouched,
Still hanging incorruptible, till men
Grow up to their provision, and more hands
Help to disburden Nature of her birth."

To whom the wily Adder, blithe and glad:
"Empress, the way is ready, and not long;
Beyond a row of myrtles, on a flat,
Fast by a fountain, one small thicket past
Of blowing myrrh and balm: if thou accept
My conduct, I can bring thee thither soon."   630
    "Lead then," said Eve. He leading swiftly rolled
In tangles, and made intricate seem straight,
To mischief swift. Hope elevates, and joy
Brightens his crest. As when a wandering fire,
Compact of unctuous vapour, which the night
Condenses, and the cold environs round,
Kindled through agitation to a flame
(Which oft, they say, some evil spirit attends),
Hovering and blazing with delusive light,
Misleads the amazed night-wanderer from his way   640
To bogs and mires, and oft through pond or pool,
There swallowed up and lost, from succour far:
So glistered the dire Snake, and into fraud
Led Eve, our credulous mother, to the Tree
Of prohibition, root of all our woe;
Which when she saw, thus to her guide she spake:
    "Serpent, we might have spared our coming hither,
Fruitless to me, though fruit be here to excess,
The credit of whose virtue rest with thee;
Wondrous indeed, if cause of such effects!   650
But of this tree we may not taste nor touch;
God so commanded, and left that command
Sole daughter of his voice: the rest, we live
Law to ourselves; our reason is our law."
    To whom the Tempter guilefully replied:
"Indeed? Hath God then said that of the fruit
Of all these garden-trees ye shall not eat,
Yet lords declared of all in Earth or air?"
    To whom thus Eve, yet sinless: "Of the fruit

Of each tree in the garden we may eat;   6
But of the fruit of this fair tree amidst
The garden, God hath said, 'Ye shall not eat
Thereof, nor shall ye touch it, lest ye die.'"
    She scarce had said, though brief, when now more bold
The Tempter, but with show of zeal and love
To Man, and indignation at his wrong,
New part puts on, and, as to passion moved,
Fluctuates disturbed, yet comely, and in act
Raised, as of some great matter to begin.
As when of old some orator renowned   6
In Athens or free Rome, where eloquence
Flourished, since mute, to some great cause addressed,
Stood in himself collected, while each part,
Motion, each act, won audience ere the tongue,
Sometimes in highth began, as no delay
Of preface brooking through his zeal of right:
So standing, moving, or to highth upgrown,
The Tempter, all impassioned, thus began:
    "O sacred, wise, and wisdom-giving Plant,
Mother of science! now I feel thy power   6
Within me clear, not only to discern
Things in their causes, but to trace the ways
Of highest agents, deemed however wise.
Queen of this Universe! do not believe
Those rigid threats of death. Ye shall not die:
How should ye? by the fruit? it gives you life
To knowledge; by the threatener? look on me,
Me who have touched and tasted, yet both live,
And life more perfect have attained than Fate
Meant me, by venturing higher than my lot.   6
Shall that be shut to Man which to the beast
Is open? or will God incense his ire
For such a petty trespass, and not praise
Rather your dauntless virtue, whom the pain

Of death denounced, whatever thing death be,
Deterred not from achieving what might lead
To happier life, knowledge of good and evil?
Of good, how just! of evil—if what is evil
Be real, why not known, since easier shunned?
God therefore cannot hurt ye, and be just;   700
Not just, not God; not feared then, nor obeyed:
Your fear itself of death removes the fear.
Why then was this forbid? Why but to awe,
Why but to keep ye low and ignorant,
His worshippers? He knows that in the day
Ye eat thereof, your eyes that seem so clear,
Yet are but dim, shall perfectly be then
Opened and cleared, and ye shall be as Gods,
Knowing both good and evil, as they know.
That ye should be as Gods, since I as Man,   710
Internal Man, is but proportion meet:
I, of brute, human; ye, of human, Gods.
So ye shall die perhaps, by putting off
Human, to put on Gods; death to be wished,
Though threatened, which no worse than this can bring!
And what are Gods, that Man may not become
As they, participating godlike food?
The Gods are first, and that advantage use
On our belief, that all from them proceeds:
I question it; for this fair Earth I see,   720
Warmed by the sun, producing every kind,
Them nothing: if they all things, who enclosed
Knowledge of good and evil in this tree,
That whoso eats thereof forthwith attains
Wisdom without their leave? and wherein lies
The offence, that Man should thus attain to know?
What can your knowledge hurt him, or this tree
Impart against his will, if all be his?
Or is it envy? and can envy dwell

In Heavenly breasts? These, these and many more   7
Causes import your need of this fair fruit.
Goddess humane, reach then, and freely taste!"
   He ended, and his words, replete with guile,
Into her heart too easy entrance won.
Fixed on the fruit she gazed, which to behold
Might tempt alone, and in her ears the sound
Yet rung of his persuasive words, impregned
With reason, to her seeming, and with truth.
Meanwhile the hour of noon drew on, and waked
An eager appetite, raised by the smell   7·
So savoury of that fruit, which with desire,
Inclinable now grown to touch or taste,
Solicited her longing eye; yet first,
Pausing a while, thus to herself she mused:
   "Great are thy virtues, doubtless, best of fruits,
Though kept from Man, and worthy to be admired,
Whose taste, too long forborne, at first assay
Gave elocution to the mute, and taught
The tongue not made for speech to speak thy praise.
Thy praise he also who forbids thy use   75
Conceals not from us, naming thee the Tree
Of Knowledge, knowledge both of good and evil;
Forbids us then to taste; but his forbidding
Commends thee more, while it infers the good
By thee communicated, and our want;
For good unknown sure is not had, or had,
And yet unknown, is as not had at all.
In plain then, what forbids he but to know?
Forbids us good, forbids us to be wise!
Such prohibitions bind not. But if death   76
Bind us with after-bands, what profits then
Our inward freedom? In the day we eat
Of this fair fruit, our doom is, we shall die!
How dies the Serpent? He hath eaten and lives,

And knows, and speaks, and reasons, and discerns,
Irrational till then. For us alone
Was death invented? or to us denied
This intellectual food, for beasts reserved?
For beasts it seems; yet that one beast which first
Hath tasted envies not, but brings with joy   770
The good befallen him, author unsuspect,
Friendly to Man, far from deceit or guile.
What fear I then? rather, what know to fear
Under this ignorance of good and evil,
Of God or death, of law or penalty?
Here grows the cure of all, this fruit divine,
Fair to the eye, inviting to the taste,
Of virtue to make wise: what hinders then
To reach, and feed at once both body and mind?"
      So saying, her rash hand in evil hour   780
Forth reaching to the fruit, she plucked, she eat.
Earth felt the wound, and Nature from her seat,
Sighing through all her works, gave signs of woe
That all was lost. Back to the thicket slunk
The guilty Serpent, and well might, for Eve,
Intent now only on her taste, naught else
Regarded; such delight till then, as seemed,
In fruit she never tasted, whether true,
Or fancied so through expectation high
Of knowledge; nor was Godhead from her thought.   790
Greedily she ingorged without restraint,
And knew not eating death. Satiate at length,
And hightened as with wine, jocund and boon,
Thus to herself she pleasingly began:
      "O sovran, virtuous, precious of all trees
In Paradise! of operation blest
To sapience, hitherto obscured, infamed,
And thy fair fruit let hang, as to no end
Created! but henceforth my early care,

Not without song, each morning, and due praise,   8
Shall tend thee, and the fertile burden ease
Of thy full branches, offered free to all;
Till, dieted by thee, I grow mature
In knowledge, as the Gods who all things know;
Though others envy what they cannot give—
For, had the gift been theirs, it had not here
Thus grown! Experience, next to thee I owe,
Best guide: not following thee, I had remained
In ignorance: thou open'st Wisdom's way,
And giv'st access, though secret she retire.   8
And I perhaps am secret; Heaven is high,
High, and remote to see from thence distinct
Each thing on Earth; and other care perhaps
May have diverted from continual watch
Our great Forbidder, safe with all his spies
About him. But to Adam in what sort
Shall I appear? Shall I to him make known
As yet my change, and give him to partake
Full happiness with me, or rather not,
But keep the odds of knowledge in my power   8
Without copartner? so to add what wants
In female sex, the more to draw his love,
And render me more equal, and perhaps,
A thing not undesirable, sometime
Superior; for, inferior, who is free?
This may be well: but what if God have seen,
And death ensue? then I shall be no more,
And Adam, wedded to another Eve,
Shall live with her enjoying, I extinct!
A death to think! Confirmed then I resolve,   8
Adam shall share with me in bliss or woe:
So dear I love him, that with him all deaths
I could endure, without him live no life."
     So saying, from the tree her step she turned,

But first low reverence done, as to the Power
That dwelt within, whose presence had infused
Into the plant sciential sap, derived
From nectar, drink of Gods. Adam the while,
Waiting desirous her return, had wove
Of choicest flowers a garland, to adorn   840
Her tresses, and her rural labours crown,
As reapers oft are wont their harvest queen.
Great joy he promised to his thoughts, and new
Solace in her return, so long delayed;
Yet oft his heart, divine of something ill,
Misgave him; he the faltering measure felt,
And forth to meet her went, the way she took
That morn when first they parted. By the Tree
Of Knowledge he must pass; there he her met,
Scarce from the tree returning; in her hand   850
A bough of fairest fruit, that downy smiled,
New gathered, and ambrosial smell diffused.
To him she hasted; in her face excuse
Came prologue, and apology to prompt,
Which, with bland words at will, she thus addressed:
   "Hast thou not wondered, Adam, at my stay?
Thee I have missed, and thought it long, deprived
Thy presence—agony of love till now
Not felt, nor shall be twice; for never more
Mean I to try, what rash untried I sought,   860
The pain of absence from thy sight. But strange
Hath been the cause, and wonderful to hear.
This tree is not, as we are told, a tree
Of danger tasted, nor to evil unknown
Opening the way, but of divine effect
To open eyes, and make them Gods who taste;
And hath been tasted such. The Serpent wise,
Or not restrained as we, or not obeying,
Hath eaten of the fruit, and is become,

Not dead, as we are threatened, but thenceforth   87
Endued with human voice and human sense,
Reasoning to admiration, and with me
Persuasively hath so prevailed, that I
Have also tasted, and have also found
The effects to correspond—opener mine eyes,
Dim erst, dilated spirits, ampler heart,
And growing up to Godhead; which for thee
Chiefly I sought, without thee can despise.
For bliss, as thou hast part, to me is bliss;
Tedious, unshared with thee, and odious soon.   88
Thou therefore also taste, that equal lot
May join us, equal joy, as equal love;
Lest, thou not tasting, different degree
Disjoin us, and I then too late renounce
Deity for thee, when fate will not permit."
    Thus Eve with countenance blithe her story told;
But in her cheek distemper flushing glowed.
On the other side, Adam, soon as he heard
The fatal trespass done by Eve, amazed,
Astonied stood and blank, while horror chill   89
Ran through his veins, and all his joints relaxed;
From his slack hand the garland wreathed for Eve
Down dropt, and all the faded roses shed.
Speechless he stood and pale, till thus at length
First to himself he inward silence broke:
    "O fairest of creation, last and best
Of all God's works, creature in whom excelled
Whatever can to sight or thought be formed,
Holy, divine, good, amiable, or sweet!
How art thou lost! how on a sudden lost,   90
Defaced, deflowered, and now to death devote!
Rather, how hast thou yielded to transgress
The strict forbiddance, how to violate
The sacred fruit forbidden? Some cursed fraud

Of enemy hath beguiled thee, yet unknown,
And me with thee hath ruined; for with thee
Certain my resolution is to die:
How can I live without thee? how forgo
Thy sweet converse and love so dearly joined,
To live again in these wild woods forlorn?   910
Should God create another Eve, and I
Another rib afford, yet loss of thee
Would never from my heart; no, no! I feel
The link of nature draw me: flesh of flesh,
Bone of my bone thou art, and from thy state
Mine never shall be parted, bliss or woe."
   So having said, as one from sad dismay
Recomforted, and, after thoughts disturbed,
Submitting to what seemed remediless,
Thus in calm mood his words to Eve he turned: 920
   "Bold deed thou hast presumed, adventurous Eve,
And peril great provoked, who thus hast dared,
Had it been only coveting to eye
That sacred fruit, sacred to abstinence;
Much more to taste it, under ban to touch.
But past who can recall, or done undo?
Not God Omnipotent, nor Fate! Yet so
Perhaps thou shalt not die; perhaps the fact
Is not so heinous now—foretasted fruit,
Profaned first by the Serpent, by him first   930
Made common and unhallowed ere our taste,
Nor yet on him found deadly; he yet lives,
Lives, as thou saidst, and gains to live, as Man,
Higher degree of life: inducement strong
To us, as likely, tasting, to attain
Proportional ascent; which cannot be
But to be Gods, or Angels, demi-gods.
Nor can I think that God, Creator wise,
Though threatening, will in earnest so destroy

Us his prime creatures, dignified so high,   9

Set over all his works, which in our fall,

For us created, needs with us must fail,

Dependent made; so God shall uncreate,

Be frustrate, do, undo, and labour lose;

Not well conceived of God, who, though his power

Creation could repeat, yet would be loth

Us to abolish, lest the Adversary

Triumph and say: 'Fickle their state whom God

Most favours; who can please him long? Me first

He ruined, now mankind; whom will he next?'   9

Matter of scorn not to be given the Foe.

However, I with thee have fixed my lot,

Certain to undergo like doom: if death

Consort with thee, death is to me as life;

So forcible within my heart I feel

The bond of nature draw me to my own,

My own in thee, for what thou art is mine.

Our state cannot be severed; we are one,

One flesh; to lose thee were to lose myself."

So Adam, and thus Eve to him replied: 9

"O glorious trial of exceeding love,

Illustrious evidence, example high!

Engaging me to emulate; but, short

Of thy perfection, how shall I attain,

Adam? from whose dear side I boast me sprung,

And gladly of our union hear thee speak,

One heart, one soul in both; whereof good proof

This day affords, declaring thee resolved,

Rather than death, or aught than death more dread,

Shall separate us, linked in love so dear,   9

To undergo with me one guilt, one crime,

If any be, of tasting this fair fruit;

Whose virtue (for of good still good proceeds,

Direct, or by occasion) hath presented

This happy trial of thy love, which else
So eminently never had been known.
Were it I thought death menaced would ensue
This my attempt, I would sustain alone
The worst, and not persuade thee, rather die
Deserted, than oblige thee with a fact   980
Pernicious to thy peace, chiefly assured
Remarkably so late of thy so true,
So faithful love unequalled; but I feel
Far otherwise the event—not death, but life
Augmented, opened eyes, new hopes, new joys,
Taste so divine, that what of sweet before
Hath touched my sense flat seems to this and harsh.
On my experience, Adam, freely taste,
And fear of death deliver to the winds."
    So saying, she embraced him, and for joy   990
Tenderly wept, much won that he his love
Had so ennobled, as of choice to incur
Divine displeasure for her sake, or death.
In recompense (for such compliance bad
Such recompense best merits), from the bough
She gave him of that fair enticing fruit
With liberal hand; he scrupled not to eat,
Against his better knowledge, not deceived,
But fondly overcome with female charm.
Earth trembled from her entrails, as again   1000
In pangs, and Nature gave a second groan;
Sky loured, and, muttering thunder, some sad drops
Wept at completing of the mortal sin
Original; while Adam took no thought,
Eating his fill, nor Eve to iterate
Her former trespass feared, the more to soothe
Him with her loved society; that now,
As with new wine intoxicated both,
They swim in mirth, and fancy that they feel

Divinity within them breeding wings   101
Wherewith to scorn the Earth. But that false fruit
Far other operation first displayed,
Carnal desire inflaming: he on Eve
Began to cast lascivious eyes; she him
As wantonly repaid; in lust they burn,
Till Adam thus 'gan Eve to dalliance move:
    "Eve, now I see thou art exact of taste,
And elegant, of sapience no small part;
Since to each meaning savour we apply,
And palate call judicious. I the praise   102
Yield thee, so well this day thou hast purveyed.
Much pleasure we have lost, while we abstained
From this delightful fruit, nor known till now
True relish, tasting; if such pleasure be
In things to us forbidden, it might be wished
For this one tree had been forbidden ten.
But come; so well refreshed, now let us play,
As meet is, after such delicious fare;
For never did thy beauty, since the day
I saw thee first and wedded thee, adorned   103
With all perfections, so inflame my sense
With ardour to enjoy thee, fairer now
Than ever—bounty of this virtuous tree!"
    So said he, and forbore not glance or toy
Of amorous intent, well understood
Of Eve, whose eye darted contagious fire.
Her hand he seized, and to a shady bank,
Thick overhead with verdant roof embowered,
He led her, nothing loth; flowers were the couch,
Pansies, and violets, and asphodel,   104
And hyacinth—Earth's freshest, softest lap.
There they their fill of love and love's disport
Took largely, of their mutual guilt the seal,
The solace of their sin, till dewy sleep

Oppressed them, wearied with their amorous play.
  Soon as the force of that fallacious fruit,
That with exhilarating vapour bland
About their spirits had played, and inmost powers
Made err, was now exhaled, and grosser sleep,
Bred of unkindly fumes, with conscious dreams   1050
Encumbered, now had left them, up they rose
As from unrest, and, each the other viewing,
Soon found their eyes how opened, and their minds
How darkened. Innocence, that as a veil
Had shadowed them from knowing ill, was gone;
Just confidence, and native righteousness,
And honour, from about them, naked left
To guilty Shame: he covered, but his robe
Uncovered more. So rose the Danite strong,
Herculean Samson, from the harlot-lap   1060
Of Philistean Dalilah, and wak'd
Shorn of his strength; they destitute and bare
Of all their virtue. Silent, and in face
Confounded, long they sat, as strucken mute;
Till Adam, though not less than Eve abashed,
At length gave utterance to these words constrained:
  "O Eve, in evil hour thou didst give ear
To that false worm, of whomsoever taught
To counterfeit Man's voice, true in our fall,
False in our promised rising; since our eyes   1070
Opened we find indeed, and find we know
Both good and evil, good lost and evil got:
Bad fruit of knowledge, if this be to know,
Which leaves us naked thus, of honour void,
Of innocence, of faith, of purity,
Our wonted ornaments now soiled and stained,
And in our faces evident the signs
Of foul concupiscence; whence evil store,
Even shame, the last of evils; of the first

Be sure then. How shall I behold the face   10
Henceforth of God or Angel, erst with joy
And rapture so oft beheld? those Heavenly shapes
Will dazzle now this earthly with their blaze
Insufferably bright. Oh, might I here
In solitude live savage, in some glade
Obscured, where highest woods, impenetrable
To star or sunlight, spread their umbrage broad,
And brown as evening! Cover me, ye pines!
Ye cedars, with innumerable boughs
Hide me, where I may never see them more!   10
But let us now, as in bad plight, devise
What best may for the present serve to hide
The parts of each from other that seem most
To shame obnoxious, and unseemliest seen;
Some tree, whose broad smooth leaves together sewed,
And girded on our loins, may cover round
Those middle parts, that this new comer, Shame,
There sit not, and reproach us as unclean."
    So counselled he, and both together went
Into the thickest wood; there soon they chose   11
The fig-tree—not that kind for fruit renowned,
But such as at this day, to Indians known,
In Malabar or Decan spreads her arms
Branching so broad and long that in the ground
The bended twigs take root, and daughters grow
About the mother tree, a pillared shade
High overarched, and echoing walks between:
There oft the Indian herdsman, shunning heat,
Shelters in cool, and tends his pasturing herds
At loop-holes cut through thickest shade. Those leaves   11
They gathered, broad as Amazonian targe,
And with what skill they had together sewed,
To gird their waist; vain covering, if to hide
Their guilt and dreaded shame! Oh how unlike

To that first naked glory! Such of late
Columbus found the American, so girt
With feathered cincture, naked else and wild
Among the trees on isles and woody shores.
Thus fenced, and, as they thought, their shame in part
Covered, but not at rest or ease of mind,   1120
They sat them down to weep; nor only tears
Rained at their eyes, but high winds worse within
Began to rise, high passions, anger, hate,
Mistrust, suspicion, discord, and shook sore
Their inward state of mind, calm region once
And full of peace, now tost and turbulent:
For Understanding ruled not, and the Will
Heard not her lore, both in subjection now
To sensual Appetite, who, from beneath
Usurping over sovran Reason, claimed   1130
Superior sway. From thus distempered breast
Adam, estranged in look and altered style,
Speech intermitted thus to Eve renewed:
    "Would thou hadst hearkened to my words, and stayed
With me, as I besought thee, when that strange
Desire of wandering, this unhappy morn,
I know not whence possessed thee! we had then
Remained still happy, not, as now, despoiled
Of all our good, shamed, naked, miserable!
Let none henceforth seek needless cause to approve   1140
The faith they owe; when earnestly they seek
Such proof, conclude, they then begin to fail."
    To whom, soon moved with touch of blame, thus Eve:
"What words have passed thy lips, Adam severe!
Imput'st thou that to my default, or will
Of wandering, as thou call'st it, which who knows
But might as ill have happened, thou being by,
Or to thyself perhaps? Hadst thou been there,
Or here the attempt, thou couldst not have discerned

Fraud in the Serpent, speaking as he spake;   11
No ground of enmity between us known,   ˙
Why he should mean me ill, or seek to harm.
Was I to have never parted from thy side?
As good have grown there still, a lifeless rib.
Being as I am, why didst not thou, the head,
Command me absolutely not to go,
Going into such danger, as thou saidst?
Too facile then, thou didst not much gainsay,
Nay, didst permit, approve, and fair dismiss.
Hadst thou been firm and fixed in thy dissent,   11●
Neither had I transgressed, nor thou with me."
    To whom, then first incensed, Adam replied:
"Is this the love, is this the recompense
Of mine to thee, ingrateful Eve, expressed
Immutable when thou wert lost, not I,
Who might have lived, and joyed immortal bliss,
Yet willingly chose rather death with thee?
And am I now upbraided as the cause
Of thy transgressing? not enough severe,
It seems, in thy restraint! What could I more?   11⁷
I warned thee, I admonished thee, foretold
The danger, and the lurking enemy
That lay in wait; beyond this had been force,
And force upon free will hath here no place.
But confidence then bore thee on, secure
Either to meet no danger, or to find
Matter of glorious trial; and perhaps
I also erred in overmuch admiring
What seemed in thee so perfect, that I thought
No evil durst attempt thee; but I rue   18●
That error now, which is become my crime,
And thou the accuser. Thus it shall befall
Him who, to worth in women overtrusting,
Lets her will rule: restraint she will not brook;

And, left to herself, if evil thence ensue,
She first his weak indulgence will accuse."
   Thus they in mutual accusation spent
The fruitless hours, but neither self-condemning;
And of their vain contest appeared no end.

PARADISE LOST

BOOK X

THE ARGUMENT

MAN's transgression known, the guardian Angels forsake Paradise, and return up to Heaven to approve their vigilance, and are approved; God declaring that the entrance of Satan could not be by them prevented. He sends his Son to judge the transgressors; who descends, and gives sentence accordingly; then in pity clothes them both, and reascends. Sin and Death, sitting till then at the gates of Hell, by wondrous sympathy feeling the success of Satan in this new World, and the sin by Man there committed, resolve to sit no longer confined in Hell, but to follow Satan, their sire, up to the place of Man. To make the way easier from Hell to this World to and fro, they pave a broad highway or bridge over Chaos, according to the track that Satan first made; then, preparing for Earth, they meet him, proud of his success, returning to Hell; their mutual gratulation. Satan arrives at Pandemonium; in full assembly relates, with boasting, his success against Man; instead of applause is entertained with a general hiss by all his audience, transformed, with himself also, suddenly into serpents, according to his doom given in Paradise; then, deluded with a show of the Forbidden Tree springing up before them, they, greedily reaching to take of the fruit, chew dust and bitter ashes. The proceedings of Sin and Death: God foretells the final victory of his Son over them, and the renewing of all things; but for the present commands his Angels to make several alterations in the heavens and elements. Adam, more and more perceiving his fallen condition, heavily bewails, rejects the condolement of Eve; she persists, and at length appeases him: then, to evade the curse likely to fall on their offspring, proposes to Adam violent ways, which he approves not, but, conceiving better hope, puts her in mind of the late promise made them, that her seed should be revenged on the Serpent, and exhorts her, with him, to seek peace of the offended Deity by repentance and supplication.

PARADISE LOST

BOOK X

MEANWHILE the heinous and despiteful act
Of Satan done in Paradise, and how
He, in the Serpent, had perverted Eve,
Her husband she, to taste the fatal fruit,
Was known in Heaven; for what can scape the eye
Of God all-seeing, or deceive his heart
Omniscient? who, in all things wise and just,
Hindered not Satan to attempt the mind
Of Man, with strength entire and free will armed,
Complete to have discovered and repulsed   10
Whatever wiles of foe or seeming friend.
For still they knew, and ought to have still remembered,
The high injunction not to taste that fruit,
Whoever tempted; which they not obeying
Incurred (what could they less?) the penalty,
And, manifold in sin, deserved to fall.

　　Up into Heaven from Paradise in haste
The Angelic guards ascended, mute and sad
For Man; for of his state by this they knew,
Much wondering how the subtle Fiend had stolen   20
Entrance unseen. Soon as the unwelcome news
From Earth arrived at Heaven-gate, displeased
All were who heard; dim sadness did not spare
That time celestial visages, yet, mixed
With pity, violated not their bliss.
About the new-arrived, in multitudes,
The ethereal people ran, to hear and know
How all befell. They towards the throne supreme
Accountable made haste to make appear
With righteous plea their utmost vigilance,   30

And easily approved; when the Most High
Eternal Father, from his secret cloud
Amidst, in thunder uttered thus his voice:
   "Assembled Angels, and ye Powers returned
From unsuccessful charge, be not dismayed,
Nor troubled at these tidings from the Earth,
Which your sincerest care could not prevent,
Foretold so lately what would come to pass,
When first this Tempter crossed the gulf from Hell.
I told ye then he should prevail and speed   4
On his bad errand; Man should be seduced
And flattered out of all, believing lies
Against his Maker; no decree of mine
Concurring to necessitate his fall,
Or touch with lightest moment of impulse
His free will, to her own inclining left
In even scale. But fallen he is; and now
What rests, but that the mortal sentence pass
On his transgression, death denounced that day?
Which he presumes already vain and void,   5
Because not yet inflicted, as he feared,
By some immediate stroke; but soon shall find
Forbearance no acquittance ere day end:
Justice shall not return, as bounty, scorned.
But whom send I to judge them? whom but thee,
Vicegerent Son? to thee I have transferred
All judgment, whether in Heaven, or Earth, or Hell.
Easy it may be seen that I intend
Mercy colleague with justice, sending thee,
Man's friend, his Mediator, his designed   6
Both ransom and Redeemer voluntary,
And destined Man himself to judge Man fallen."
   So spake the Father; and, unfolding bright
Toward the right hand his glory, on the Son
Blazed forth unclouded deity; he full

Resplendent all his Father manifest
Expressed, and thus divinely answered mild:
  "Father Eternal, thine is to decree,
Mine both in Heaven and Earth to do thy will
Supreme, that thou in me, thy Son beloved,   70
May'st ever rest well pleased. I go to judge
On Earth these thy transgressors; but thou know'st,
Whoever judged, the worst on me must light,
When time shall be; for so I undertook
Before thee, and, not repenting, this obtain
Of right, that I may mitigate their doom
On me derived; yet I shall temper so
Justice with mercy, as may illustrate most
Them fully satisfied, and thee appease.
Attendance none shall need, nor train, where none   80
Are to behold the judgment but the judged,
Those two; the third best absent is condemned,
Convict by flight, and rebel to all law:
Conviction to the Serpent none belongs."
  Thus saying, from his radiant seat he rose
Of high collateral glory; Him Thrones and Powers,
Princedoms, and Dominations ministrant
Accompanied to Heaven-gate, from whence
Eden and all the coast in prospect lay.
Down he descended straight; the speed of Gods   90
Time counts not, though with swiftest minutes winged.
  Now was the sun in western cadence low
From noon, and gentle airs due at their hour
To fan the Earth now waked, and usher in
The evening cool, when he, from wrath more cool,
Came, the mild Judge and Intercessor both,
To sentence Man. The voice of God they heard
Now walking in the garden, by soft winds
Brought to their ears, while day declined; they heard,
And from his presence hid themselves among   100

The thickest trees, both man and wife, till God,
Approaching, thus to Adam called aloud:
  "Where art thou, Adam, wont with joy to meet
My coming seen far off? I miss thee here,
Not pleased, thus entertained with solitude,
Where obvious duty erewhile appeared unsought.
Or come I less conspicuous, or what change
Absents thee, or what chance detains? Come forth."
  He came, and with him Eve, more loth, though first
To offend, discountenanced both, and discomposed;   110
Love was not in their looks, either to God
Or to each other, but apparent guilt,
And shame, and perturbation, and despair,
Anger, and obstinacy, and hate, and guile.
Whence Adam, faltering long, thus answered brief:
  "I heard thee in the garden, and of thy voice
Afraid, being naked, hid myself." To whom
The gracious Judge without revile replied:
  "My voice thou oft hast heard, and hast not feared,
But still rejoiced; how is it now become   120
So dreadful to thee? That thou art naked, who
Hath told thee? Hast thou eaten of the tree,
Whereof I gave thee charge thou shouldst not eat?"
  To whom thus Adam, sore beset, replied:
  "O Heaven! in evil strait this day I stand
Before my Judge—either to undergo
Myself the total crime, or to accuse
My other self, the partner of my life;
Whose failing, while her faith to me remains,
I should conceal, and not expose to blame   130
By my complaint; but strict necessity
Subdues me, and calamitous constraint,
Lest on my head both sin and punishment,
However insupportable, be all
Devolved; though should I hold my peace, yet thou

Wouldst easily detect what I conceal.
This woman, whom thou mad'st to be my help,
And gav'st me as thy perfect gift, so good,
So fit, so acceptable, so divine,
That from her hand I could suspect no ill,   140
And what she did, whatever in itself,
Her doing seemed to justify the deed;
She gave me of the tree, and I did eat."
   To whom the Sovran Presence thus replied:
   "Was she thy God, that her thou didst obey
Before his voice? or was she made thy guide,
Superior, or but equal, that to her
Thou didst resign thy manhood, and the place
Wherein God set thee above her, made of thee
And for thee, whose perfection far excelled   150
Hers in all real dignity? Adorned
She was indeed, and lovely, to attract
Thy love, not thy subjection; and her gifts
Were such as under government well seemed,
Unseemly to bear rule; which was thy part
And person, hadst thou known thyself aright."
   So having said, he thus to Eve in few:
"Say, Woman, what is this which thou hast done?"
   To whom sad Eve, with shame nigh overwhelmed,
Confessing soon, yet not before her Judge   160
Bold or loquacious, thus abashed replied:
"The Serpent me beguiled, and I did eat."
   Which when the Lord God heard, without delay
To judgment he proceeded on the accused
Serpent, though brute, unable to transfer
The guilt on him who made him instrument
Of mischief, and polluted from the end
Of his creation; justly then accursed,
As vitiated in nature. More to know
Concerned not Man (since he no further knew),   170

Nor altered his offence; yet God at last
To Satan, first in sin, his doom applied,
Though in mysterious terms, judged as then best;
And on the Serpent thus his curse let fall:
    "Because thou hast done this, thou art accursed
Above all cattle, each beast of the field;
Upon thy belly grovelling thou shalt go,
And dust shalt eat all the days of thy life.
Between thee and the Woman I will put
Enmity, and between thine and her seed;   18
Her seed shall bruise thy head, thou bruise his heel."
    So spake this oracle, then verified
When Jesus, son of Mary, second Eve,
Saw Satan fall like lightning down from Heaven,
Prince of the air; then, rising from his grave,
Spoiled Principalities and Powers, triumphed
In open show, and with ascension bright
Captivity led captive through the air,
The realm itself of Satan long usurped,
Whom he shall tread at last under our feet;   19
Even he who now foretold his fatal bruise,
And to the Woman thus his sentence turned:
    "Thy sorrow I will greatly multiply
By thy conception; children thou shalt bring
In sorrow forth; and to thy husband's will
Thine shall submit; he over thee shall rule."
    On Adam last thus judgment he pronounced:
"Because thou hast hearkened to the voice of thy wife,
And eaten of the tree, concerning which
I charged thee, saying, 'Thou shalt not eat thereof,'   20
Curs'd is the ground for thy sake; thou in sorrow
Shalt eat thereof all the days of thy life;
Thorns also and thistles it shall bring thee forth
Unbid; and thou shalt eat the herb of the field;
In the sweat of thy face shalt thou eat bread,

Till thou return unto the ground; for thou
Out of the ground wast taken: know thy birth,
For dust thou art, and shalt to dust return."
  So judged he Man, both Judge and Saviour sent,
And the instant stroke of death, denounced that day,   210
Removed far off; then, pitying how they stood
Before him naked to the air, that now
Must suffer change, disdained not to begin
Thenceforth the form of servant to assume;
As when he washed his servants' feet, so now,
As father of his family, he clad
Their nakedness with skins of beasts, or slain,
Or as the snake with youthful coat repaid;
And thought not much to clothe his enemies.
Nor he their outward only with the skins   220
Of beasts, but inward nakedness, much more
Opprobrious, with his robe of righteousness
Arraying, covered from his Father's sight.
To him with swift ascent he up returned,
Into his blissful bosom reassumed
In glory as of old; to him appeased,
All, though all-knowing, what had passed with Man
Recounted, mixing intercession sweet.
  Meanwhile, ere thus was sinned and judged on Earth,
Within the gates of Hell sat Sin and Death,   230
In counterview within the gates, that now
Stood open wide, belching outrageous flame
Far into Chaos, since the Fiend passed through,
Sin opening; who thus now to Death began:
  "O Son, why sit we here each other viewing
Idly, while Satan, our great author, thrives
In other worlds, and happier seat provides
For us, his offspring dear? It cannot be
But that success attends him; if mishap,
Ere this he had returned, with fury driven   240

By his avengers, since no place like this
Can fit his punishment, or their revenge.
Methinks I feel new strength within me rise,
Wings growing, and dominion given me large
Beyond this Deep, whatever draws me on,
Or sympathy, or some connatural force,
Powerful at greatest distance to unite
With secret amity things of like kind
By secretest conveyance. Thou, my shade
Inseparable, must with me along;   25
For Death from Sin no power can separate.
But, lest the difficulty of passing back
Stay his return perhaps over this gulf
Impassable, impervious, let us try
Adventurous work, yet to thy power and mine
Not unagreeable, to found a path
Over this main from Hell to that new World
Where Satan now prevails; a monument
Of merit high to all the infernal host,
Easing their passage hence, for intercourse   26
Or transmigration, as their lot shall lead.
Nor can I miss the way, so strongly drawn
By this new-felt attraction and instinct."
    Whom thus the meagre Shadow answered soon:
"Go whither fate and inclination strong
Leads thee; I shall not lag behind, nor err
The way, thou leading; such a scent I draw
Of carnage, prey innumerable, and taste
The savour of death from all things there that live.
Nor shall I to the work thou enterprisest   27
Be wanting, but afford thee equal aid."
    So saying, with delight he snuffed the smell
Of mortal change on Earth. As when a flock
Of ravenous fowl, though many a league remote,
Against the day of battle, to a field,

Where armies lie encamped, come flying, lured
With scent of living carcases designed
For death the following day in bloody fight:
So scented the grim Feature, and upturned
His nostril wide into the murky air,   280
Sagacious of his quarry from so far.
Then both, from out Hell-gates, into the waste
Wide anarchy of Chaos damp and dark
Flew diverse, and with power (their power was great)
Hovering upon the waters, what they met
Solid or slimy, as in raging sea
Tossed up and down, together crowded drove,
From each side shoaling, towards the mouth of Hell;
As when two polar winds, blowing adverse
Upon the Cronian sea, together drive   290
Mountains of ice, that stop the imagined way
Beyond Petsora eastward, to the rich
Cathaian coast. The aggregated soil
Death with his mace petrific, cold and dry,
As with a trident smote, and fixed as firm
As Delos, floating once; the rest his look
Bound with Gorgonian rigour not to move,
And with asphaltic slime; broad as the gate
Deep to the roots of Hell the gathered beach
They fastened, and the mole immense wrought on   300
Over the foaming Deep high-arched, a bridge
Of length prodigious, joining to the wall
Immovable of this now fenceless World,
Forfeit to Death; from hence a passage broad,
Smooth, easy, inoffensive, down to Hell.
So, if great things to small may be compared,
Xerxes, the liberty of Greece to yoke,
From Susa, his Memnonian palace high,
Came to the sea, and, over Hellespont
Bridging his way, Europe with Asia joined,   310

And scourged with many a stroke the indignant waves.
Now had they brought the work by wondrous art
Pontifical, a ridge of pendent rock,
Over the vexed Abyss, following the track
Of Satan, to the self-same place where he
First lighted from his wing, and landed safe
From out of Chaos, to the outside bare
Of this round World. With pins of adamant
And chains they made all fast, too fast they made
And durable; and now in little space   3
The confines met of empyrean Heaven
And of this World, and on the left hand Hell
With long reach interposed; three several ways,
In sight, to each of these three places led.
And now their way to Earth they had descried,
To Paradise first tending, when, behold
Satan, in likeness of an Angel bright,
Betwixt the Centaur and the Scorpion steering
His zenith, while the sun in Aries rose!
Disguised he came; but those his children dear   3
Their parent soon discerned, though in disguise.
He, after Eve seduced, unminded slunk
Into the wood fast by, and, changing shape
To observe the sequel, saw his guileful act
By Eve, though all unweeting, seconded
Upon her husband, saw their shame that sought
Vain covertures; but when he saw descend
The Son of God to judge them, terrified
He fled, not hoping to escape, but shun
The present, fearing guilty what his wrath   3
Might suddenly inflict; that past, returned
By night, and listening where the hapless pair
Sat in their sad discourse and various plaint,
Thence gathered his own doom; which understood
Not instant, but of future time, with joy

And tidings fraught, to Hell he now returned,
And at the brink of Chaos, near the foot
Of this new wondrous pontifice, unhoped
Met who to meet him came, his offspring dear.
Great joy was at their meeting, and at sight   350
Of that stupendous bridge his joy increased.
Long he admiring stood, till Sin, his fair
Enchanting daughter, thus the silence broke:
    "O Parent, these are thy magnific deeds,
Thy trophies, which thou view'st as not thine own;
Thou art their author and prime architect;
For I no sooner in my heart divined
(My heart, which by a secret harmony
Still moves with thine, joined in connexion sweet)
That thou on Earth hadst prospered, which thy looks   360
Now also evidence, but straight I felt,
Though distant from thee worlds between, yet felt
That I must after thee with this thy son;
Such fatal consequence unites us three.
Hell could no longer hold us in her bounds,
Nor this unvoyageable gulf obscure
Detain from following thy illustrious track.
Thou hast achieved our liberty, confined
Within Hell-gates till now; thou us empowered
To fortify thus far, and overlay   370
With this portentous bridge the dark Abyss.
Thine now is all this World; thy virtue hath won
What thy hands builded not, thy wisdom gained
With odds what war hath lost, and fully avenged
Our foil in Heaven: here thou shalt monarch reign,
There didst not; there let him still victor sway,
As battle hath adjudged, from this new World
Retiring, by his own doom alienated,
And henceforth monarchy with thee divide
Of all things, parted by the empyreal bounds,   380

His quadrature, from thy orbicular World,
Or try thee now more dangerous to his throne."
　Whom thus the Prince of Darkness answered glad:
"Fair daughter, and thou son and grandchild both,
High proof ye now have given to be the race
Of Satan (for I glory in the name,
Antagonist of Heaven's Almighty King),
Amply have merited of me, of all
The infernal empire, that so near Heaven's door
Triumphal with triumphal act have met,　　　　　　　3
Mine with this glorious work, and made one realm
Hell and this World—one realm, one continent
Of easy thoroughfare. Therefore, while I
Descend through darkness, on your road with ease,
To my associate Powers, them to acquaint
With these successes, and with them rejoice,
You two this way, among these numerous orbs,
All yours, right down to Paradise descend;
There dwell and reign in bliss; thence on the Earth
Dominion exercise and in the air,　　　　　　　　　4
Chiefly on Man, sole lord of all declared;
Him first make sure your thrall, and lastly kill.
My substitutes I send ye, and create
Plenipotent on Earth, of matchless might
Issuing from me: on your joint vigour now
My hold of this new kingdom all depends,
Through Sin to Death exposed by my exploit.
If your joint power prevail, the affairs of Hell
No detriment need fear; go, and be strong."
　So saying, he dismissed them; they with speed　　4
Their course through thickest constellations held,
Spreading their bane; the blasted stars looked wan,
And planets, planet-struck, real eclipse
Then suffered. The other way Satan went down
The causey to Hell-gate; on either side

Disparted Chaos over-built exclaimed,
And with rebounding surge the bars assailed,
That scorned his indignation. Through the gate,
Wide open and unguarded, Satan passed,
And all about found desolate; for those   420
Appointed to sit there had left their charge,
Flown to the upper World; the rest were all
Far to the inland retired, about the walls
Of Pandemonium, city and proud seat
Of Lucifer, so by allusion called
Of that bright star to Satan paragoned;
There kept their watch the legions, while the Grand
In council sat, solicitous what chance
Might intercept their Emperor sent; so he
Departing gave command, and they observed.   430
As when the Tartar from his Russian foe,
By Astracan, over the snowy plains
Retires, or Bactrian Sophi, from the horns
Of Turkish crescent, leaves all waste beyond
The realm of Aladule, in his retreat
To Tauris or Casbeen: so these, the late
Heaven-banished host, left desert utmost Hell
Many a dark league, reduced in careful watch
Round their metropolis, and now expecting
Each hour their great adventurer from the search   440
Of foreign worlds. He through the midst unmarked,
In show plebeian Angel militant
Of lowest order, passed; and, from the door
Of that Plutonian hall, invisible
Ascended his high throne, which, under state
Of richest texture spread, at the upper end
Was placed in regal lustre. Down a while
He sat, and round about him saw unseen.
At last, as from a cloud, his fulgent head
And shape star-bright appeared, or brighter, clad   450

With what permissive glory since his fall
Was left him, or false glitter. All amazed
At that so sudden blaze, the Stygian throng
Bent their aspect, and whom they wished beheld,
Their mighty Chief returned: loud was the acclaim.
Forth rushed in haste the great consulting peers,
Raised from their dark divan, and with like joy
Congratulant approached him, who with hand
Silence, and with these words attention, won:
     "Thrones, Dominations, Princedoms, Virtues, Powers!
For in possession such, not only of right,
I call ye, and declare ye now, returned,
Successful beyond hope, to lead ye forth
Triumphant out of this infernal pit
Abominable, accursed, the house of woe,
And dungeon of our tyrant! Now possess,
As lords, a spacious World, to our native Heaven
Little inferior, by my adventure hard
With peril great achieved. Long were to tell
What I have done, what suffered, with what pain
Voyaged the unreal, vast, unbounded Deep
Of horrible confusion, over which
By Sin and Death a broad way now is paved,
To expedite your glorious march; but I
Toiled out my uncouth passage, forced to ride
The untractable Abyss, plunged in the womb
Of unoriginal Night and Chaos wild,
That, jealous of their secrets, fiercely opposed
My journey strange, with clamorous uproar
Protesting Fate supreme; thence how I found
The new-created World, which fame in Heaven
Long had foretold, a fabric wonderful,
Of absolute perfection; therein Man
Placed in a Paradise, by our exile
Made happy. Him by fraud I have seduced

From his Creator, and, the more to increase
Your wonder, with an apple! He, thereat
Offended—worth your laughter!—hath given up
Both his beloved Man and all his World
To Sin and Death a prey, and so to us,   490
Without our hazard, labour, or alarm,
To range in, and to dwell, and over Man
To rule, as over all he should have ruled.
True is, me also he hath judged, or rather
Me not, but the brute serpent, in whose shape
Man I deceived: that which to me belongs
Is enmity, which he will put between
Me and mankind; I am to bruise his heel;
His seed—when is not set—shall bruise my head:
A world who would not purchase with a bruise,   500
Or much more grievous pain? Ye have the account
Of my performance; what remains, ye Gods,
But up and enter now into full bliss?"
    So having said, a while he stood, expecting
Their universal shout and high applause
To fill his ear; when, contrary, he hears,
On all sides, from innumerable tongues,
A dismal universal hiss, the sound
Of public scorn. He wondered, but not long
Had leisure, wondering at himself now more;   510
His visage drawn he felt to sharp and spare,
His arms clung to his ribs, his legs entwining
Each other, till, supplanted, down he fell
A monstrous serpent on his belly prone,
Reluctant, but in vain; a greater power
Now ruled him, punished in the shape he sinned,
According to his doom. He would have spoke,
But hiss for hiss returned with forked tongue
To forked tongue; for now were all transformed
Alike, to serpents all, as accessories   520

5

To his bold riot. Dreadful was the din
Of hissing through the hall, thick-swarming now
With complicated monsters, head and tail,
Scorpion, and asp, and amphisbæna dire,
Cerastes horned, hydrus, and ellops drear,
And dipsas (not so thick swarmed once the soil
Bedropt with blood of Gorgon, or the isle
Ophiusa); but still greatest he the midst,
Now dragon grown, larger than whom the sun
Engendered in the Pythian vale on slime,   5
Huge Python; and his power no less he seemed
Above the rest still to retain. They all
Him followed, issuing forth to the open field,
Where all yet left of that revolted rout,
Heaven-fallen, in station stood or just array,
Sublime with expectation when to see
In triumph issuing forth their glorious Chief;
They saw, but other sight instead, a crowd
Of ugly serpents! Horror on them fell,
And horrid sympathy; for what they saw   5
They felt themselves now changing: down their arms,
Down fell both spear and shield; down they as fast,
And the dire hiss renewed, and the dire form
Catched by contagion, like in punishment,
As in their crime. Thus was the applause they meant
Turned to exploding hiss, triumph to shame
Cast on themselves from their own mouths. There stood
A grove hard by, sprung up with this their change,
His will who reigns above, to aggravate
Their penance, laden with fair fruit, like that   5
Which grew in Paradise, the bait of Eve
Used by the Tempter. On that prospect strange
Their earnest eyes they fixed, imagining
For one forbidden tree a multitude
Now risen, to work them further woe or shame;

Yet, parched with scalding thirst and hunger fierce,
Though to delude them sent, could not abstain,
But on they rolled in heaps, and, up the trees
Climbing, sat thicker than the snaky locks
That curled Megæra. Greedily they plucked   560
The fruitage fair to sight, like that which grew
Near that bituminous lake where Sodom flamed;
This, more delusive, not the touch, but taste
Deceived; they, fondly thinking to allay
Their appetite with gust, instead of fruit
Chewed bitter ashes, which the offended taste
With spattering noise rejected. Oft they assayed,
Hunger and thirst constraining; drugged as oft,
With hatefulest disrelish writhed their jaws,
With soot and cinders filled; so oft they fell   570
Into the same illusion, not as Man
Whom they triumphed once lapsed. Thus were they
        plagued
And worn with famine long, and ceaseless hiss,
Till their lost shape, permitted, they resumed;
Yearly enjoined, some say, to undergo
This annual humbling certain numbered days,
To dash their pride, and joy for Man seduced.
However, some tradition they dispersed
Among the heathen of their purchase got,
And fabled how the Serpent, whom they called   580
Ophion, with Eurynome (the wide
Encroaching Eve perhaps), had first the rule
Of high Olympus, thence by Saturn driven
And Ops, ere yet Dictæan Jove was born.
    Meanwhile in Paradise the Hellish pair
Too soon arrived; Sin there in power before,
Once actual, now in body, and to dwell
Habitual habitant; behind her Death,
Close following pace for pace, not mounted yet

On his pale horse; to whom Sin thus began: 5ᵍ

"Second of Satan sprung, all-conquering Death!
What think'st thou of our empire now, though earned
With travail difficult? not better far
Than still at Hell's dark threshold to have sat watch,
Unnamed, undreaded, and thyself half-starved?"

Whom thus the Sin-born Monster answered soon:
"To me, who with eternal famine pine,
Alike is Hell, or Paradise, or Heaven;
There best, where most with ravin I may meet;
Which here, though plenteous, all too little seems   6c
To stuff this maw, this vast unhide-bound corpse."

To whom the incestuous Mother thus replied:
"Thou therefore on these herbs, and fruits, and flowers,
Feed first; on each beast next, and fish, and fowl,
No homely morsels; and whatever thing
The scythe of Time mows down devour unspared;
Till I, in Man residing, through the race,
His thoughts, his looks, words, actions, all infect,
And season him thy last and sweetest prey."

This said, they both betook them several ways,   61
Both to destroy, or unimmortal make
All kinds, and for destruction to mature
Sooner or later; which the Almighty seeing,
From his transcendent seat the Saints among,
To those bright Orders uttered thus his voice:

"See with what heat these dogs of Hell advance
To waste and havoc yonder World, which I
So fair and good created, and had still
Kept in that state, had not the folly of Man
Let in these wasteful furies, who impute   62
Folly to me (so doth the Prince of Hell
And his adherents), that with so much ease
I suffer them to enter and possess
A place so heavenly, and conniving seem

To gratify my scornful enemies,
That laugh, as if, transported with some fit
Of passion, I to them had quitted all,
At random yielded up to their misrule;
And know not that I called and drew them thither,
My Hell-hounds, to lick up the draff and filth   630
Which Man's polluting sin with taint hath shed
On what was pure; till, crammed and gorged, nigh burst
With sucked and glutted offal, at one sling
Of thy victorious arm, well-pleasing Son,
Both Sin, and Death, and yawning Grave at last,
Through Chaos hurled, obstruct the mouth of Hell
For ever, and seal up his ravenous jaws.
Then Heaven and Earth, renewed, shall be made pure
To sanctity that shall receive no stain:
Till then the curse pronounced on both precedes."   640
   He ended, and the Heavenly audience loud
Sung Halleluiah, as the sound of seas,
Through multitude that sung: "Just are thy ways,
Righteous are thy decrees on all thy works;
Who can extenuate thee?" Next, to the Son,
Destined restorer of mankind, by whom
New Heaven and Earth shall to the ages rise,
Or down from Heaven descend. Such was their song,
While the Creator, calling forth by name
His mighty Angels, gave them several charge,   650
As sorted best with present things. The sun
Had first his precept so to move, so shine,
As might affect the Earth with cold and heat
Scarce tolerable, and from the north to call
Decrepit winter, from the south to bring
Solstitial summer's heat. To the blanc moon
Her office they prescribed; to the other five
Their planetary motions and aspects,
In sextile, square, and trine, and opposite,

Of noxious efficacy, and when to join   6(
In synod unbenign; and taught the fixed
Their influence malignant when to shower;
Which of them rising with the sun, or falling,
Should prove tempestuous. To the winds they set
Their corners, when with bluster to confound
Sea, air, and shore; the thunder when to roll
With terror through the dark aerial hall.
Some say he bid his Angels turn askance
The poles of Earth twice ten degrees and more
From the sun's axle; they with labour pushed   67
Oblique the centric globe: some say the sun
Was bid turn reins from the equinoctial road
Like distant breadth to Taurus with the seven
Atlantic Sisters, and the Spartan Twins,
Up to the Tropic Crab; thence down amain
By Leo and the Virgin and the Scales,
As deep as Capricorn; to bring in change
Of seasons to each clime: else had the spring
Perpetual smiled on Earth with vernant flowers,
Equal in days and nights, except to those   68
Beyond the polar circles; to them day
Had unbenighted shone, while the low sun,
To recompense his distance, in their sight
Had rounded still the horizon, and not known
Or east or west; which had forbid the snow
From cold Estotiland, and south as far
Beneath Magellan. At that tasted fruit
The sun, as from Thyestean banquet, turned
His course intended: else how had the World
Inhabited, though sinless, more than now   6(
Avoided pinching cold and scorching heat?
These changes in the heavens, though slow, produced
Like change on sea and land, sideral blast,
Vapour, and mist, and exhalation hot,

Corrupt and pestilent. Now from the north
Of Norumbega, and the Samoed shore,
Bursting their brazen dungeon, armed with ice
And snow and hail and stormy gust and flaw,
Boreas and Cæcias and Argestes loud
And Thrascias rend the woods and seas upturn;   700
With adverse blasts upturns them from the south
Notus and Afer black with thundrous clouds
From Serraliona; thwart of these, as fierce
Forth rush the Levant and the Ponent winds,
Eurus and Zephyr with their lateral noise,
Sirocco, and Libecchio. Thus began
Outrage from lifeless things; but Discord first,
Daughter of Sin, among the irrational
Death introduced through fierce antipathy:
Beast now with beast 'gan war, and fowl with fowl,   710
And fish with fish; to graze the herb all leaving
Devoured each other; nor stood much in awe
Of Man, but fled him, or with countenance grim
Glared on him passing. These were from without
The growing miseries, which Adam saw
Already in part, though hid in gloomiest shade,
To sorrow abandoned, but worse felt within,
And, in a troubled sea of passion tost,
Thus to disburden sought with sad complaint:
    "O miserable of happy! is this the end   720
Of this new glorious World, and me so late
The glory of that glory? who now, become
Accursed of blessed, hide me from the face
Of God, whom to behold was then my highth
Of happiness! Yet well, if here would end
The misery; I deserved it, and would bear
My own deservings; but this will not serve:
All that I eat or drink, or shall beget,
Is propagated curse. O voice, once heard

Delightfully, 'Increase and multiply';   7
Now death to hear! for what can I increase
Or multiply, but curses on my head?
Who, of all ages to succeed, but, feeling
The evil on him brought by me, will curse
My head? 'Ill fare our Ancestor impure!
For this we may thank Adam!' but his thanks
Shall be the execration; so, besides
Mine own that bide upon me, all from me
Shall with a fierce reflux on me redound,
On me, as on their natural centre, light   7
Heavy, though in their place. O fleeting joys
Of Paradise, dear bought with lasting woes!
Did I request thee, Maker, from my clay
To mould me Man? did I solicit thee
From darkness to promote me, or here place
In this delicious garden? As my will
Concurred not to my being, it were but right
And equal to reduce me to my dust,
Desirous to resign and render back
All I received, unable to perform   7
Thy terms too hard, by which I was to hold
The good I sought not. To the loss of that,
Sufficient penalty, why hast thou added
The sense of endless woes? inexplicable
Thy justice seems. Yet, to say truth, too late
I thus contest; then should have been refused
Those terms whatever, when they were proposed.
Thou didst accept them: wilt thou enjoy the good,
Then cavil the conditions? And though God
Made thee without thy leave, what if thy son   7
Prove disobedient, and, reproved, retort,
'Wherefore didst thou beget me? I sought it not!'
Wouldst thou admit for his contempt of thee
That proud excuse? yet him not thy election,

But natural necessity, begot.
God made thee of choice his own, and of his own
To serve him; thy reward was of his grace;
Thy punishment then justly is at his will.
Be it so, for I submit; his doom is fair,
That dust I am, and shall to dust return.   770
O welcome hour whenever! Why delays
His hand to execute what his decree
Fixed on this day? Why do I overlive?
Why am I mocked with death, and lengthened out
To deathless pain? How gladly would I meet
Mortality, my sentence, and be earth
Insensible! how glad would lay me down
As in my mother's lap! There I should rest
And sleep secure; his dreadful voice no more
Would thunder in my ears; no fear of worse   780
To me and to my offspring would torment me
With cruel expectation. Yet one doubt
Pursues me still, lest all I cannot die;
Lest that pure breath of life, the spirit of Man
Which God inspired, cannot together perish
With this corporeal clod; then, in the grave,
Or in some other dismal place, who knows
But I shall die a living death? O thought
Horrid, if true! Yet why? It was but breath
Of life that sinned: what dies but what had life   790
And sin? the body properly hath neither.
All of me then shall die: let this appease
The doubt, since human reach no further knows.
For though the Lord of all be infinite,
Is his wrath also? Be it, Man is not so,
But mortal doomed. How can he exercise
Wrath without end on Man, whom death must end?
Can he make deathless death? That were to make
Strange contradiction; which to God himself

Impossible is held, as argument   80
Of weakness, not of power. Will he draw out,
For anger's sake, finite to infinite
In punished Man, to satisfy his rigour
Satisfied never? That were to extend
His sentence beyond dust and Nature's law;
By which all causes else according still
To the reception of their matter act,
Not to the extent of their own sphere. But say
That death be not one stroke, as I supposed,
Bereaving sense, but endless misery   81
From this day onward, which I feel begun
Both in me and without me, and so last
To perpetuity—Ay me! that fear
Comes thundering back with dreadful revolution
On my defenceless head! Both Death and I
Am found eternal, and incorporate both:
Nor I on my part single; in me all
Posterity stands cursed. Fair patrimony
That I must leave ye, sons! Oh, were I able
To waste it all myself, and leave ye none!   82
So disinherited, how would ye bless
Me, now your curse! Ah, why should all mankind,
For one man's fault, thus guiltless be condemned,
If guiltless? But from me what can proceed
But all corrupt, both mind and will depraved
Not to do only, but to will the same
With me? How can they then acquitted stand
In sight of God? Him, after all disputes,
Forced I absolve; all my evasions vain
And reasonings, though through mazes, lead me still   83
But to my own conviction: first and last
On me, me only, as the source and spring
Of all corruption, all the blame lights due;
So might the wrath! Fond wish! couldst thou support

That burden, heavier than the Earth to bear;
Than all the World much heavier, though divided
With that bad woman? Thus, what thou desir'st,
And what thou fear'st, alike destroys all hope
Of refuge, and concludes thee miserable
Beyond all past example and future;   840
To Satan only like, both crime and doom.
O Conscience! into what abyss of fears
And horrors hast thou driven me; out of which
I find no way, from deep to deeper plunged!"
    Thus Adam to himself lamented loud
Through the still night, not now, as ere Man fell,
Wholesome and cool and mild, but with black air
Accompanied, with damps and dreadful gloom;
Which to his evil conscience represented
All things with double terror. On the ground   850
Outstretched he lay, on the cold ground, and oft
Cursed his creation; Death as oft accused
Of tardy execution, since denounced
The day of his offence. "Why comes not Death,"
Said he, "with one thrice-acceptable stroke
To end me? Shall Truth fail to keep her word,
Justice divine not hasten to be just?
But Death comes not at call; Justice divine
Mends not her slowest pace for prayers or cries.
O woods, O fountains, hillocks, dales, and bowers!   860
With other echo late I taught your shades
To answer, and resound far other song."
Whom thus afflicted when sad Eve beheld,
Desolate where she sat, approaching nigh,
Soft words to his fierce passion she assayed;
But her with stern regard he thus repelled:
    "Out of my sight, thou serpent! that name best
Befits thee, with him leagued, thyself as false
And hateful: nothing wants, but that thy shape,

Like his, and colour serpentine, may show   8
Thy inward fraud, to warn all creatures from thee
Henceforth; lest that too heavenly form, pretended
To hellish falsehood, snare them. But for thee
I had persisted happy, had not thy pride
And wandering vanity, when least was safe,
Rejected my forewarning, and disdained
Not to be trusted, longing to be seen,
Though by the Devil himself, him overweening
To overreach; but, with the Serpent meeting,
Fooled and beguiled; by him thou, I by thee,   8
To trust thee from my side, imagined wise,
Constant, mature, proof against all assaults;
And understood not all was but a show,
Rather than solid virtue, all but a rib
Crooked by nature—bent, as now appears,
More to the part sinister—from me drawn;
Well if thrown out, as supernumerary
To my just number found! Oh, why did God,
Creator wise, that peopled highest Heaven
With Spirits masculine, create at last   8
This novelty on Earth, this fair defect
Of Nature, and not fill the World at once
With men, as Angels, without feminine;
Or find some other way to generate
Mankind? This mischief had not then befallen,
And more that shall befall—innumerable
Disturbances on Earth through female snares,
And strait conjunction with this sex. For either
He never shall find out fit mate, but such
As some misfortune brings him, or mistake;   9
Or whom he wishes most shall seldom gain,
Through her perverseness, but shall see her gained
By a far worse, or, if she love, withheld
By parents; or his happiest choice too late

Shall meet, already linked and wedlock-bound
To a fell adversary, his hate or shame:
Which infinite calamity shall cause
To human life, and household peace confound."
  He added not, and from her turned; but Eve,
Not so repulsed, with tears that ceased not flowing,   910
And tresses all disordered, at his feet
Fell humble, and, embracing them, besought
His peace, and thus proceeded in her plaint:
  "Forsake me not thus, Adam! witness Heaven
What love sincere and reverence in my heart
I bear thee, and unweeting have offended,
Unhappily deceived! Thy suppliant
I beg, and clasp thy knees; bereave me not,
Whereon I live, thy gentle looks, thy aid,
Thy counsel in this uttermost distress,   920
My only strength and stay: forlorn of thee,
Whither shall I betake me, where subsist?
While yet we live, scarce one short hour perhaps,
Between us two let there be peace; both joining,
As joined in injuries, one enmity
Against a foe by doom express assigned us,
That cruel Serpent. On me exercise not
Thy hatred for this misery befallen;
On me already lost, me than thyself
More miserable. Both have sinned; but thou   930
Against God only; I against God and thee,
And to the place of judgment will return,
There with my cries importune Heaven, that all
The sentence, from thy head removed, may light
On me, sole cause to thee of all this woe,
Me, me only, just object of His ire."
  She ended weeping; and her lowly plight,
Immovable till peace obtained from fault
Acknowledged and deplored, in Adam wrought

Commiseration. Soon his heart relented
Towards her, his life so late and sole delight,
Now at his feet submissive in distress,
Creature so fair his reconcilement seeking,
His counsel, whom she had displeased, his aid;
As one disarmed, his anger all he lost,
And thus with peaceful words upraised her soon:
  "Unwary, and too desirous, as before
So now, of what thou know'st not, who desir'st
The punishment all on thyself! Alas!
Bear thine own first, ill able to sustain
His full wrath, whose thou feel'st as yet least part,
And my displeasure bear'st so ill. If prayers
Could alter high decrees, I to that place
Would speed before thee, and be louder heard,
That on my head all might be visited,
Thy frailty and infirmer sex forgiven,
To me committed, and by me exposed.
But rise; let us no more contend, nor blame
Each other, blamed enough elsewhere, but strive
In offices of love, how we may lighten
Each other's burden, in our share of woe;
Since this day's death denounced, if aught I see,
Will prove no sudden, but a slow-paced evil,
A long day's dying, to augment our pain,
And to our seed (O hapless seed!) derived."
  To whom thus Eve, recovering heart, replied:
"Adam, by sad experiment I know
How little weight my words with thee can find,
Found so erroneous, thence by just event
Found so unfortunate; nevertheless,
Restored by thee, vile as I am, to place
Of new acceptance, hopeful to regain
Thy love, the sole contentment of my heart,
Living or dying from thee I will not hide

What thoughts in my unquiet breast are risen,
Tending to some relief of our extremes,
Or end, though sharp and sad, yet tolerable,
As in our evils, and of easier choice.
If care of our descent perplex us most,
Which must be born to certain woe, devoured   980
By Death at last (and miserable it is
To be to others cause of misery,
Our own begotten, and of our loins to bring
Into this cursed World a woeful race,
That after wretched life must be at last
Food for so foul a monster), in thy power
It lies, yet ere conception, to prevent
The race unblest, to being yet unbegot.
Childless thou art, childless remain; so Death
Shall be deceived his glut, and with us two   990
Be forced to satisfy his ravenous maw.
But if thou judge it hard and difficult,
Conversing, looking, loving, to abstain
From love's due rites, nuptial embraces sweet,
And with desire to languish without hope,
Before the present object languishing
With like desire, which would be misery
And torment less than none of what we dread;
Then, both our selves and seed at once to free
From what we fear for both, let us make short,   1000
Let us seek Death, or, he not found, supply
With our own hands his office on ourselves.
Why stand we longer shivering under fears
That show no end but death, and have the power,
Of many ways to die the shortest choosing,
Destruction with destruction to destroy?"
    She ended here, or vehement despair
Broke off the rest; so much of death her thoughts
Had entertained as dyed her cheeks with pale.

But Adam, with such counsel nothing swayed,
To better hopes his more attentive mind
Labouring had raised, and thus to Eve replied:
   "Eve, thy contempt of life and pleasure seems
To argue in thee something more sublime
And excellent than what thy mind contemns;
But self-destruction therefore sought refutes
That excellence thought in thee, and implies,
Not thy contempt, but anguish and regret
For loss of life and pleasure overloved.
Or if thou covet death, as utmost end
Of misery, so thinking to evade
The penalty pronounced, doubt not but God
Hath wiselier armed his vengeful ire than so
To be forestalled; much more I fear lest death
So snatched will not exempt us from the pain
We are by doom to pay; rather such acts
Of contumacy will provoke the Highest
To make death in us live. Then let us seek
Some safer resolution, which methinks
I have in view, calling to mind with heed
Part of our sentence, that thy seed shall bruise
The Serpent's head: piteous amends! unless
Be meant, whom I conjecture, our grand foe,
Satan, who in the serpent hath contrived
Against us this deceit. To crush his head
Would be revenge indeed; which will be lost
By death brought on ourselves, or childless days
Resolved as thou proposest; so our foe
Shall scape his punishment ordained, and we
Instead shall double ours upon our heads.
No more be mentioned then of violence
Against ourselves, and wilful barrenness,
That cuts us off from hope, and savours only
Rancour and pride, impatience and despite,

Reluctance against God and his just yoke
Laid on our necks. Remember with what mild
And gracious temper he both heard and judged,
Without wrath or reviling; we expected
Immediate dissolution, which we thought
Was meant by death that day; when, lo! to thee   1050
Pains only in child-bearing were foretold,
And bringing forth, soon recompensed with joy,
Fruit of thy womb; on me the curse aslope
Glanced on the ground: with labour I must earn
My bread; what harm? Idleness had been worse;
My labour will sustain me; and, lest cold
Or heat should injure us, his timely care
Hath, unbesought, provided, and his hands
Clothed us unworthy, pitying while he judged;
How much more, if we pray him, will his ear   1060
Be open, and his heart to pity incline,
And teach us further by what means to shun
The inclement seasons, rain, ice, hail, and snow!
Which now the sky with various face begins
To show us in this mountain, while the winds
Blow moist and keen, shattering the graceful locks
Of these fair spreading trees; which bids us seek
Some better shroud, some better warmth to cherish
Our limbs benumbed, ere this diurnal star
Leave cold the night, how we his gathered beams   1070
Reflected may with matter sere foment,
Or by collision of two bodies grind
The air attrite to fire; as late the clouds,
Justling or pushed with winds, rude in their shock,
Tine the slant lightning, whose thwart flame driven down
Kindles the gummy bark of fir or pine,
And sends a comfortable heat from far,
Which might supply the sun. Such fire to use,
And what may else be remedy or cure

To evils which our own misdeeds have wrought,   108
He will instruct us praying, and of grace
Beseeching him; so as we need not fear
To pass commodiously this life, sustained
By him with many comforts, till we end
In dust, our final rest and native home.
What better can we do, than, to the place
Repairing where he judged us, prostrate fall
Before him reverent, and there confess
Humbly our faults, and pardon beg, with tears
Watering the ground, and with our sighs the air   109
Frequenting, sent from hearts contrite, in sign
Of sorrow unfeigned and humiliation meek?
Undoubtedly he will relent, and turn
From his displeasure; in whose look serene,
When angry most he seemed and most severe,
What else but favour, grace, and mercy shone?"
   So spake our father penitent; nor Eve
Felt less remorse. They, forthwith to the place
Repairing where he judged them, prostrate fell
Before him reverent, and both confessed   1100
Humbly their faults, and pardon begged, with tears
Watering the ground, and with their sighs the air
Frequenting, sent from hearts contrite, in sign
Of sorrow unfeigned and humiliation meek.

NOTES

Abbreviations:

M. = Milton, or Milton's poetry, as distinguished from his prose.

G. = Glossary.

P. R. = *Paradise Regained.*

S. A. = *Samson Agonistes.*

Other books of *Paradise Lost* are indicated by Roman numerals; thus in the first note "v. 331–450" means book v, lines 331 to 450.

The edition of Milton's prose works to which reference is made under the abbreviation "*P. W.*" is that published in "Bohn's Standard Library".

Note. The action of the whole poem is sketched in the *Introduction*, and should be studied by any reader who is not familiar with them.

BOOK IX

1–5. This introduction refers mainly to Raphael's colloquy with Adam in the four preceding books of *Paradise Lost*. We were told in them how the Archangel came down to Eden, partook with Adam of the "rural repast" which Eve prepared (v. 331–450), and then held long "talk" with him; narrating the rebellion of Satan and his followers, their expulsion from Heaven (v. 577–907, vi. 1–892), and the Creation of the World (book vii), explaining other points on which Adam asks questions (book viii), and admonishing him against his Enemy (vi. 900–12, viii. 635–43). Raphael is referred to several times in books v–viii as Adam's "Angel-guest" (v. 328), "godlike guest" (v. 351), "Heavenly guest" (vii. 69, viii. 646), and it is to him that the description in lines 2–4 is meant to apply.

1. *No more of talk*, i.e. there will be no more of this friendly conversation in the rest of the poem. In book xi the Messenger sent from Heaven is not Raphael "the affable Archangel" (vii. 41), but the stern, warlike Michael, who has to announce to Adam and Eve their banishment from Eden and to lead them forth.

where God; understand from what follows some words like 'conversed', 'spoke'. The reference is to book viii, where Adam says that the Almighty gave him possession of the Garden of

Eden, warned him not to touch the Tree of Knowledge (VIII. 316–33), and then promised him a helpmate in Eve (VIII. 437–51).

2. *as with his friend.* Cf. *Exodus* xxxiii. 11, "And the Lord spake unto Moses face to face, as a man speaketh unto his friend".

6. *tragic,* i.e. "notes", to which the nouns "distrust", "breach", etc., are in apposition.

9. *distance,* coldness.

11. *a world of,* much of, a deal of. For the verbal quibble see 648, and cf. XI. 627, "The world ere long a world of tears must weep".

12. *Sin. . .Death*; see X. 230, note. *shadow,* inseparable companion; cf. "shade", X. 249. There is perhaps in both cases an allusion to the description of Death's appearance—"that shadow seemed", II. 669; "the meagre shadow", X. 264.

Misery, all kinds of physical pain and disease—the "harbingers" (see G.), i.e. forerunners, of death. Cf. the vision revealed to Adam in XI. 477–90 of the "diseases dire" that Eve's disobedience brought upon men.

13–19. He means that as regards the "argument" (see G.), i.e. subject, with which it is now about to deal, his poem has an advantage over the three great classical epics: (i) the *Iliad,* which commences with the line "Sing, O Muse, the wrath of Achilles", and describes in book XXII his pursuit of Hector ("his foe") thrice round the wall of Troy; (ii) the *Odyssey,* which relates the wanderings that Odysseus ("the Greek") experienced on his homeward journey after the Trojan war because Neptune was hostile to him; and (iii) the *Æneid,* which tells of the hostility of Juno to Æneas, the son of Cytherea, i.e. Venus, and of his betrothal to Lavinia (daughter of Latinus, king of Latium), who had previously been promised in marriage to Turnus.

There is a similar summary of the themes of the three classical epics in his *Second Defence of the People of England,* where he writes: "The epic poet who adheres at all to the rules of that species of composition does not profess to describe the whole life of the hero whom he celebrates, but only some particular action of his life, as the resentment of Achilles at Troy, the return of Ulysses, or the coming of Æneas into Italy", *P.W.* I. 299. It is remarkable, I think, how much more repetition of thought and expression there is in Milton than in Shakespeare.

This claim to moral, not artistic, superiority, as of Christianity over Paganism, occurs in the two other great passages of invocation in *Paradise Lost*; cf. I. 12–16 and VII. 1–12. In Milton's view

the great poet is a teacher in the first place, a singer in the second, and he seems to have regarded himself as literally an inspired teacher.

"Wrath", (14), "rage" (16), "ire" (18) all point back to "anger" in l. 10. "The anger that he is about to sing is an 'argument' more heroic not only than the anger of men, of Achilles and Turnus, but than that even of the gods, of Neptune and Juno. The anger of the true God is a more noble subject than [the anger] of the false gods" (Newton).

20. *answerable*, corresponding; a style equal to the dignity of his subject.

21. *my celestial patroness*, i.e. the "Heavenly Muse" whose aid he invokes at the beginning of the poem (I. 6); she is the divine power, he says, who "taught" Moses on Sinai (I. 6–10) and inspired David on Sion (III. 29–32) and the other prophets and singers of Israel. He calls her (VII. 1) "Urania" = "the Heavenly one" (Gk. οὐρανία); cf. "*celestial* patroness". Milton's references to this Muse of Sacred Song which gave him inspiration have a reality that is lacking in the conventional poetical appeals to the 'Muses'. In *P.R.* I. 8–17 he seems to identify the "Heavenly Muse" with the Holy Spirit.

22. *nightly*; cf. 47. He elsewhere speaks of himself as best inspired at night or just at dawn; cf. III. 29–32 and VII. 28–30,

> "thou (i.e. the Muse)
> Visit'st my slumbers nightly, or when morn
> Purples the east."

Newton in his *Life* of M. says that the poet's widow, "being asked...who the Muse was, replied it was God's grace, and the Holy Spirit that *visited him nightly*". (Cf. Shakespeare's famous 86th *Sonnet*.) And Johnson, on the authority of Richardson's *Life* (1734), relates that M. "would sometimes lie awake whole nights...and on a sudden his poetical faculty would rush upon him with an *impetus*, and his daughter was immediately called to secure what came".

24. The trochee ("eásy") in the first foot is intended to give an easy flow of rhythm corresponding with the sense.

25. *Since first*, i.e. about 1640; some lines of *Paradise Lost* (IV. 32–41) were written as early as 1642.

this subject for heroic song. See the *Appendix*, pp. 143, 144.

26. *long choosing and beginning late*; see *Introduction*, pp. xxvi–xlii.

29. I.e. *the* chief mastery *being* to, etc. *dissect*; referring to the detailed descriptions of wounds in Homer and Virgil.

30, 31. *fabled. . .feigned*. A mythical subject would not appeal
to M. Probably one of his reasons for abandoning the story of
King Arthur which he at one time intended to take as the subject
of his great poem was that he found the story to be "fabled" and
"feigned"; see *Introduction*. His three great poems all had a
solid basis; so had *Lycidas*, and perhaps *Comus* in a minor degree
(see Pitt Press ed. p. xxxvi).

33. *races and games*. The allusion is to the classical poets; cf.
especially the description of the games in *Iliad* XXIII and *Æneid* V.
M. makes the Angels who keep guard over the entrance to Paradise "exercise heroic games" (IV. 551, 552), but does not describe
them. See also II. 528–38.

34–8. The allusion is to the Italian poets—e.g. Boiardo,
Ariosto and Tasso—and Spenser, who describe tournaments and
scenes of chivalry.

34. *tilting furniture*, all the equipments of a tournament.
imblazoned, with coats of arms portrayed on them.

35. *Impresses*, devices on shields; see G.

36. The *base* was a skirt or kilt, reaching from the waist to the
knees, worn by a knight on horseback. See G. Keightley quotes
the *Faerie Queene*, III. 1. 15:

"Her garments all were wrought of beaten gold,
    And all her steed with tinsell trappings shone."

37, 38. "The *marshal* placed the guests according to their rank
and saw that they were properly served; the *sewer* marched in
before the meats, and arranged them on the table; the *seneshal*
was the household steward" (Todd). See *sewer* and *seneshal* in
G.

39. *The skill*; in apposition to "to describe", 33.

41, 43. *me. . .remains* = *me manet*.

43, 44. *to raise That name*, i.e. to raise up, create, for my poem
the title "heroic".

44. *an age too late*; i.e. in the world's history; implying that
the conditions favourable to epic poetry had passed away. It is,
I suppose, true that no great epic poem (unless Tennyson's *Idylls
of the King* be an exception) has been written, at any rate in
English, since *Paradise Lost*.

In his *Life* of Milton Johnson says: "There prevailed in his
time an opinion, that the world was in its decay.... It was
suspected that the whole creation languished, that neither trees
nor animals had the height or bulk of their predecessors, and that
everything was daily sinking by gradual diminution. Milton
appears to suspect that souls partake of the general degeneracy,

and is not without some fear that his book is to be written in 'an age too late' for heroic poesy." The opinion to which Johnson refers "is said to have been first propagated by Dr Gabriel Goodman, Bishop of Gloucester, in a work entitled 'The Fall of Man, or the Corruption of Nature proved by Natural Reason', 1616" (C. H. Firth).

44, 45. *or cold Climate.* Here he touches on what was a lifelong opinion. Thus in his poem *Mansus* (1638) he apologises for his Latin poems on the ground that his Muse was reared in the chill north; while in the *History of Britain* he complains that the English lack "the sun [which] ripens wits as well as fruits" (*P. W.* v. 240). We find the same idea in the *Reason of Church Government* ("if there be nothing adverse in our *climate*, or the fate of this age", i.e. adverse to the composition of a great poem) and in the *Areopagitica*; see *P. W.* II. 53, 479.

or years; perhaps not far short of sixty; see p. xliv.

wing; his favourite emblem of inspiration; cf. III. 13, VII. 4.

46. *depressed*; used proleptically, and with an antithesis to "raise", 43.

53. The close of the fourth book describes how Satan was driven out of Eden by Gabriel. In the intervening books, V–VIII there is very little advance in the action of the poem, except that Adam receives warning of his Enemy through Raphael. See "The Story of the Poem", *Introduction*, p. lx.

54, 55. At his first entrance into Eden Satan had overheard Adam and Eve speaking about the Tree of Knowledge and thus learned the one thing in which to tempt them and compass their ruin (IV. 408–535).

fraud; in the general sense 'deceit, guile'; see 89, 285. Cf. *The Prayer-Book*, "Whatsoever hath been decayed by the fraud and malice of the devil" (the Collect in 'The Visitation of the Sick').

59. *From compassing the Earth.* Cf. *Job* i. 7, "And the Lord said unto Satan, Whence comest thou? Then Satan answered the Lord, and said, From going to and fro in the earth, and from walking up and down in it."

cautious of day, i.e. avoiding it; cf. "rode with darkness", 63, 64.

60–2. Cf. IV. 549–88, where Uriel is described as coming to warn Gabriel, who guarded the eastern gate of Paradise with Cherubim, that one of the outcast evil angels has found his way into the "garden".

Uriel; supposed to be one of "the seven Spirits of God sent forth into all the earth", *Revelation* v. 6; "which are before his

throne", I. 4. Cf. *Paradise Lost*, III. 648–58. Uriel is mentioned
in 2 *Esdras* iv. 1, v. 20, x. 28. Tradition identified him with the
angel whom John saw "standing in the sun", *Rev.* xix. 17, and
regarded him as the "regent of the sun" (III. 690) and dispenser
of heat. Thus Heywood says that the four quarters of the world
are assigned to the government of four angelic beings, and "The
South, whence Auster comes, rules Uriel" (*Hierarchie of the
Blessed Angells*, 1635 ed., p. 214). Cf. too Henry More:

> "The fiery scorching shafts which Uriel
>   From Southern quarter darted with strong hand,"

(*Song of the Soul*, Cambridge ed., 1647, p. 53). Possibly the
whole conception of his attributes originated in the meaning of
his name, viz. 'fire of God'.

63–6. First he gives an astronomical, then a geographical (76–
82), account of Satan's wanderings.

"Of the seven days during which Satan went round and round
the Earth, always keeping himself on its dark side, three were
spent in moving from east to west on the equatorial line; four in
moving round from pole to pole, [i.e.] from north to south and
back,—in which second way of moving he would traverse (or go
along) the two colures,—viz. two great circles, so named by astronomers, drawn from the poles. Originally all great circles passing
through the poles were called *colures* (κόλουροι, curtailed); but
the term was at length confined to the two great circles drawn
from the poles through the equinoxes and the solstices respectively. The one was called the Equinoctial colure, the other the
Solstitial" (Masson).

67. *the coast averse*, the side of Paradise away from the gate
where the Cherubim kept watch (IV. 542–4); that this was the
north side is shown, as Keightley noted, by the position assigned
to the Tigris in IV. 223–32. *coast*; see G.

69–73. He identifies the Tigris with the river that "went out
of Eden to water the garden", *Genesis* ii. 10.

71. *of Paradise*; which is situated on the level summit of a hill
(IV. 132–5, X. 1065): a tradition due to *Ezekiel* xxviii. 13, 14.
Gk. παράδεισος, a park; a word of Persian origin.

"Eden", it should be noticed, means the whole district of Asia
in which the first inhabitants of the Earth dwelt: "Paradise"
being the "garden" in the east of this district (*Genesis* ii. 8).
After Adam and Eve were banished from "Paradise" they still
"Through Eden took their solitary way", XII. 649.

73. *Rose up*. We have the same rhythm expressing the same
effect in I. 10 and IV. 229.

75. *involved in*, wrapped in. Lat. *involvere*.

76–82. "The Fiend, on leaving Eden, had gone northward over the Pontus Euxinus or Black Sea, and over the Palus Mæotis or Sea of Azof, and so still northward, over what is now Russian territory, as far as beyond the Siberian river Ob or Obe, which flows into the Arctic sea; whence, continuing round the pole and descending on the other side of the globe, he had gone southward again as far as the Antarctic sea and pole. So much for his travels north and south. In *length*, i.e. measured as longitude in an equatorial direction, his journeys had extended from the Syrian river Orontes, west of Eden, to the Isthmus of Darien, and so still west, completing the great circle [of the world] to India on the east of Eden. Observe how true to the imagined reality is the mention of Ganges here before Indus. In the circuit described Satan would come upon the Ganges first" (Masson).

77. *pool*, i.e. inland sea; used in allusion to its classical name, ἡ Μαιῶτις λίμνη, *Mæotis Palus*. So in *P.R.* iv. 79 he calls it "the Tauric pool". Cf. "the Asphaltic pool"=the Dead Sea, i. 411. The river *Ob* is mentioned several times in Milton's *History of Moscovia* (i.e. Russia), one of his minor prose works, not published till 1682.

79. *antarctic*, south. "No particular place is mentioned near the South pole, there being [there] all sea or land unknown" (Newton).

81. *Darien*, i.e. the Isthmus of Panama.

82. *the orb*, the whole world—*orbis terrarum*.

83. *narrow*, careful, scrutinising closely.

86. "Now the Serpent was more subtil than any beast of the field which the Lord God had made", *Genesis* iii. 1. Cf. 560.

87, 88. *irresolute Of thoughts revolved*, i.e. a debate that for a long time came to no decision in regard to—no settlement of—the thoughts pondered over. *sentence*, decision, Lat. *sententia*.

89. *imp*, evil spirit.

90. *suggestions*, temptations; see G.

95. *doubt*, suspicion.

98. *passion*; deep feeling, emotion. The alliteration emphasises the intensity of his emotion.

99. Cf. vii. 328, 329 (part of the account of the Creation):
"Earth now
Seemed like to Heaven, a seat where gods might dwell."

100. *seat*, abode, dwelling-place; cf. the similar use of Lat. *sedes*.

103. M. is fond of comparing the motions of the stellar bodies

(="other heavens") to a "dance"; cf. v. 178, 620–4, VIII. 125.

104. *officious*, that serve thee; see G.

105. *as seems*. Cf. VIII. 15–38, where dealing with the same thought M. uses the same cautious language—e.g. "that seem", 19, "for aught appears", 30. Probably his reason was that he thought that some of the heavenly bodies might be inhabited (VIII. 148–76): especially the Moon (III. 459–62, VIII. 142–8).

107. *sacred*; used in reference to "light"; see 192, note.
influence; see G.

110. *virtue*, power, efficacy; see G.

112. *animate*; see G.

113. *growth, sense, reason*. "The three kinds of life rising as it were by steps ['gradual', 112], the vegetable, animal and rational; of all which Man partakes, and he only; he grows as plants...he lives as all other animated creatures, but is over and above indued with reason" (Richardson). See note on v. 469.

115. *joy in aught*. One joy is left to him, but only one (477–9).

119. *place*; implying '*fit* place to dwell in'. *refuge*, i.e. from his misery.

126–8. Cf. the sentiment of the proverbial line *solamen miseris socios habuisse doloris*. Contrast *P. R.* I. 397–402.

130. *him destroyed*; a *dative* absolute construction. In Elizabethan, as in modern, English the absolute case is the nominative, but in Old English it was the dative. Morris quotes Wyclif, *Matthew* xxviii. 13, "Thei han stolen him *us slepinge*". With the present participle M. always uses the nominative absolute—cf. 312, 1147: so usually with the past participle; but in his fondness for classical constructions he *sometimes* employs the old idiom as suggesting more the Latin ablative absolute. Thus "*me* overthrown", *S. A.* 463, has more of a Latin sound than "*I* overthrown". Cf. again VII. 141–3:

> "This inaccessible high strength, the seat,
>   Of Deity supreme, *us* dispossessed,
>   He trusted to have seized."

(It is, I think, just possible from the punctuation of the original editions that M. intended "him destroyed" as an ordinary accusative after "follow" in 133; but apparently no editor takes the passage so.)

133. *Follow*, i.e. fall, like man himself, into destruction.

139–54. Cf. VII. 131–67.

140–51. Cf. the "Argument" of book VII: "God, after the expelling of Satan and his Angels out of Heaven, declared His

pleasure to create another World, and other creatures to dwell therein."

140. *in one night*; that in which the rebellion in Heaven began; see v. 642–717, 743 *et seq.*

141. *well nigh half*; rather, "a third part", *Revelation* xii. 4. The number of the outcast Angels was a point much disputed among the Schoolmen.

142. *name*; cf. Lat. *nomen* in the sense 'race, stock'.

145. *virtue*, efficacy, power; see G.

146, 147. *if they...are his created*; which he denies when addressing his followers, v. 859–63, telling them that they are "self-begot, self-raised", 860. Yet he knew and elsewhere (IV. 42, 43) admitted to himself the truth.

147–51. Cf. Satan's words at his first sight of Adam and Eve (IV. 358–60):

> "O Hell! what do mine eyes with grief behold?
> Into our room of bliss thus high advanced
> Creatures of other mould, Earth-born perhaps."

150. *base original*, mean origin; referring to "earth", 149.

155. "He shall give his angels charge over thee", *Psalm* xci. 11.

156. *flaming ministers*, the Cherubim (61, 62); cf. IV. 797, 798:

> "So saying, on he led his radiant files,
> Dazzling the moon" (i.e. the ranks of Cherubim).

157. *earthy*; so the original editions; the mis-reading *earthly* occurs often in modern texts.

166. *This essence*, i.e. the fiery ether of which M. conceived the Angelic forms to consist, as is shown by passages like I. 117, V. 499, VI. 330, 433, and the discourse on Angels in his *Christian Doctrine*, I. VII.—*P. W.* IV. 185, 186. After their rebellion the "liquid texture" (VI. 348) of the forms of the evil Angels degenerated into a "gross" substance (VI. 661), which tended more and more to "imbody and imbrute" (*Comus*, 468). That the forms of the fallen Angels changed was a doctrine taught by many of the Church Fathers.

to incarnate and imbrute; probably, I think, intransitive, in apposition to "foul descent", with "this essence" as their subject; but they may be transitive, dependent on "constrained", with "this essence" as the object.

170. *obnoxious*; in the sense of Lat. *obnoxius*, 'liable, exposed to'.

172. Cf. IV. 17, 18.

174. *higher*, i.e. aiming higher, against the Almighty himself.

175–8. Jealousy is one of the motives that animate Satan against man, but the strongest is desire "to spite the great Creator" (II. 384). Cf. 178 and X. I, "the...despiteful act".

176. *son of despite*; modelled on Hebraic phrases like 'sons of valour', 2 *Samuel* ii. 7, 'sons of Belial', I *Samuel* ii. 12.

180. *Like a...mist*; the simile is used again, XII. 629–31.

192. *whenas*, when; so *whereas*, where; both are common in Elizabethan writers, and may perhaps have been originally rather more emphatic than the simple forms, though the distinction, if it existed, was soon lost.

sacred; because "God is light", I *John* i. 5. Cf. the invocation ("Hail, holy Light") in III. 1–6.

193, 194. The origin of Gray's line, "The breezy call of incense-breathing Morn", *Elegy*, 17.

196, 197. Cf. passages like *Genesis* viii. 21, *Leviticus* i. 9.

198, 199. Cf. their "Morning Hymn", v. 153–208.

200. Newton aptly notes that M. himself was an early riser, quoting the passage to that effect in the *Apology for Smectymnuus*, *P. W.* III. 112. Cf. *L'Allegro*, 41–68. Among the Milton MSS. found at Netherby Hall in Cumberland and printed by the Camden Society was a piece of Latin verse in praise of early rising.

212. *wild*, wildness.

213. *hear*; so the First Ed.; the Second misprints (?) *bear*.

218. *spring*, clump, thicket; commonly 'a sprig, single shoot of a tree', as in *Venus and Adonis*, 656, "This canker that eats up Love's tender spring".

219. *redress*, set right.

228. *Compare*; used as a noun in III. 138, v. 467; so in Shakespeare.

229. *motioned*, proposed; cf. *motion* = 'proposal' in politics.

233. *to study household good*. Cf. *S. A.* 1046–9. Milton brought up his daughters on this principle. Apparently he had good reason to be satisfied in this respect with his third wife, "a genteel person", says Aubrey, "of a peaceful and agreeable humour", who, according to tradition, was careful "in providing such dishes" as he liked best.

241. *not the lowest end*, i.e. the highest object, since "without love no happiness", as Raphael tells Adam (VIII. 621).

not the lowest; a *meiosis*.

245. *wilderness*, wildness.

247. Scan *convérse*; cf. 909. So in *Hamlet*, II. 1. 42.

249. Cf. Cicero's saying which has become proverbial, *nun-*

quam minus solus quam cum solus; and the familiar lines in *Childe Harold* IV, "There is a pleasure", etc.

The verse is noticeable as having two extra syllables; see *Introduction*, p. lxviii.

264. *envy*; cf. 175, note, and IV. 502, 503.

265. *Or this, or worse*; whether this, or worse, *be his design* (261).

265, 266. The creation of Eve (*Genesis* ii. 21, 22) is described in VIII. 465–71. Cf. the allusion in 1153, 1154.

270. *virgin*, sinless, innocent. *majesty of Eve*; an abstract expression for the concrete.

276. *the parting Angel*, Raphael, whose last words to Adam were a warning to "beware" and "stand fast" in his obedience (VIII. 633–43).

281. *May*, i.e. who may.

282. *thou fear'st not*. "Adam had not said so expressly, but had implied as much in enlarging particularly upon [their Enemy's] 'sly assault', 256" (Newton).

288. *thoughts which*; the abrupt transition to the interrogative form "how found they?" marks the agitation of the speaker.

harbour, dwelling-place, lodging; cf. 2 *Henry VI*, III. 1. 335, 336:

"Let pale-faced fear keep with the mean-born man,
    And find no harbour in a royal heart."

289. *misthought*, not rightly thought; a participle. *so dear*; cf. 228.

290. *healing words*; again in *S. A.* 605.

292. *entire*; in the literal sense of Lat. *integer* (from which *entire* is derived), 'untouched by, free from'. Lat. *in*, not + the root of *tango*, 'to touch'.

293. *Not diffident of thee*. 'It is not because I do not feel confidence in thee that I', etc.

304. *dare*, i.e. to offer; cf. "offered wrong", 300.

310. *Access in*, an increase of.

314. *raised unite*, concentrate it when raised.

320. *Less attributed to*, too little credit given to. *Less*, i.e. than she deserved. Apparently M. scanned *áttribúted*; cf. VIII. 12.

325. *like defence*, i.e. equal to, a match for, his force or fraud.

327. *only our foe*; she quotes Adam's argument (296–9) and then (329) endeavours to answer it.

330. *front*, brow, forehead (Lat. *frons*); used with quibbling allusion to "affronts" in 328.

334. *event*, issue, result, Lat. *eventus*; cf. 405, 984.

336. *Alone*; emphatic. 'What is the value of these qualities till they have been tested and stood the test by their own unaided merits?' The sentiment is that of the fine passage in the *Areopagitica* where M. says, "I cannot praise a cloistered virtue", i.e. one that does not go out into the world and face evil (*P. W.* II. 68).

339. *As not secure*, i.e. as not *to be* secure. *to single or combined*, to *us*, whether separated or together.

341. *no Eden*, i.e. "no place of happiness, not what its name denotes" (Keightley). "Eden" means 'pleasure'.

351. *But God left free the will*. On this point, as might be expected, M. dwells often; cf. X. 9, III. 96–128, V. 524–34. There is much bearing on the subject in chapters III and IV—on "The divine Decrees" and "Predestination"—of the 1st book of his discourse on *Christian Doctrine*.

351, 352. *what obeys Reason is free*; cf. XII. 83–101.

353. *ware*, i.e. wary. *still erect*, always on the alert.

358. *mind*, remind.

361. *suborned*, procured for an evil purpose; qualifying "object".

367. *approve*, give proof of, demonstrate; see G.

371. *securer*, less on our guard, "less prepared" (381). See G. *thou seem'st*, to be, i.e. "secure".
'It may be (says Adam) that if we remain together and let the trial come to us, instead of going to meet it, we shall not be so well prepared for it when it does come as you appear to be after my warning: if you think so, then go.'

372–5. The rapid, rather abrupt style is meant, apparently, to indicate some displeasure on the part of Adam.

372. Newton thought that Milton here had in mind the incident of his own wife's leaving him soon after their marriage; see *Introduction*, p. xvi.

377. I.e. for all her submissiveness she has the last word. It is in these side-touches that M. shows his own estimate of women. Indeed the picture he draws of Eve in this book is not agreeable. She is self-willed; easily flattered by the Serpent; disobedient of command (780, 781); selfish enough to drag down Adam in her fall (831); deceitful (877, 878); and so mean-spirited as to reproach him (1155–61).

387. *Oread*, a nymph of the mountain (Gk. ὄρος, a mountain). *Dryad*, a nymph of the wood—literally of the trees (Gk. δρῦς, an oak or any tree). *Delia*, Artemis or Diana, who was born in the island of *Delos*; the goddess of the chase, in which capacity

she was attended by a "train" of nymphs. M. refers to her in
Comus, 441, 442, as

> "the huntress Dian...
> Fair silver-shafted queen for ever chaste."

392. *Guiltless of fire*. The conception of fire and its uses occurs
to Adam later (x. 1070–8).

Guiltless of; cf. the similar use of 'innocent of'.

393–5. *Pales*, a Roman divinity of flocks and shepherds.
Pomona, the goddess of fruit (Lat. *pomum*); cf. v. 378. The story
of Pomona's being wooed by *Vertumnus*, one of the lesser rustic
deities of Roman mythology, is told by Ovid in *Metamorphoses*,
XIV. 623, *et seq.*

394. *Likest*; misprinted *Likeliest* in the Second Ed. Newton
restored the true reading.

395, 396. *Ceres*, the goddess of agriculture. *Yet virgin of*, i.e.
before she had become the mother of Proserpine by Jupiter.

Prosérpina, the Latin form; in IV. 269 he uses the Englished
form Proserpíne.

On the appositeness of the comparisons in 386–96 Pearce has
an excellent note. "She [Eve] was likened to the Nymphs and
Delia in regard to her gait; but now that Milton has mentioned
her being 'armed with garden tools,' he beautifully compares
her to Pales, Pomona, and Ceres, all three Goddesses like to each
other [and to Eve] in these circumstances, that they were hand-
some, that they presided over gardening and cultivation of
ground, and that they are usually described by the ancient poets
as carrying tools of gardening or husbandry in their hands."

401, 402. I.e. to be returned and *to have* all things, etc.; an
instance of *zeugma*.

409. *hellish rancour imminent*. The word-order, a noun between two qualifying epithets, is common in M.; cf. 5, 1047. We
find it in Greek; cf. Euripides, *Phœnissæ*, 234, νιφόβολον ὄρος
ἱρόν.

418. *more pleasant*, i.e. especially pleasant.

419. *tendance*, that which they tended; the abstract word
being used in a concrete sense, as often in M.

423. *to*, agreeably to, in harmony with. Cf. *S. A.* 1539, "And
to our wish I see one hither speeding", i.e. just as we wanted.

426. *bushing*; there is no authority for *blushing*, as some texts
print.

429. *Carnation*; an adjective; perhaps 'crimson'.

436. *voluble*; in the literal sense of Lat. *volubilis* = rolling.

438. *Imbordered*, planted so as to form a border.

each bank, i.e. either side of the "walk" (434).   *hand*, handi-
work; she had planted and tended the shrubs and flowers.

439, 440. There is a fuller allusion to the legend of the 'Garden
of Adonis' in *Comus*, 998–1002. No doubt, M. knew the long
description of the 'Garden' in the *Faerie Queene*, III. 6. 29–49,
which Keats in turn followed in *Endymion* II. The allusion is not
uncommon in Elizabethan writers. Cf. Ben Jonson, *Cynthia's
Revels*, v. 3, "I pray thee, light honey-bee, remember that thou
art not now in Adonis' garden, but in Cynthia's presence, where
thorns lie in garrison about the roses"; and Giles Fletcher,
Christ's Victorie on Earth, 40, "Adonis' garden was to this but
vayne". The chief classical authority for the legend is Pliny,
Natural History, XIX. 4, where the gardens of Adonis *and Alcinous*
are mentioned in the same sentence.

revived, i.e. after he was slain by the boar. According to the
myth, the prayers of Aphrodite (Venus) moved the gods of the
lower world to allow Adonis to return to the earth every year and
pass six months with the goddess. Spenser treats the story as an
allegory of the immortality of love and says (*Faerie Queene*, III.
6. 46–8) that after his restoration to life Aphrodite would not
let Adonis descend to the nether world but kept him in the
'Garden':

> "By her hid from the world, and from the skill
> Of Stygian Gods which doe her love envy."

440. *renowned*, i.e. through Homer's mention of him.

441. *Alcinous*, the king of the Phæacians in the island of
Scheria, who entertained Odysseus ("Laertes' son") in his
wanderings—*Odyssey* VII–XIII. The gardens and vineyard of his
palace are described in *Odyssey* VII. 112–32, a description which
made them proverbial for beauty. Hence the references to them
here and in v. 340, 341 and in Milton's third *Elegy*, 43, 44 (*non
dea tam variis ornavit floribus hortos | Alcinoi. . .Chloris*).

442, 443. Referring to the Garden of Solomon ("the sapient
king") mentioned in the *Song of Solomon*, VI. 2. By "fair Egyptian spouse" M. means "Pharaoh's daughter", 1 *Kings* iii. 1, to
whom the *Song* alludes in VII. 1 ("O prince's daughter"). Some
critics regard the *Song of Solomon* as an *epithalamium* on Solomon's marriage with this princess.

not mystic. M. inserts these words as the allusion is to Scripture—not as before, to classical legend. Contrast "feigned",
439.

445–54. Perhaps "only a narrative of what befell the poet in
his younger days, when living in his father's house in Bread

Street, in the City" (Keightley). Cf. the seventh of his Latin
Elegies, where, speaking of his youth, M. says:

> Et modo qua nostri spatiantur in urbe Quirites
> et modo villarum proxima rura placent:

lines which Cowper renders:

> "I shunned not, therefore, public haunts, but strayed
> Careless in city, or suburban shade."

(Probably the "public haunt" specially meant was Gray's Inn
Walk, then the fashionable promenade, and not far from Milton's
home.)

446. *annoy*, make *noisome*, pollute; see G.

450. *tedded*, mown and spread out to dry. Thomson, who
imitated M. much, has the word in his *Summer*, "Wide flies the
tedded grain", i.e. the corn-sheaves are scattered to dry. Of
Scandinavian origin.

453. *for her*, because of her.

454. *sums*, sums *up* (cf. 113).

456. *plat* = plot; see G.

458. *more soft*, i.e. than those *of Angels* (implied in "Angelic").

463. *That space*, i.e. for that space of time.

467, 468. Cf. the sentiment of the famous lines (I. 254, 255):

> "The mind is its own place, and in itself
> Can make a Heaven of Hell, a Hell of Heaven."

Though in, i.e. even if he were in.

471. *recollects*; in the literal sense 're-collects', i.e. gathers
together again; cf. I. 528 ("his wonted pride soon recollecting").

476. *for Hell*, i.e. as a substitute for, instead of.

476–8. I.e. not hope of enjoying pleasure but hope of destroying all pleasure, save such as lies in the work of destroying.

479, 480. *pass Occasion*, let slip the opportunity.

483. *intellectual*, intellect; see 606, note.

485. *of terrestrial mould*, i.e. "formed of earth" (149), a "man
of clay" (176). *mould* = material, substance; as often in M.

488. *to*, compared with.

489. Cf. Tennyson's description of Helen of Troy in *A Dream
of Fair Women*:

> "A daughter of the gods, divinely tall,
> And most divinely fair."

490, 491. I.e. love and beauty inspire a certain awe unless
there is a still stronger influence of hate to counteract them.

not approached, i.e. if not; the metaphor is continued in "way"
and "tend" (='direct my course'), 493.

496. *indented*; "going in and out like the teeth of a saw", says

6

Newton, who refers to the description of the snake in *As You Like It*, IV. 3. 113:

> " it unlink'd itself,
> And with indented glides did slip away."

502. *spires*, coils; Lat. *spira*, a coil, wreath. Cf. Pope, *Rape of the Lock*, 509, " Now glaring fiends, and snakes on rolling spires ".

505. "He here enumerates all the transformed serpents of which antiquity had told, viz. those into which Cadmus and his wife Harmonia were changed in Illyria; that which accompanied the Roman ambassadors from Epidaurus to Rome; and those which were regarded as the sires of Alexander the Great and of Scipio Africanus; of which the former ['he '] was said to have been Jupiter Ammon, the latter Jupiter Capitolinus" (Keightley).

not those that. . .changed, i.e. not those *serpents* that changed *into themselves* Hermione and Cadmus. This interpretation—Keightley's—seems the best; but some editors insert a comma after "changed", taking it intransitively and treating "Hermione and Cadmus" as in apposition to "those".

506. *Hermione*; the name usually given is Harmonia. The story how Cadmus, king of Thebes, and his wife Harmonia came to Illyria and were changed into serpents is told by Ovid in the *Metamorphoses*, IV. 562–602; a passage which M. seems to have had again in his mind when he described the final change of Satan, X. 511–32. The *Metamorphoses* was one of Milton's favourite books, according to his daughter's statement; see Johnson's *Life*.

506, 507. *the god*, Æsculapius, the god of medicine, whose chief seat of worship was at Epidaurus. At the time of a great pestilence at Rome the oracle of Delphi bade the Romans seek the aid of Æsculapius; so they sent ambassadors to Epidaurus and the god appeared to them in the form of a serpent which accompanied them back and stayed the pestilence at Rome, where Æsculapius was thenceforth worshipped. This legend also is told by Ovid, *Metamorphoses*, XV. 622–744.

507. *nor to which*, i.e. nor *those serpents* into which Jupiter Ammon was changed and was seen (i.e. by mortals).

The story that Jupiter Ammon—the "Libyan Jove", IV. 277, so called in allusion to his shrine in the Libyan desert—was the father of Alexander the Great occurs in Plutarch's *Life* of Alexander. Dryden uses it, with obvious reference to this passage, in *Alexander's Feast*, 21–9. A similar fable represented Jupiter *Capitolinus* (i.e. of the *Capitol*) as the father of Scipio Africanus,

the vanquisher of Hannibal. *Olympias*; the wife of Philip of Macedon.

510. *the highth*; the glory, pride; or perhaps 'the greatest man'.

516. *So*; his habitual way of introducing the completion of a simile; cf. 643, 677, 1059.

522. An allusion to the legend of the sorceress Circe who bewitched men with magic drugs, and then by a touch of her wand transformed them into animals (cf. "herd disguised") which she kept in subjection. Cf. the account in *Odyssey* x. how Odysseus came to the island of Æa where she dwelt, and how she changed some of his followers into swine. Milton represents Comus as the son of Circe and assigns to him the attributes of the Enchantress. See *Comus*, 50–77.

525. *turret*, towering. *enamelled*, smooth and variegated like enamel. Perhaps M. recollected *A Midsummer Night's Dream*, II. 1. 255, "And there the snake throws her enamell'd skin" (i.e. throws off, casts).

529, 530. I.e. either he actually used the serpent's tongue as an instrument of speech (although "not made" for it, 749), or he caused a voice to sound by impression of the air.

532. This description of the temptation should be compared with Eve's account of the dream in which she supposed herself to be tempted, v. 35–93.

533. *sole wonder*; cf. Comus's address to 'the Lady' in *Comus*, 265, "Hail foreign wonder"; and *The Tempest*, I. 2. 426, 427.

544. *shallow to*, without sufficient intelligence to; rather a favourite epithet of contempt with M.

549. *glozed*, spoke flatteringly; see G. *proem*, introduction; Gk. προοίμιον, a prelude in music (cf. "tuned"), hence a preface to a poem or speech.

553. *may*, can; the original use; cf. Germ. *mag*. So *might* = 'could', 598.

558. *The latter I demur*; 'as to the latter—"sense", 554—I am doubtful whether it was denied to brutes, for' etc. Probably this is an expression of Milton's own opinion; cf. VIII. 373, 374:
"They also know,
And reason not contemptibly";
where "they" = the brute creation. *demur*; see G.

560, 561. I.e. thee I knew *to be* the subtlest beast; because Raphael had so described the serpent when speaking with Adam and Eve (VII. 494, 495).

563. *speakable*; used actively, 'able to speak'.

of mute, from being mute; an imitation of the use of ἐκ in Greek and *ex* in Latin to express change from one condition to another; cf. the oft-quoted examples τυφλὸς ἐκ δεδορκότος (Sophocles, *Œdipus Rex*, 454) and Horace's *ex humili potens* (*Odes*, III. 30. 12). So in 712, X. 720, XI. 56, 57, XII. 167, and in Milton's prose works, e.g. in the *Tenure of Kings*, "raised them to be high and rich of poor and base", *P. W.* II. 47. Cf. Wordsworth, *The Recluse*, "Happier of happy though I be".

574. *apprehended*, understood.

575. *roving the field*; cf. *Comus*, 60, "Roving the Celtic and Iberian fields". So 'roam' is transitive in I. 521.

581, 582. *fennel*; of which serpents were supposed to be fond; cf. Pliny, *Natural History*, XIX. 9, *feniculum anguibus gratissimum*. They were also thought to suck the teats of sheep and goats. (From Newton's note.)

586–8. Cf. 740, 741.

599, 600. *to degree Of reason*, to the extent of giving me the faculty of reason.

inward; cf. "internal man", 711; externally there was no change in him, 601.

601. *Wanted not*, was not lacking. *retained*; in somewhat loose agreement with *me* (599).

605. *or middle*, in the air.

606. *fair*; similarly used as a noun by Shakespeare; cf. *Sonnet* XVI. 11, "Neither in inward worth nor outward fair". In Elizabethan writers the use of an adj. = a noun is common; cf. 'good', 'sweet', 986, 'deep', X. 844, 'pale', X. 1009.

612. *universal Dame*, mistress (*domina*) of all. Cf. "Empress", 568; "Queen of this universe", 684.

613. For a more striking instance of the same alliterative effect (*s...s*), designed to suggest the serpent's hiss, see X. 520–6.

spirited, possessed by a spirit.

615, 616. *thy overpraising*, i.e. of herself. She thinks that in his excessive compliments (cf. 605–12) he has scarcely shown such "reason" (600) as he said that the fruit conferred.

616. *virtue*, efficacy, power; cf. 649 and see G.

621. *greater*, i.e. than is touched. *store*, abundance, supply.

623. *to their provision*, to enjoy what is provided for them.

624. *birth*, produce—'what she *bears*'; *birth* is from A.S. *beran*, 'to bear', and in the original editions of *P. L.* the word is here spelt *bearth*. As in the passages where the word occurs in its ordinary sense it has its ordinary form, some editors think that M. intended the peculiar form *bearth* to indicate the some-

NOTES

what peculiar sense, and retain the form. The *New English Dictionary* (which does not recognise *bearth* as an independent form) quotes Dryden's translation of *Georgic* I. 196:

"The fruitful Earth
Was free to give her unexacted birth."

629. *blowing*, blossoming; see G. *balm*, i.e. the balsam-tree (Gk. βάλσαμος), to which "myrrh", a kind of thorny shrub, is akin. Of course 'balm' and 'balsam' are the same word in origin.

630. *conduct*, guidance, escort.

634. *wandering fire*, an *ignis fatuus*; cf. the German *elf-licht*.

635. *Compact of*, composed of; cf. *Titus Andronicus*, v. 3. 88, "My heart is not compact of flint nor steel".

638–42. Cf. Burton, *Anatomy of Melancholy*, "Fiery spirits or devils are such as commonly work by blazing Stars, Firedrakes, 'or *Ignes Fatui*'; which lead men often *in flumina*, aut *præcipitia*" (9th ed., 1800, I. 65). The chief of these spirits were Will-o'-the-Wisp and Jack-o'-the-Lanthorn. M. alludes to the superstition in *L'Allegro*, 104 (see Pitt Press note) and *Comus*, 433, but whether he himself believes in it we do not know as he is careful to add the qualifying words "they say". Cf. *Comus*, 432–7:

"*Some say* no evil thing that walks by night,
In fog or *fire*, by lake or moorish fen,

.   .   .   .

Hath hurtful power o'er true virginity."

640. M. recollected *A Midsummer-Night's Dream*, II. 1. 39, "Mislead night-wanderers, laughing at their harm" (said of the mischievous Puck; cf. also III. 1. 112).

643. *fraud*, offence, crime (Lat. *fraus*); or 'hurt', 'damage'.

645. *root*, source; used perhaps with a grim, quibbling allusion to "tree".

648. *Fruitless...fruit.* There are not a few of these jingling phrases in M. See note on l. 11, and cf. "beseeching or besieging", v. 869, "feats of war defeats", *S. A.* 1278. Generally he expresses sarcasm or contempt by them. The use of this figure of speech (*paronomasia*), is specially common in late Latin writers; see Mayor's note on Cicero's 2nd *Philippic* XI. 13. M. uses it in his Latin writings; cf. the *Christian Doctrine*, I. 11, "*Natura natam* se fatetur...et *fatum* quid nisi *effatum* divinum omnipotentis cujuspiam numinis potest esse?" Something similar is found in Hebrew.

653. *Sole*; because it was the only recorded command laid upon Adam and Eve; cf. IV. 421, 433.

daughter of his voice; a literal rendering of a Hebrew phrase
which implies 'a voice from Heaven'. Wordsworth describes
Duty as "Stern daughter of the Voice of God", *Ode to Duty*.

the rest, for the rest—'in all else' (Lat. *cetera*).

654. Cf. *Romans* ii. 14, "these . . . are a law unto themselves".

655–63. See *Genesis* iii. 1–3, the words of which M. follows
very closely.

655. *guilefully*; because he knew that only one tree—not "all"
—was forbidden them.

667. *New part puts on*, assumes a new character, i.e. feigning
indignant sympathy with man.

669. *Fluctuates*; used literally; 'undulates' (Lat. *fluctuat*) with
his body.

670. *some orator*; such as Demosthenes, to whom M. refers
in *P. R.* iv. 268–71; or Isocrates, the "old man eloquent" of his
Sonnet (x) "Daughter to that good Earl", and author of the
λόγος 'Αρεοπαγιτικός whence the title of the *Areopagitica* was
adapted; or Cicero (cf. 675, note). In *P. R.* iv. 356–60 he makes
the Saviour speak of the Prophets of Israel as better teachers of
the true principles of statesmanship "Than all the oratory of
Greece and Rome" (i.e. orators).

672. *since mute*, i.e. not merely in Greece and Rome, but
altogether, as though eloquence were an extinct quality.

addressed, ready to discuss. *addressed*; see G.

673. *in himself collected*, i.e. completely master of himself.

673, 674. *each part, Motion, each act*, the orator's whole form,
and every movement and gesture.

won audience, i.e. attention; cf. the picture of Satan addressing
his followers, x. 458, 459.

675. *in highth began*, plunged right into the subject (*in medias
res*). Probably (as Thyer remarked) M. had in mind the abrupt
commencement of Cicero's first Oration against Catiline—*quous-
que tandem abutere, Catilina, patientia nostra?*

680. *science*; in its original wide sense 'knowledge' (*scientia*);
cf. Gray's *Elegy*, 119, "Fair Science frown'd not on his humble
birth".

681, 682. Cf. Virgil's line *felix qui potuit rerum cognoscere
causas* (*Georgic* II. 490).

685–712. See *Genesis* iii. 4, 5.

687. *To knowledge*, i.e. in addition to.

698. *how just!* how right and proper, i.e. is knowledge of good.

700. *ye*; wrongly changed to *you* in some editions. Originally
ye was used for the nominative only and *you* for the objective

cases; cf. "Ye have not chosen me, but I have chosen you", *John* xv. 16. Elizabethan writers, however, often disregarded the distinction.

701. *not feared*, i.e. not to be feared.

702. *the fear*, i.e. of God. The Serpent's argument is—'Your fear of death implies injustice on the part of God: but if He is "not just", then is He "not God", and so not to be feared' (701).

710–12. So Adam also reasons; cf. 932–7.

710. *should*; so the original editions; *shall*, which some modern texts print, is obviously due to 708.

711. *Internal Man*; though externally he is still a serpent; cf. 601.

712. *of brute...of human*; the same idiom as in 563.

713. *So ye shall die perhaps*, i.e. *this* perhaps will be the death meant for you, of which you spoke (663).

713, 714. *put off...on*; cf. the New Testament often, e.g. *Colossians* iii. 9, 10, "ye have put off the old man...and have put on the new man".

Human = humanity; 606, note.

719. *On*, over; so as to influence our belief.

722. *if they*, i.e. produce.

729, 730. *can envy dwell*, etc.; a variation of Virgil's *tantæne animis cælestibus iræ*—*Æneid* I. 11. So in VI. 788; see also IV. 118, 119.

732. *humane*; a complimentary term, 'gracious'. Some editors interpret it = 'human', a sense which it does not bear in the two other places where M. uses it, viz. II. 109, *P. R.* I. 221.

735, 736. I.e. merely to behold which might tempt.

737. *impregned*, filled; Lat. *imprægnare*; cf. IV. 500.

740, 741. Cf. 586–8; V. 84–6. *with desire*; cf. *Genesis* iii. 6, "a tree to be desired".

742. *Inclinable*; leaning to, inclined towards (Lat. *inclinabilis*).

754. *Commends*, is recommendation of; 'makes thee seem more desirable'. *infers*, proves.

758. *In plain*; cf. "in few", i.e. words, X. 157.

768. *intellectual*; cf. "wise and wisdom-giving plant", 679.

771. *author*, informant. *unsuspect*, not to be suspected.

773, 774. 'Being ignorant of good and evil, how can I know what is to be feared?'

777. Cf. *Genesis* iii. 6, "good for food, and...pleasant to the eyes".

778. *Of virtue to*, with efficacy to; cf. 865, "of divine effect to".

781. *eat*; a preterite = *ate*; so often in Shakespeare; cf. *Macbeth*, II. 4. 18.

782-4. The introduction of "signs" and omens after the manner of classical writers occurs at several important points in the action of the poem. Cf. 1000-3; VIII. 513, 514; XI. 182-207. Similarly Grotius in his *Adamus Exul*, the tragedy on the Fall of Man with which M. is thought to have been acquainted, represents Eve's disobedient act as accompanied by portents—*arborque trepido tota subsiluit solo.*

783. The pathetic effect of the alliteration is noticeable; cf. the *Nativity Ode*, 186.

792. *knew not eating*, i.e. that she was eating; an imitation of the Greek use of a participle after verbs of knowledge or perception, as e.g. in Euripides, *Hecuba*, 397, οὐ γὰρ οἶδα δεσπότας κεκτημένος. So in *S. A.* 840, "Knowing, as needs I must, by thee betrayed", i.e. that I was betrayed.

793. *boon*, gay, cheerful; cf. 'boon companion'.

795. *virtuous...precious*; equivalent to superlatives. Ben Jonson in his *English Grammar*, book II, chapter IV, refers to this use of the positive, which may have been imitated from the Greek and Latin idiom. Editors quote δῖα θεάων, *Iliad* V. 381, and *sancte deorum*, *Æneid* IV. 576.

796. *operation*, effect; cf. 1012.

797. *To sapience*, even to the point of conferring wisdom; cf. 599 ("to degree of"). *infamed*, without fame, unknown.

800. *Not without*, with (Lat. *non sine*).

803-5. I.e. she intends to eat of the fruit till she equals the gods ("others"), however much they may grudge ("envy") her the knowledge.

805-7. The Serpent had argued that the tree was not the gift of the gods, 718-28.

807. *Experience*, making trial. *owe*, am under an obligation.

811-13. Cf. texts like *Psalms* x. 11, xciv. 7, *Job* xxii. 13, 14.

815. *safe*, not dangerous, not likely to harm; cf. the colloquial phrase 'safe out of the way'. *Macbeth* (III. 4. 25) asks the murderer, "But Banquo's safe?", i.e. disposed of, so as not to cause trouble.

818. *give him to partake*; cf. the Latin idiom, as in *Æneid* I. 66, *tibi divum pater...mulcere dedit fluctus.*

820. *odds*, balance, advantage; cf. x. 374.

821. *to add what wants*, to supply what is deficient.

823. *more equal*. Cf. Milton's earliest description (IV. 296) of Adam and Eve, "Not equal, as their sex not equal seemed".

Johnson says, "The superiority of Adam is diligently sustained" (*Life* of Milton). Cf. IV. 295–9, 635–8; VIII. 540–75; X. 145–56, 888–98: passages which, taken together, are evidence of Milton's own conception of the difference between man and woman. There is indeed something curiously personal in the references to woman in his poems, as though he could not refrain from expressing his own views; cf. 1182–6.

830. *to think*, i.e. of.

832, 833. Cf. Horace's *tecum vivere amem, tecum obeam libens* (*Odes* III. 9. 24).

837. *sciential*, conferring knowledge, i.e. on those who partake of it; see G. There is a happy allusion to Milton in Lamb's essay *Oxford in the Long Vacation*, where he describes his visits to the libraries: "I seem to inhale learning...; and the odour of their [the books'] old moth-scented coverings is fragrant as the first bloom of those sciential apples which grew amid the happy orchard" (i.e. of Eden).

845. *divine of*, foreboding = Lat. *divinus* in the sense 'prophetic of', as in Horace, *Ars Poetica* 218, *divina futura... sententia*.

846. *the faltering measure*, the tremulous, uneven 'beat' of his heart.

851. *smiled*; cf. Lat. *ridere* in the sense 'to look pleasant'.

852. *ambrosial*; see G.

853, 854. I.e. the pleading expression in her face, showing that she was conscious of guilt, served to introduce the apology she was about to make. The construction seems to be, 'excuse came as prologue and (came) to lead up to apology'—*prompt* being a verb. The alteration "*too* prompt" (adj.) is tempting, but has no authority.

864. *tasted*, if tasted.

867. *tasted such*, i.e. tasted and found such.

872. *to admiration*; cf. F. *à merveille*, admirably, wonderfully well.

875. *to correspond*, to be the same in me as in the Serpent. *opener mine eyes*; cf. 706–8, 985.

877–85. A deceitful argument; contrast her reasoning in 823–5.

890. *Astonied*, astonished; cf. *Job* xvii. 8, "Upright men shall be astonied at this". See G. *horror chill*; cf. Virgilian expressions like *gelidus tremor* and *frigidus horror* (*Æneid* II. 120, 121, III. 29).

899. *amiable*, lovely, pleasing to the eye; of the five epithets

in the line it is the only one that carries on the notion in " fairest ",
896, and " to sight ", 898. See G.

901. The alliteration seems to emphasise the certainty and
hopelessness of her doom. *to death devote*; from Horace's line
devota morti pectora liberæ (*Odes* IV. 14. 18). *devote*; see G.

910. *wild.* The epithet well marks Adam's distress: even Paradise has suddenly lost its beauty in his eyes and become " wild "
and dreary.

914, 915. "And Adam said, This is now bone of my bones,
and flesh of my flesh: she shall be called Woman " (*Genesis* ii. 23).

922. *hast*; so the First Ed.; the Second *hath*.

922, 923. The original editions have a comma after " dared ",
with the sense—'who hast been so daring, had it been only in
gazing on the fruit covetously '. Some editors remove the comma
after " dared " and make the construction " dared to eye ": a
needless change, I think. *sacred to*, devoted to (= Lat. *sacer*).

927. *so*, even so, i.e. though what is done cannot be undone.

928. *fact*; in the literal sense 'deed', Lat. *factum*; cf. 980.

929. *heinous*; see G. *foretasted fruit*, the fruit having been
tasted already, i.e. " by the serpent ", 930.

932–7. This was the Serpent's argument to Eve; cf. 710–12.

939. *in earnest*, really.

940. *prime*, chief; Lat. *primus*, first.

944. *frustrate*, frustrated, baffled in his design; see *animate* in
the Glossary.

945. *Not well conceived of*, i.e. it is not to be supposed that the
Almighty would act thus. Cf. " Nor can I think that ", 938.

947, 948. *lest the Adversary…say.* Cf. *Deuteronomy* xxxii.
27. For " the Adversary " = Satan, according to the meaning of
the name, cf. *Job* i. 6 (margin), 1 *Peter* v. 8.

951. *Matter of*, material, or occasion, for; cf. 1177.

953. *Certain to*, resolved to. An imitation of Lat. *certus*, with
infinitive or gerund, = 'determined to'; cf. *certus eundi* and *certa
mori* (*Æneid* IV. 554, 564).

964. *attain*, i.e. to it, viz. Adam's " perfection ".

965. *I boast me sprung*; cf. the Homeric εὔχομαι εἶναι.

967. Cf. VIII. 604 and the definition of friendship—" one soul
in two bodies ".

974. *by occasion*, indirectly.

977–81. Again her deceitfulness is marked; contrast 826–31.

980. *oblige*; in the sense of Lat. *obligare*, to render liable to
punishment, make guilty. *fact*; cf. 928.

986. *Taste*, the sense of taste, palate. *sweet*; cf. 606, note.

989. Cf. the proverbial phrase 'to scatter to the winds'. Newton compares Horace, *Odes* I. 26. 1–3.

998. *not deceived*; as Eve was by the serpent; Adam sinned wilfully. Cf. 1 *Timothy* ii. 14, "And Adam was not deceived, but the woman being deceived was in the transgression".

999. Cf. x. 151–3. *fondly*, foolishly.

1000–4. Cf. 782–4 (with note).

1003, 1004. It has been remarked that this is the only passage in the poem where M. uses the phrase 'Original Sin'; the doctrine expressed by it he discusses in the treatise on *Christian Doctrine*, I. VII, XI (*P. W.* IV. 193–5, 260–2).

1007. *that*, so that.

1009. *swim*, revel; cf. XI. 625, "swim in joy". So in the *Faerie Queene*, I. 12. 41, "Yet swimming in that sea of blissful joy".

1011. Cf. Horace's *spernit humum fugiente penna* (*Odes* III. 2. 24).

1018. *elegant*; in the sense of Lat. *elegans*, 'refined in taste', 'fastidious'. Cf. v. 335, "tastes…inelegant".

1019, 1020. "Since we use the word *savour* in both senses [physical and moral], and apply it to the understanding as well as to the palate" (Newton). In this rather far-fetched thought M. is really playing upon the two senses of Lat. *sapere*, 'to taste' and 'to have discernment, be wise'—both *sapience* (1018) and *savour* (through the French) coming from *sapere*. Newton quotes the same quibble from Cicero's *de Finibus* II. 8, *nec enim sequitur ut cui cor sapiat ei non sapiat palatum*. "Taste", e.g. 'man of taste', lends itself to the same sort of word-play.

1026. *For*, instead of.

1027. Cf. *Exodus* xxxii. 6.

1034. *toy*, caress.

1042. Cf. *Proverbs* vii. 18.

1046–52. Contrast the earlier description of Adam's sleep (v. 4, 3) as

> "aery light, from pure digestion bred,
> And temperate *vapours bland*."

1050. *unkindly*, not natural. *fumes*, vapours, as of intoxication; cf. Dryden, *Aurengzebe*:

> "Power like new *wine* does your weak brain surprise,
> And its mad *fumes* in hot discourses rise."

1056, 1057. *confidence…righteousness…honour*, i.e. "were gone".

1058. *Shame*; personified, as in 1097. In the original editions the sense was obscured by the omission of a stop after "shame".

1058, 1059. *he covered*; cf. *Psalm* cix. 29, "Let mine adversaries be clothed with shame".

but his robe Uncovered more, i.e. Shame, till then unknown to them (IV. 313–18), made them conscious of their nakedness. The thought is worked out in his *Christian Doctrine*, I. XII (*P. W.* IV. 264).

1059–62. See *Judges* xvi. 4–20; and cf. *Samson Agonistes* almost *passim*. There is a striking application of the story in *The Reason of Church Government*, book II (*P. W.* II. 506); cf. also the allusion in *Eikonoklastes* XXII.

the Danite; cf. the description of Samson's father Manoah in *Judges* xiii. 2, "a man of Zorah, of the family of the Danites", i.e. of the Tribe of Dan.

1061. Some editors have put forward the view that here and in the three lines of *S. A.* where the name occurs M. treated the second syllable of *Dalilah* as short or unaccented, e.g. *Dalīlah*, a scansion which seems to me as unpleasant as it is needless. The correct accentuation is *Dalīlah* (=Daleelah), and the last two syllables form a trochee or "inversion of rhythm" such as M. admits into any foot of his blank verse; see p. lxiii. Thus the present line, I think, runs

"Of Phíl|isté|an Da|lílah, | and wák'd,"

the third foot having no stress or accent; see p. lxiv.

The lines in *S. A.* in which the name comes are:

"Was in the vale of Sorec, Da|líla," 229:

"Than Da|líla | thy wife," 723 (a short verse):

"The sump|tuous Da|líla | floating this way," 1072.

In each verse the trochee is rhythmical and quite regular. 'Dalilah' follows the first syllable of the Greek form; the form in the Authorised Version, 'Delilah', is nearer to the Hebrew. As printed in *S. A.* the name has no *h*, perhaps an intentional difference, M. being extremely particular where *sound* was affected.

1062. *they*, i.e. "waked".

1064. *strucken*; cf. *The Comedy of Errors*, I. 2. 45, "The clock hath strucken twelve upon the bell". The forms of the preterite and past participle of *strike* vary greatly in Elizabethan English.

1068. *worm*, serpent; cf. *Antony and Cleopatra*, V. 2. 243, where Cleopatra asks for the asp or serpent to kill herself, "Hast thou the pretty worm of Nilus there?"

1069. *true in*, i.e. in regard to.

1079. *the last*, the worst, greatest; cf. Lat. *extremus*, *ultimus*. *of the first*, i.e. lesser evils, which they may well expect, seeing

that they have already experienced the greatest of evils, viz. shame.

1080–2. Cf. X. 723–5, XI. 315–17.

1083. *this earthly*, i.e. shape; or "earthly" might be a noun = 'mortal nature', as in VIII. 453, "My earthly by his Heavenly overpowered".

1086–8. Cf. IV. 244–6:

"Both where the morning sun first warmly smote
The open field, and where the unpierced shade
Imbrowned the noontide bowers—"

'unpierced', i.e. by the sun.

1087. *To star*. Newton quotes Statius, *Thebais* X. 85, 86, *nulli penetrabilis astro | lucus iners*, which perhaps suggested Spenser's description of the grove "Not perceable with power of any starr", *Faerie Queene*, I. I. 7. Cf. *Arcades*, 88, 89:

"Under the shady roof
Of branching elm star-proof."

1088. *brown*, dark; see G. *cover me*; cf. *Revelation* vi. 16.

1090. *them*; the "Heavenly shapes", 1082.

1091. *as in*, seeing that we are in; Lat. *ut*; cf. X. 978.

1101–11. The reference is to the banyan-tree or Indian fig (*Ficus indica*). Warton pointed out that M. has followed closely —cf. the numerous verbal similarities—the account of this tree in Gerard's *Herball*, 1597 (the standard Elizabethan work on botany), where it is called "the arched Indian Fig-tree". Gerard, who took his information on the subject from Pliny, *Natural History*, XII. 5, says:

"The ends [of its branches] hang doune, and touch the ground, where they take roote and grow in such sort that theyr twigs become great trees; and these, being grown up unto the like greatnesse, do cast their branches or twiggy tendrels into the earth, where they likewise take hold and roote; by means whereof it cometh to passe that of one tree is made a great wood or desart of trees, which the Indians do use for coverture against the extreme heat of the sun. Some likewise use them for pleasure, cutting doune by a direct line a long walke, or as it were a vault, through the thickest part, from which also they cut certain loop-holes or windowes in some places, to the end to receive thereby the fresh cool air that entreth thereat, as also for light that they may see their cattell that feed thereby.... From which vault or close walke doth rebound such an admirable echo or answering voice.... The first or mother of this wood is hard to be known from the children."

The description of the size of the leaves of this tree—"broad as Amazonian targe", 1111—is due to the same source, Gerard reproducing Pliny's mis-statement that *foliorum latitudo peltæ effigiem Amazonicæ habet*. The description is inaccurate as the leaves of the *banyan* are small: it is the *banana* or plaintain tree that has large leaves which "are used, on the coast of Malabar, in the same manner as here by Adam and Eve" (Keightley). Pliny in describing the *Ficus indica* evidently united the characteristics of the *banyan* and *banana*, and apparently writers even later than M. repeat the confusion. The banyan from its peculiar character is described in many early travels, e.g. in Sir Thomas Herbert's (1634) and Tavernier's (1684).

1103. *Decan*; the name was often applied to the Indian peninsula in general, i.e. so as to include Malabar.

1111. Cf. Virgil's reference to the 'crescent-shaped shields' (*lunatæ peltæ*) of the Amazons, *Æneid* 1. 490. *targe*; see G.

1113. Cf. the marginal rendering in *Genesis* iii. 7, "things to gird about".

1115. *of late*, i.e. as compared with the remote events of which the poem treats; not strictly "of late" in relation to Milton's own time, because the date of Columbus's discovery was 1492.

1117. *With feathered cincture*. Hence Gray's phrase, "feather-cinctur'd chiefs", spoken of the Indians of South America, *The Progress of Poetry*, 62.

1127-31. Cf. 351-6.

1140, 1141. Cf. Eve's words "what is *faith*...unassayed?" 335. *approve*; cf. 367. *owe*, possess; see G.

1144. Cf. Homer's ποῖόν σε ἔπος φύγεν ἕρκος ὀδόντων.

1154. Cf. 265, 266, note.

1155. *the head*. An allusion to 1 *Corinthians* xi. 3, "the head of the woman is the man". So in IV. 443.

1158. *facile*, yielding. *gainsay*, oppose my wish.

1159. Alluding to 372-5.

1163, 1164. *the love*, i.e. that you have to offer me; "*thy* love" is a needless change. *the recompense*, i.e. that you make *for my love* to you.

1164, 1165. *expressed Immutable*, shown to be unchanging; the words refer to Adam's love for Eve, which he had "expressed", i.e. demonstrated, so strikingly; cf. 961, 962.

1175. *secure*, feeling sure.

1182-6. No doubt, an expression of Milton's own opinion.

1183. *women*; he may have dictated *woman*.

1189. *contest.* M. accents both noun and verb (x. 756), as we do the verb alone, *contést*; cf. XI. 800, " In sharp *contést* of battle found no aid ".

BOOK X

1. *heinous*; cf. IX. 929. *despiteful*, full of spite, i.e. against the Almighty; see IX. 175, note.

5–7. Contrast IX. 811–16.

9. *with. . .free will armed.* Cf. 46 and see IX. 351, note.

10. *Complete to*, fully equipped so as to; qualifying " mind " or " Man ". Some editors remove the comma of the original editions after " armed ", which they connect with " complete ". But the rhythm seems to me to favour a slight pause at the end of verse 9.

12. *they*, i.e. " Man ", 9, used collectively, as in *Genesis* i. 26.

14. *which*, i.e. " injunction ", 13.

16. *manifold in sin.* " The Divines. . .reckon up several sins as included in this one act of eating the forbidden fruit, namely, pride, uxoriousness, wicked curiosity, infidelity, disobedience, etc." (Newton). M. has a passage to this effect in the *Christian Doctrine*, I. XI (*P. W.* IV. 254).

18. *The Angelic guards*, i.e. the Cherubim; cf. IX. 61, 62, 156, 157.

19. *by this*, i.e. time; cf. *Julius Cæsar*, I. 3. 125, "And I do know, by this, they stay for me ".

20. 21. *had stolen Entrance*; as is described in IX. 69–76.

29. I.e. to make appear accountable = to explain, justify.

accountable; in the sense 'that can be accounted for'; not, as more often, 'liable to render account'.

32. *his secret cloud.* The description is based on passages like *Exodus* xxxiii. 9, 10; 1 *Kings* viii. 10, 11; *Ezekiel* x. 4: to which (and others) M. refers in the chapter, I. 11, of his *Christian Doctrine* that treats " Of God " (*P. W.* IV. 29). Cf. the fuller allusion in III. 378–81.

33. "And out of the throne proceeded lightnings and thunderings and voices", *Revelation* iv. 5. Where he is describing Heaven M. draws largely on the Book of *Revelation*, as we should expect.

35. *charge*, duty, office, viz. of guarding Man; cf. IX. 157.

38. *Foretold*, having been warned. *so lately*; see III. 80 *et seq.*

39. *the gulf*, of Chaos; cf. 253, 366, III. 70.

40. *speed*, be successful in.

42. *flattered*; cf. IX. 532–48, 606–12.

lies; cf. IX. 703–9, 716–30.

45. *moment*, force = Lat. *momentum*, the metaphor being taken from a balance; cf. "inclining" (46), "even scale" (47). So in VI. 239.

48. *rests*, remains, Lat. *restat*; cf. 3 *Henry VI*, V. 7. 42, 43:

> "And now what rests but that we spend the time
> With stately triumphs?"

pass, should be pronounced.

50. *presumes…vain*, i.e. to be vain; cf. Adam's words, IX. 928–37.

52. *By some immediate stroke*; see 210. Cf. the *Christian Doctrine*, I. XII, "Under the head of death, in Scripture, all evils whatever, together with everything which in its consequences tends to death, must be understood as comprehended; for mere bodily death did not follow the sin of Adam on the selfsame day, as God had threatened" (*P. W.* IV. 263).

54. *as bounty*, i.e. has been scorned. Man had shown scorn of the gifts of the Almighty by seeking something more which was forbidden him.

55–7. Cf. *John* v. 22, "For the Father judgeth no man, but hath committed all judgment unto the Son".

Vicegerent, i.e. ruling in place of the Father.

58. *may*; so the First Ed.; the Second has *might*.

59. *Mercy…justice*. Cf. *Psalm* lxxxv. 10 and see the *Nativity Ode*, 141–4.

60. *his Mediator*. M. discusses the "Mediatorial office" of Christ in the *Christian Doctrine*, I. XV.

63–7. For similar passages see III. 138–42, 384–9, VI. 680–2, 719–21; and cf. *Hebrews* i. 3, "Who being the brightness of his glory, and the express image of his person,…sat down on the right hand of the Majesty on high".

67. *Expressed*, showed forth.

70, 71. Cf. *Matthew* xvii. 5, "This is my beloved Son, in whom I am well pleased".

74. *time*, i.e. the appointed time; cf. III. 284, "Made flesh, when time shall be, of virgin seed".

for so I undertook; as was related in III. 222–65. See "The Story of the Poem", *Introduction*, p. lx.

77. *derived*, turned aside. Lat. *derivare*, 'to divert a stream from its channel', hence figuratively, 'to turn aside', 'divert'.

79. *Them*; "Justice" and "Mercy".

80. *need*, be necessary; cf. the intransitive use of "want", 869. *train*, i.e. of Angels to accompany him.

82. *the third*, the Serpent.

83. *Convict*, convicted; see *animate* in the Glossary.

84. *Conviction*, proving guilty; this is not necessary because the Serpent has admitted his own guilt by flight. The line emphasises the words "convict by flight".

86. *Of high collateral glory.* Cf. 64 ("Toward the right hand").

86–8. Compare the description of the Son accompanied to the gate of Heaven by a host of Angelic beings as he goes forth to create the Universe, VII. 192–209. *Thrones...Powers*, etc.; titles of the Heavenly beings; see *Appendix*, pp. 144–6.

88, 89. Cf. VII. 617–25. *coast*, region; see G.

90, 91. Cf. Raphael's account of his descent from Heaven to Paradise, VIII. 110–14.

92. The time is determined by *Genesis* iii. 8 ("in the cool of the day").

94. *usher*; see G.

95. *more cool*, i.e. than "the evening cool": not a very happy play on words.

96. *Intercessor.* "And he saw that there was no man, and wondered that there was no intercessor", *Isaiah* lix. 16. Cf. III. 219, XI. 19. Milton deals with the subject of Christ's intercession for man, as one aspect of his office as 'Mediator', in *Christian Doctrine*, I. xv (*P. W.* IV. 301, 302).

97–223. The whole scene follows *Genesis* iii. 8–21 closely, the words of the Scripture being worked into the text, just as in Shakespeare's Roman historical plays the language of North's *Plutarch* is constantly reproduced. In many passages of the poem, especially where he represents the Deity as speaking, M. reproduces the Scripture thus, merely adapting it to the form of blank verse.

106. *obvious*; in the sense of Lat. *obvius*, coming to meet; see G.

112. *apparent*, clear, manifest; see G.

120. *still*, ever, always.

121, 122. Cf. IX. 1051–9, 1070–98.

128. *My other self* = ἕτερος αὐτός, *alter ego*, applied to a very intimate friend. Cf. VIII. 450, "Thy likeness, thy fit help, thy other self" (spoken to Adam in reference to Eve).

131, 132. The lines are suggestive of *Lycidas*, 6, 7.

135. *should I*, i.e. *even* if I should.

145. *she...her*; emphatic.

146. *Before*, in preference to.

149, 150. See IX. 265, 266 (note), and cf. IV. 440, 441.

150–6. We have the same sentiments—no doubt, Milton's own—expressed more fully in VIII. 537–42, 567–76. See also IX. 823, note.

154. I.e. such as were seemly while subject to her husband's government.

155, 156. *part*...*person*; terms drawn from the stage. 'It was for you to play the part (cf. IX. 667) and character (Lat. *persona*) of ruler.' Cf. the expression *dramatis personæ*. So in *P. R.* II. 240.

157. *in few*, i.e. words; cf. *Henry V*, I. 2. 245. So "in plain", IX. 758.

161. *Bold*; as when she plucked the forbidden fruit (IX. 780, 781).

loquacious; as in her argument with Adam (IX. 273 *et seq.*).

165. *unable*; qualifying "Serpent".

166. *on him*, Satan. *made him*, the Serpent.

167. *end*, object.

169. *More to know*, i.e. that the Serpent was only the instrument of Satan.

173. *mysterious*, because they had an inner application, viz. to Satan, which, for the time, was to be hidden from Adam, who would suppose that they referred to the Serpent. Later (1033–5) Adam perceives the application.

judged as then best; an inversion of order; 'as was then thought best'.

175–81. See *Genesis* iii. 14, 15.

181. *Her seed*, i.e. in the person of the Son of Man (183).

182. *then verified*. The 'verification' described (183–90) is of the last and most significant words of the whole curse, viz. "Her seed shall bruise", etc. (180).

183. *Mary, second Eve*; repeated from v. 387. The thought is similar to that which makes Christ "the last Adam", 1 *Corinthians* xv. 45.

184. "And he said unto them, I beheld Satan as lightning fall from heaven", *Luke* x. 18.

185. Cf. *Ephesians* ii. 2, "the prince of the power of the air", referring to Satan.

It should be remembered that tradition identified the fallen Angels with the "dæmons" of classical mythology who were supposed to inhabit the four "elements" of air, earth, fire and water. M. alludes to this belief in various passages; cf. II. 274, 275, 397–402 (notes), and *P. R.* II. 121–6. It is, however, especially as the "dæmons" or rulers of "the air" that he represents Satan and his followers (i.e. after the Fall of Man). Cf. 188, 189

and *P. R.* I, where Satan summons a council of his followers in "mid air" (39), and addresses them, 44–6:

> "O ancient powers of air and this wide world
> (For much more willingly I mention air,
> This our old conquest, than remember Hell)."

185–90. Based on the following texts: *Colossians* ii. 15; *Psalm* lxviii. 18; *Romans* xvi. 20. Cf. III. 247–56.

191. *his fatal bruise*, i.e. Satan's.

207. *birth*, origin.

213. *suffer change*; cf. 651 *et seq.*

214, 215. See *Philippians* ii. 7; *John* xiii. 5.

217. *slain*; apparently for the purpose, as hitherto it has been implied that the beasts were not killed by each other (see 710, note) or by Adam.

218. *repaid*, i.e. for the loss of their old skin. "Pliny mentions some lesser creatures shedding their skins in the manner of snakes, but that is hardly authority sufficient for such a notion as this" (Newton).

219. *thought not much*; cf. *The Tempest*, I. 2. 252.

his enemies; because it was their sin that necessitated His sacrifice.

222. *robe of righteousness*; see *Isaiah* lxi. 10.

225. "The only-begotten Son, which is in the bosom of the Father", *John* i. 18.

229. *was sinned and judged*; for the use of the impersonal construction cf. VI. 335, 336:

> "Forthwith on all sides to his aid was run
> By Angels many and strong" (i.e. Lat. *cursum est*).

230. Sin as a personified figure is introduced under the title Hamartia (Gk. ἁμαρτία, fault, sin) in Phineas Fletcher's *Purple Island*, XII. 27; cf. too his *Apollyonists*, I. 10 *et seq.*, and Spenser's description of Error, *Faerie Queene*, I. 1. 14 *et seq.* For the personification of Death we may remember *Revelation* vi. 8, and the θάνατος of Euripides' *Alcestis*. Death is found too among the allegorical figures of the Morality plays, and in Spenser, *Faerie Queene*, VII. 7. 46.

231. *In counterview*, i.e. opposite each other, one "on either side" (II. 649) of the entrance; *vis-à-vis*. Cf. 235.

231, 232. *the gates...Now open wide.* Cf. the description in II. 871–89 how Sin, "the Portress of Hell-gate", opened "the infernal doors" to let Satan pass out on his journey through Chaos to the new-created World and then could not shut them. *Now*; emphatic.

232. *outrageous*; see the noun in the Glossary.

235. *O Son.* M. makes Sin the daughter of Satan, and Death ("the sin-born monster", 596) the offspring of Satan and Sin ("the incestuous mother", 602). See II. 727–814. The allegory is based partly on *James* i. 15, "Then when lust hath conceived, it bringeth forth sin: and sin, when it is finished, bringeth forth death".

236. *author*, parent. *thrives*, succeeds, prospers; cf. 360.

241. *avengers*; so the Second Ed.; the First Ed. has *avenger*; but cf. "*their* revenge", 242.

like this, i.e. so well as this; qualifying "can fit".

246. Cf. 263, 358, 359, and the "Argument" of the book, ll. 6, 7 ("by wondrous sympathy").

249. *secretest*; cf. *Macbeth*, III. 4. 126, "the secret'st man of blood".

Thou, my shade, i.e. shadow; cf. IX. 12, note. Sin and Death are always introduced together in the poem: an allegory of their connection.

253. *Stay*, hinder. *his*, Satan's.

256. *unagreeable*, unsuitable. *found*, build; Lat. *fundare*, to lay the foundation of.

257. *this main*, the "sea" (286) of Chaos; "the foaming Deep", 301.

260, 261. "*Intercourse*, passing frequently backward and forward; *transmigration*, quitting Hell once for all to inhabit the new creation; they were uncertain which their lot should be" (Richardson).

264. *meagre*; in the literal sense 'lean', F. *maigre*; cf. the conventional representation of Death as a skeleton.

266, 267. *err The way*, i.e. miss; or wander from.

274. *ravenous fowl.* "Of vultures particularly it is said by Pliny, that they will fly three days beforehand to places where there are future carcases—*triduo antea volare eos ubi cadavera futura sunt* [*Nat. Hist.* x. 6]. And (what probably gave occasion to this similitude in Milton) Lucan has described [VII. 831–5] the ravenous birds that followed the Roman camps, and scented the battle of Pharsalia" (Newton). Cf. *Julius Cæsar*, V. 1. 85–7, where on the morning of the battle Cassius says:

> "ravens, crows, and kites
> Fly o'er our heads, and downward look on us,
> As we were sickly prey," (i.e. as if).

though; the reading *through* has no authority.

279. *So*; see IX. 516, note. *Feature*, shape, form; as com-

monly in Shakespeare, from the literal meaning 'make', O.F. *faiture*, Lat. *factura*. M. purposely uses rather a vague word which leaves much to the imagination; cf. the description of Death in II. 666–8:

> "The other Shape—
> If shape it might be called that shape had none
> Distinguishable in member, joint or limb."

279, 280. Cf. *Georgic* I. 376, *suspiciens patulis captavit naribus auras*.

281. *Sagacious of*, scenting (Lat. *sagax*). *quarry*, prey; see G.

282, 283. *waste Wide*; one of his favourite alliterative effects, here suggestive of desolation.

anarchy, disordered realm; an abstract word in a concrete sense; cf. VI. 873. In II. 988 Chaos is personified as "the Anarch old".

284–302. Lines 284–8 describe how Sin and Death collected towards the mouth of Hell the materials for their causeway: ll. 293–8 how Death made the materials coalesce into solid masses suitable for the purposes mentioned in the next verses: ll. 299–302 how the materials were used partly to form the foundation of the whole structure, partly to construct the bridge raised on those foundations. "Aggregated soil" in 293 and "gathered beach" in 299 refer to the "solid" elements mentioned in 286, while "asphaltic slime" in 298 refers to the "slimy" elements, 286. By "the rest" in 296 he means, I think, all such "solid" elements as are not included under "soil" in 293: the "slime", i.e. pitch, helps to bind these elements together: the "soil" may be conceived as coalescing more easily under the petrifying stroke of Death's sceptre. In 296–8 the sense obviously is that Death bound the elements together by means of his look and by means of the slime; the manner of expression is rather strained but, as it seems to me, quite Miltonic, the combination of an abstract word like "rigour" and a literal word like "slime" being somewhat similar to I. 502, "flown with insolence and wine".

288. *shoaling*; apparently transitive; 'driving it in a shoal or bank'.

290. *the Cronian sea*, the Arctic Ocean; from the Lat. name *Cronium Mare* (Pliny, *Natural History* IV. 16), less used than *Mare Concretum*.

291. *the imagined way*, i.e. the north-east passage, then thought to be practicable and made the object of many voyages of discovery to India and the East. Cf. a similar allusion in the *Areopagitica*, "a passage far easier and shorter than an Indian

voyage, though it could be sailed. . . by the north of *Cataio* eastward" (i.e. even though it could) (*P. W.* II. 69).

292. *Petsora*, the gulf of Petchora in the Arctic Ocean, at the mouth of the river of that name. M. speaks of the river "Pechora or Petzora", and of the town of the same name in his *History of Moscovia*, quoting as his authority the narratives of certain merchants of Hull who had wintered in those parts in the year 1611; see *P. W.* v. 396, 431.

292, 293. *the. . .Cathaian coast*; commonly explained 'the coast of China'—with doubtful correctness, however. Strictly 'Cathay' was identical with China, *Cathay* being a corruption of *Kitai*, the name by which China is still known in Russia and in many Asiatic countries. But formerly, till some time after 1600, the opinion prevailed that 'Cathay' was a great region distinct from China, lying north of it and stretching right up to the Arctic Ocean; comprehending, in fact, East Siberia. Cathay is marked so in many old maps, and its capital was supposed to be Cambalu—i.e. Cambalu was regarded as a different city from Pekin, the capital of China, though properly they were the same. I believe that this was Milton's notion of Cathay, from the references to it in the *History of Moscovia* and from the fact that in *P. L.* XI. 388 and 390 he treats "Cambalu, seat of *Cathaian* Can" and "Paquin [*Pekin*] of *Sinæan* kings" as two distinct cities. (*Sinæan*: cf. *Tsin*, the title of the great dynasty from which the country derived the name *Tsina* = *China*.)

rich. In the *History of Moscovia* he touches several times on the wealth and trade of the cities of Cathay (*P. W.* v. 407). Indeed the wealth of this mysterious land had become proverbial through the reports of travellers from the time of Marco Polo onwards. See chapter XX in Mandeville's *Voiage*.

294. *mace*, sceptre; cf. *Henry V*, IV. I. 278, "The sword, the mace, the crown imperial". Todd quotes from the play *Dido, Queen of Carthage*, by Marlowe and Nash, "like pale Death's stony mace" (II. I. 116, Bullen's ed. II. 320). Burke has an effective allusion to this line in the *Reflections on the Revolution in France*, part II, section v—"sooner thaw the eternal ice of his atlantic regions, than restore the central heat to Paris, whilst it remains 'smitten with the cold, dry petrifick mace' of a false and unfeeling philosophy" (Payne's ed., p. 288).

296. *Delos*; one of the Cyclades Islands, in the Ægean Sea. "According to a legend, founded perhaps on some tradition of its late volcanic origin, it was called out of the deep by the trident [cf. 'as with a trident', 295] of Poseidon [= Neptune], but was a

floating island until Zeus fastened it by adamantine chains to the bottom of the sea, that it might be a secure resting-place to Leto, for the birth of Apollo and Artemis" (*Classical Dictionary*).

296, 297. *his look*, i.e. like the look of the Gorgons which turned men into stone.

Gorgonian, petrifying; cf. II. 611, "Gorgonian terror".

298. *asphaltic slime*, i.e. asphalt or bitumen (cf. 562), such as that which floated on the surface of the Dead Sea—thence called 'Lake *Asphaltites*', and by M. "the Asphaltic pool" (I. 411), or simply "Asphaltis" (see 561, 562, note). Probably he here had in mind *Genesis* xi. 3, where the Hebrew word used for this bituminous substance is rendered 'slime'. See XII. 41, note.

299, 300. *Deep to the roots...They fastened*, i.e. laid the foundation of the structure.

mole, causeway = Latin *moles*, used of any massive structure, e.g. a dam or pier.

305. *inoffensive*, free from obstacles (Lat. *inoffensus*); literally, not causing one to offend, i.e. stumble against (Lat. *offendere*).

306. *if great things...* Virgil's *si parva licet componere magnis* (*Georgic* IV. 176). Cf. also *Eclogue* I. 24. M. has the allusion in II. 921, 922, VI. 310, 311, *P. R.* IV. 563, 564.

307–11. Alluding to the invasion of Greece by Xerxes, 480 B.C.

308. *Susa*; a Persian city of the province of Susiana and winter residence of the kings of Persia; see *P. R.* III. 288. According to tradition, Susa was founded by Tithonus, the father of Memnon (see *Il Penseroso*, 18), and Memnon built its acropolis, called after him the *Memnonium*. Susa is the Shushan of *Esther* i. 2 and *Daniel* viii. 2, passages of which perhaps we have an echo in "Memnonian *palace*".

310. *Bridging*; with the bridge of boats described by Herodotus, VII. 36. See Mayor's notes on Juvenal, x. 173–6, for a mass of illustrations.

311. The reference is to the story told by Herodotus (VII. 35), that Xerxes in his anger at the destruction of his first bridge by a storm ordered the Hellespont to receive three hundred lashes from a "scourge"—τριηκοσίας ἐπικέεσθαι μάστιγι πληγὰς—and to have a pair of fetters thrown into it. Cf. Johnson's *Vanity of Human Wishes*, 232, "The waves he lashes, and enchains the wind" (said of Xerxes).

indignant; cf. *Georgic* II. 162, *Æneid* VIII. 728 (*pontem indignatus Araxes*).

313. *Pontifical*; literally bridge-making (Lat. *pons + facere*); cf. *pontifice*, 348. It has been suggested that M. used the word

with a sarcastic allusion to its other sense 'belonging to the Pontiff, i.e. the Pope'.

314. *vexed*, storm-tost; cf. I. 306 and see VII. 211–13. Cf. the similar use of Lat. *vexare*, e.g. by Virgil, *Eclogue* VI. 76.

316. *First lighted*. See III. 418. *wing*, flight.

317. The original editions have no comma after "Chaos" and the construction intended might be "landed to the outside", i.e. on to; but it seems better to regard the words "to the outside" as a kind of explanation of "to the self-same place where": taken thus, they define the place.

318. *adamant*; see G.

320–4. See *Appendix*, pp. 133–5.

323. *interposed*, i.e. between "the confines" of Heaven and those of the World. The bridge from Hell touched the outer surface of this World at the point where (i) the stair from Heaven also touched the surface, and where (ii) the passage led down to the interior of the World. The bridge therefore resembles the middle one of three roads which form a junction.

327. *in likeness*, i.e. "disguised" (330), as in III. 634–44, 694.

328, 329. "Satan, to avoid being discovered (as he had been before, IV. 569 *et seq*.) by Uriel regent of the Sun [see IX. 60–2, note], takes care to keep at as great a distance as possible, and therefore, 'while the sun rose in Aries', he steers his course directly upwards 'betwixt the Centaur and the Scorpion', two constellations which lay in a quite different part of the heavens from Aries" (Newton).

steering, steering *to*. *His zenith*, i.e. straight upwards, towards that opening in the surface of the globe through which he had descended into the interior (III. 526 *et seq*.) and Sin and Death were about to descend.

332. *after Eve seduced*, after the temptation and disobedience of Eve: a Latinised turn of phrase which M. uses often. Cf. I. 573, "since created man", *post hominem creatum*; *S. A.* 1433, "after his message told". See 577, 687.

unminded, unnoticed, i.e. by Eve.

335. *unweeting*, ignorant, i.e. of the results of her action, or of Satan's proximity. See G. *seconded*, repeated.

336, 337. Cf. IX. 1113, 1114.

344, 345. *understood*, i.e. *being* understood. The original editions have a full stop after "time" in 345, making "understood" a past tense, instead of participle, with the subject 'he' omitted. The correction (Tickell's) seems certain and is generally adopted now.

345, 346. *joy And tidings*; probably meant as a hendiadys = 'joyful tidings'.

347, 348. *the foot*; meaning, of course, the top of the bridge ("pontifice"); cf. 315–26.

351. *stupendous*; in the original editions 'stupend*i*ous'.

357–60. Cf. 236–9, 245–9.

361. *evidence*, prove; rare as verb.

364. *consequence*, connection.

368. *our liberty, confined*, i.e. the liberty *of us*, confined.

370. *fortify*, build.

372. *virtue*, courage (Lat. *virtus*).

374. *odds*, advantage.

375. *foil*; see G.

378. *doom*, judgment, decree.

379. Cf. Satan's own words, IV. 110–12:

"Evil, be thou my good: by thee at least
  Divided empire with Heaven's king I hold,
  By thee, and more than half perhaps will reign";

where he means that he rules Hell already and hopes to rule the World, leaving Heaven to the Almighty.

380. *parted*, separated; qualifying "him" (376), not "things".

380, 381. *the empyreal bounds*, the confines of the Empyrean or Heaven, which M. here treats as a square ("quadrature") in allusion to the description of the New Jerusalem in *Revelation* xxi. 16; previously he left its shape an undecided question ("undetermined square or round", II. 1048).

orbicular; the World is always spoken of in the poem as a globe.

382. *try*, i.e. and find.

384. See note on 235.

386, 387. Alluding to the meaning of the name *Satan*, viz. 'Adversary'.

389. *empire* = "powers" in 395; abstract for concrete.

389–91. The sense is—'That have met my triumphal act, my work, viz. the discovery and conquest of the new World, with your triumphal act, your glorious work, viz. the construction of this bridge'.

392. *continent*, i.e. continuous, unbroken, tract.

394. *your*, i.e. made by you.

397, 398. See the account in III. 560–742 of Satan's own descent to the Earth, "amongst innumerable stars" (III. 565) = "these numerous orbs" (397).

399–402. Cf. Satan's promise to Sin in II. 840–4, where he tells her of the new World to which he is journeying:

> "thou and Death
> Shall dwell at ease, and up and down unseen
> Wing silently the buxom air, embalmed
> With odours: there ye shall be fed and filled
> Immeasurably; all things shall be your prey."

402. *thrall*; see G.

408, 409. An allusion to the formula conferring supreme power on the Consuls at Rome in times of great crisis, namely, *videant* (or *dent operam*, etc.) *consules ne quid respublica detrimenti capiat*.

affairs; cf. Lat. *res*.

413. "Strike" (='to blast') was the word applied to the evil "influence" which astrologers supposed the planets to exercise on the earth. Cf. *Hamlet*, I. I. 162, "The nights are wholesome; then no planets strike". The belief survives in 'moon-struck'. M. says that the planets themselves were 'blasted' by bad "influence" as Sin and Death passed near them.

415. *causey*, see G.

418. *his indignation*, i.e. of Chaos; cf. 311.

420, 421. *those*; Sin and Death. *to sit there*; cf. 230.

424. *Pandemonium*, 'the home of all the demons'; cf. I. 756:

425, 426. Cf. VII. 131–4. The name *Lucifer*, 'light-bringer' (Gk. φωσφόρος), is properly a Latin title of the morning-star, but it was applied by patristic writers to Satan, in allusion perhaps to the tradition of the original "brightness" of his person. Cf. the common misinterpretation of *Isaiah* xiv. 12 ("How art thou fallen from heaven, O Lucifer"), where "thou" refers to "Babylon", not to Satan, and the Hebrew word translated "Lucifer" should be rendered "day-star", as in the Revised Version.

M. says that all the names of the rebel angels in the poem, e.g. "Satan" (v. 658), were titles given to them *after* their expulsion from Heaven; their former names being "blotted out and rased ...from the Books of Life" (I. 361–3). *Lucifer* was one of these later names: what the arch-rebel was called in Heaven we do not know (v. 658, 659). See I. 361–75, note. In each of the early drafts of Milton's contemplated drama of *Paradise Lost* the name "Lucifer", not "Satan", is assigned to him; see *Introduction*.

426. *paragoned*, compared.

427. *the Grand*, the great ones (Ital. *i grandi*), being "the great consulting peers" (456) who held the council in book II.

430. *observed*, obeyed; cf. I. 588.

431, 432. Cf. his *History of Moscovia*, "The Empire of

Moscovia, or as others call it Russia, is bounded...on the east by the river Ob, or Oby [see IX. 78], and the Nagayan *Tartars* on the Volga as far as *Astracan*" (*P. W.* v. 395).

433. *Bactrian*, Persian, the ancient Bactria or Bactriana having been a province of the Persian empire; cf. *P. R.* III. 285.

Sophi, Shah; see G.

from the horns, i.e. retreats before the Turkish armies. "During the sixteenth century there was continual warfare between the Persians and the Ottoman Turks, who were the masters of Asia Minor and Syria" (Keightley).

horns; alluding to the shape—a half-moon or "crescent"—of the ensign of the Turks; cf. Sylvester's *Du Bartas*, "The moony Standards of proud Ottoman" (Grosart's ed. I. 31; see also II. 42).

435. *Aladule*; the Greater Armenia, so called by the Turks from *Aladules*, the last king of the country, slain by the emperor Selím I (from Hume's note). A province of "Aliduli" is marked in the map of the "Turkish Empire" in Hexham's English edition (1636) of *Mercator's Atlas*. There is, I think, reason to believe that M. made use of this particular *Atlas* (which has full descriptions as well as maps), and took from it the names "Namancos" and "Bayona" in *Lycidas*, 162; see note thereon in the Pitt Press ed., pp. 156, 157.

436. *Tauris*, the modern Tabriz, in the north of Persia; not far from the Armenian frontier.

Casbeen, Kazvin, north of Teheran, the capital of Persia.

438. *reduced*, led back; Lat. *reducere*, 'to lead back', e.g. troops.

442. I.e. in appearance he was like one of the rank and file of the host of rebel Angels.

443. *from*, i.e. passing up the hall from.

444–50. Editors compare *Æneid* I. 439, 440, 586–9.

his high throne; described II. 1–4.

445. *state*, canopy; see G.

450–2. M. dwells more than once on the "*faded* splendour" (IV. 870) of Satan's form. See *Appendix*, p. 142.

451. *permissive*. Elizabethan writers treat the termination *ive* as passive in various adjectives. Cf. *As You Like It*, III. 2. 10, "The fair, the chaste and unexpress*ive* she", i.e. 'inexpress*ible*'. So 'insuppressive', not to be suppressed, *Julius Cæsar*, II. 1. 134; and 'uncomprehensive', *Troilus and Cressida*, III. 3. 198.

453. Cf. "the Stygian council" (II. 506), used similarly of Satan's followers. In describing "Hell" and its inmates M. uses

terms associated with the netherworld of classical mythology, e.g. "Plutonian" (444), "Acheron" (II. 578), "Lethe" (II. 583), "Erebus" (II. 883). His whole conception of "Hell" owes much to the classics; cf. especially II. 575–86 with *Æneid* VI. 295 *et seq.*

454. M. always scans *aspéct*, the ordinary Elizabethan accentuation; cf. 658.

456. *Forth rushed*; since they sat in council "far within" the palace, away from the inferior Angels who thronged "the hall" (I. 791, 792).

457. "The Devils are frequently described by metaphors taken from the Turks. Satan is called the 'Sultan', I. 348, as here the council is styled the 'Divan'" (Newton).

divan, council; see G. and cf. Dryden's *State of Innocence*:

"'tis not fit
Our dark Divan in public view should sit."

The *State of Innocence* was based on *P. L.*

458, 459. Cf. the picture of a great orator in IX. 670–4.

460. See *Appendix* pp. 144–6.

461. *such*, i.e. as he has described them in 460. They have, he says, a double claim to these titles implying lordship and power: (i) the claim of possession, since they are now to "possess a spacious World" (466, 467) and be lords thereof; (ii) the claim of ancient right, since these titles belonged to them in Heaven. The form of the commencement of the speech resembles II. 11–14, v. 361, 362.

465. *the house of woe*; repeated from VI. 877; cf. also II. 823. Similar descriptions of Hell are found in the Italian poets, e.g. in Tasso ("the house of grief and pain", Fairfax's translation, IX. 59).

469. *Long were to tell*; cf. I. 507, XII. 261. Like Lat. *longum est*, as in Lucretius IV. 1166, *cetera de genere hoc longum est si dicere coner.*

470–80. Cf. the description of Satan's journey through Chaos (="the Deep", 471, "the Abyss", 476) in book II. 629 *et seq.*

475. *uncouth*, unknown, strange; see G. M. always accents *úncouth.*

477. *unoriginal*, having no originator, being itself "*eldest* of things", II. 962.

478–80. An exaggeration, since Chaos, far from "opposing" his journey, directed him on his course, II. 1004–9. He magnifies his exploits to win "transcendent glory...above his fellows", II. 427, 428.

480. *Protesting Fate*, i.e. objecting that Fate did not mean the "secrets" of their realm to be explored thus. *how*, i.e. to tell how.

481, 482. Cf. Beelzebub's speech at the infernal council in II. 345–8:

> "There is a place
> (If ancient and prophetic fame in Heaven
> Err not), another world, the happy seat
> Of some new race called Man."

499. *when is not set*, i.e. the time when this is to happen is not fixed.

512. *clung*; probably a participle = 'pressed tight'.

513. *supplanted*; in the literal sense 'tripped up'; from Lat. *supplantare*, to trip up, throw a man off his feet—a wrestler's term.

515. *Reluctant*; also used literally = 'struggling against'; Lat. *reluctari*.

517. *his doom*; as pronounced on the serpent in 175–7. Cf. the "Argument" of the book.

521. *riot*, i.e. rebellion in Heaven; cf. Lat. *tumultus*.

521–9. This passage is perhaps the most striking example of alliteration in the poem, the effect being designed partly to suggest to the ear the actual sound described, partly to convey to the imagination a sense of the terror of the whole scene. Thus the repeated sibilant represents the hissing; cf. IX. 613, and I. 768, "Brushed with the hiss of rustling wings. As bees." On the other hand, the repetition of sound in "*d*readful", "*d*in", "*d*ire", "*d*rear", etc., seems to intensify the horror of the event. A similar, though less striking, instance of the same effect occurs in XI. 489–92.

523. *complicated*, twisted, twined together; Lat. *complicare*, to tie up.

524. *amphisbæna*; see G.

525. *Cerastes*; Gk. κεράστης, a horned snake, from κέρας, a horn. *hydrus*, a water-snake; cf. Gk. ὕδωρ, water.

ellops; Gk. ἔλλοψ, mute; an epithet of fish; then used substantively for a certain sea-fish (probably the swordfish or sturgeon) and later = 'serpent'. *drear*; in allusion to the literal meaning of ἔλλοψ, viz. mute.

526. *dipsas*; a serpent whose bite caused great thirst (Gk. δίψος).

526, 527. *the soil*, i.e. Libya in Africa. An allusion to the legend that as Perseus was bringing back the head of Medusa, one of the Gorgons, who had hissing snakes instead of hair, drops

of her blood fell on the soil and caused the country to abound
with serpents. Ovid touches on the story, *Metamorphoses*, IV.
613–19, while Lucan enumerates the kinds of serpents, and his
account (*Pharsalia*, IX. 699–733) was probably in Milton's
thoughts.

528. *Ophiusa*; the island of serpents = Gk. ὀφιοῦσσα, i.e.
ὀφιόεσσα, 'abounding in serpents'; a small island in the Mediterranean, to which the Romans gave the similar name 'Colu-
braria', from *coluber*, a snake, adder. Now Formentera, one of
the Balearic group.

529. *dragon*; cf. "the dragon" = Satan in *Revelation* xii. Gk.
δράκων, serpent.

529–31. Ovid speaks of the monstrous serpent Python, born
from the slime left on the earth by the flood of Deucalion—
Metamorphoses, I. 434 *et seq.*

535. *in station...or just array*; "either on guard or drawn up
in military array to receive and do him honour" (Keightley).
Lat. *in statione*, a military term = 'on guard'; cf. "stations" =
'sentinels', 'pickets', II. 412. *just*, regular, due (Lat. *justus*);
cf. 888.

536. *Sublime* = Lat. *sublimis* in its figurative sense 'uplifted'.
Cf. *S. A.* 1669, "While their hearts were jocund and sublime".

541. *changing*, i.e. changing *into*.

541–5. The partial repetition of the alliterative effect of 521–9,
to recall and point the likeness to the previous scene of trans-
formation, is surely a very happy device.

546. *exploding*, driving off the scene; see G.

549. *His will*, as he willed; in opposition to "sprung up".
aggravate, make worse, heavier to bear; Lat. *gravis*, heavy.

550. *fair*; accidentally omitted in the Second Ed.: hence a
wrong reading "like *to* that", current in later editions till Newton
restored the true text.

560. *Megæra*; one of the Eumenides or Furies, who are described as having serpents twined in their hair.

561, 562. Alluding to the apples of the Dead Sea = "that bituminous lake". Cf. *Eikonoklastes*, XXIV, "these pious flourishes
and colours [i.e. excuses], examined thoroughly, are like the
apples of Asphaltis [see 298, note] appearing goodly to the sudden
eye; but look well upon them, or at least but touch them, and
they turn into cinders" (*P. W.* I. 461).

lake; cf. the other common name for the Dead Sea, viz. 'Lake
Asphaltites'.

565. *with gust*; as we say, 'with gusto', i.e. pleasure in tasting.

567–70. The sound is meant to echo the sense.

568. *drugged*, nauseated as "with the hateful taste usually found in drugs" (Richardson).

572. *triumphed* i.e. over. *once*; emphatic. Man was deceived (by the Serpent) but "once"; the serpents were duped "oft".

lapsed; a preterite, I think; 'fell into error'.

572, 573. The original editions read:

> "Thus were they plagu'd
> And worn with famin, long and ceaseless hiss."

It seems to me simplest to suppose that the printer misplaced the comma after "famine"; if we put it after "long", then "famine" and "hiss" (a noun) are balanced with their respective epithets, and the balance gives an admirable rhythm, while the turn of phrase "worn with famine, and hiss" is quite characteristic. Keightley printed:

> "Thus were they plagued;
> And, worn with famine, long and ceaseless hiss";

taking "hiss" as a verb. Other editors have followed him (some placing a comma instead of a semicolon after "plagued"). This interpretation appears to me to be open to several objections. It rather implies that the "famine" was the cause of the hissing; involves a most awkward change from the past tense in 572 to the present in 573 and then back to the past in 574, and yields, surely, an unpleasant rhythm.

575–7. No doubt, M. had some authority for this tradition, but editors have failed to find it. The nearest approach to it known to Bishop Newton was the speech of the Fairy Manto in Ariosto's *Orlando Furioso*, xliii. 98:

> "Each sev'nth day we constrained are to take
> Upon ourselves the person of a snake." (Harington's trans.)

575. *some say*; a convenient phrase, under cover of which he can mention theories, yet avoid the responsibility of accepting them. Cf. 668, 671 and see IX. 638–42, note.

577. *for Man seduced*. See 332 (note), 687.

578. We must remember that according to the ordinary patristic and mediæval belief which M. accepted (I. 358–75), the fallen Angels became the gods of classical mythology: hence there might well be among "the heathen" some tradition of the story of Eve and the Serpent. So M. identifies the Serpent (Satan) with Ophion (cf. Gk. ὄφις, a serpent), one of the Titans and the first ruler of Olympus; and suggests that Eurynome, the daughter of Oceanus and wife of Ophion, may have been the same as Eve. Newton shewed that in the allusion to Ophion and

Eurynome M. had in his thoughts a passage of the *Argonautica* (I. 503, *et seq.*) of Apollonius Rhodius. (On the supposed identity of the fallen Angels and the classical gods see Appendix C to books I, II in this edition.)

579. *purchase*, acquisition; see G.

581, 582. *wide Encroaching.* "Some epithet should be added to *Eve* to shew the similitude between her and *Eurynome*, and why he takes the one for the other; and therefore in allusion to the name *Eurynome* [='wide-ruling'] he styles Eve 'the wide-encroaching', as extending her rule and dominion farther than she should over her husband, and affecting godhead"(Newton).

584. *Ops*, the wife of Saturn. *Dictæan*, Cretan, from Dicte, a mountain of Crete in which island Jupiter was brought up. The legend that Zeus (Jupiter) expelled Cronos (Saturn) from the rule of Olympus, the 'heaven' of classical mythology, and from sovereignty over gods and men, is touched on in *Il Penseroso*, 30.

587. *Once*, i.e. when man was tempted.

actual, the cause of an act, viz. Eve's act of disobedience. No doubt, M. is alluding to the theological term "actual sin", which he defines as "crime itself, or the act of sinning", and discusses, *Christian Doctrine*, I. XI—*P. W.* IV. 262. Cf. the *Prayer-Book*, 'Articles of Religion', XXXI.

589, 590. Cf. *Revelation* vi. 8, "And I looked, and behold a pale horse: and his name that sat on him was Death."

591. *Second*; Sin herself was first; see 235, note.

593. *not better*, is it (="our empire") not better?

599. *ravin*, prey; see G.

601. *unhide-bound*, with the skin hanging loose about it, hence capable of containing much.

606. *scythe*; the traditional attribute of Time and Death. Cf. Shakespeare, *Sonnet* 12, "And nothing 'gainst Time's scythe can make defence."

610. *several*, different; Lat. *separabilis*.

612. *kinds*, species; all forms of life; cf. 603–9.

615. *those bright Orders*, the Cherubim, Seraphim and others.

616–40. This speech is noticeable as not being so Biblical in character as most of those which M. assigns to the Almighty.

616, 617. M. seems to have had in his thoughts *Julius Cæsar*, III. 1. 273, "Cry 'Havoc', and let slip the dogs of war". The phrase 'cry "havoc"', imitated from O.F. *crier havot*, was an old military term for 'giving no quarter', i.e. it was the signal for indiscriminate slaughter; so that "to *havoc* yonder world" was an even stronger expression then than it is now.

622. *that*, because.

623. *enter and possess*; "terms of English law" (Keightley). For *possess* = 'take possession of' cf. *Romeo and Juliet*, III. 2. 27.

624. *conniving*, tolerating, permitting, them; see G.

626. *That laugh*; cf. 487–90.

633. *glutted*; Lat. *glutire*, to swallow; cf. F. *engloutir*. *offal*; see G.

638. *Heaven and Earth* = the World, as often in Scripture.

made pure, i.e. by fire, according to 2 *Peter* iii. 7, 12, 13. Cf. III. 334, 335:

"The World shall burn, and from her ashes spring
    New Heaven and Earth, wherein the just shall dwell."

See also XI. 900, 901, XII. 547–51. In the *Christian Doctrine*, I. XXXIII he treats of "the destruction of the present unclean and polluted world, namely, its final conflagration" (*P. W.* IV. 488, 489).

639. *To sanctity*, i.e. to the degree of, up to.

640. *both*, viz. Heaven and Earth.

precedes; "shall go before those ravagers Sin and Death, and shall direct and lead them on" (Newton). But might not the sense be 'has precedence = prevails', the notion being that "the curse" has power for a time but will in the end be annulled? Bentley suggested *proceeds*, i.e. goes on, continues.

642. *halleluiah* = 'praise ye the Lord'.

as the sound, resembling the sound, by reason of the multitude of voices; being even "as the voice of many waters", *Revelation* xix. 6. Cf. v. 872, 873:

"He said; and, as the sound of waters deep,
    Hoarse murmur echoed to his words applause."

643, 644. Cf. *Revelation* xv. 3, xvi. 7. To "justify the ways of God to men" (I. 26) was Milton's aim in composing *Paradise Lost*.

645. *extenuate*, weaken; properly 'make slight' (Lat. *tenuis*). *Next*, i.e. they sang.

647, 648. "And I saw a new heaven and a new earth...And the holy city, new Jerusalem, coming down from God out of heaven" (*Revelation* xxi. 1, 2); see also verse 10 and note "descending".

to the ages, i.e. for the succeeding ages. *rise*, i.e. from the conflagration; cf. III. 334 (quoted above); contrasted with "descend".

650. *His mighty Angels*; meaning, probably, "the seven Spirits" of God "which are before his throne" and execute his

7   P L

commands on Earth. See the description of them in III. 648-58, based on passages like *Zechariah* iv. 10, *Revelation* i. 4, viii. Of these Uriel was one; see IX. 60, note.

651. *sorted*, fitted, suited; cf. VIII. 384.

In *Christian Doctrine*, I. XIII he says, "All nature is subject to mortality and a curse on account of man"; and that thought is the basis of this long passage (651-716) dealing with the deterioration in the physical Universe which followed the Fall of Man. The main Scriptural authority for this thought which M. quotes is *Genesis* iii. 17, "cursed is the ground for thy sake". See *P. W.* IV. 269.

656-62. *blanc* ('pale'), *influence, malignant*; see each in G. *the other five* (i.e. planets), *the fixed* (i.e. stars); see p. 136.

On the astrological terms in 658-62, see pp. 146-7.

663. *Which of them*; e.g. Orion "with fierce winds armed", I. 305.

665. *Their corners*, their respective quarters. *when*, i.e. and also the times when. *confound*, mingle, make undistinguishable.

666. The winds are said to "roll the thunder" because they "roll" the clouds which cause the thunder; at least, I suppose this to be his meaning.

668-78. Dr Masson explains: "It is poetically assumed here that, before the Fall, the ecliptic or Sun's path was in the same plane as the Earth's equator, and that the present obliquity of the two planes, or their intersection at an angle of $23\frac{1}{2}°$, was a modification of the physical Universe for the worse, consequent upon the moral evil introduced by sin. But this physical alteration might be produced in either of two ways: either by pushing askance the axis of the Earth the required distance, leaving the Sun undisturbed; or by leaving the Earth undisturbed and compelling the Sun to deviate the required distance ('like distant breadth') from his former equatorial or equinoctial path. To indicate what 'the distant breadth' would amount to, Milton follows the Sun in imagination after his deviation from the equatorial line: tracing him, first, in his ascent north of the equator, through the constellations Taurus (in whose neck are the Pleiades, called the Seven Atlantic Sisters, as being mythologically the daughters of Atlas) and Gemini (called 'the Spartan twins', as representing Castor and Pollux, the twin sons of Tyndarus, king of Sparta), up to his extreme distance from the equator at the Crab, in the Tropic of Cancer; then returning with him in his descending path by Leo and Virgo, till he again touches the equator at Libra; and, for the rest, simply suggesting

his similar deviation from the equator to the south by naming the Tropic of Capricorn as the farthest point reached on that side.... He [Milton] gives the larger space to the hypothesis of a change of the Sun's path."

668, 671. *Some say*; cf. 575.

the centric globe, the Earth, the centre of the Universe, according to the Ptolemaic system.

676. *the Scales* = Libra (III. 558).

678, 679. He has previously said that before the Fall only one season was known in Eden, viz. "eternal spring", IV. 268: a view held by some of the Church Fathers. See also v. 394, 395.

680–4. "If the sun were to be always in the equator, there could never be night at the poles, the sun going round and round continually in the horizon" (Keightley).

682. *unbenighted*, without any night.

685–7. I.e. the sun would have prevented the snow stretching so far southward from the North Pole as it does at present, and conversely an equal distance northward from the South Pole.

Estotiland; an old name, applied not very precisely, to the part of North America lying between Baffin Bay and Hudson Bay. The description (II. 436) of the chief provinces of North America in Hexham's *Mercator* (1636) mentions both "Estotilandia" and "Norumbega" (see 696).

Magellan, i.e. the Strait of, in South America; named after the Portuguese navigator Magalhaens.

687. *that tasted fruit*, the tasting of that fruit; see 332, note.

688. An allusion to the story of the revenge taken by Atreus, king of Mycenæ, on his brother Thyestes, who had wronged him and been banished: how "Atreus, pretending to be reconciled to Thyestes, recalled him to Mycenæ, killed his two sons, and placed their flesh before their father at a banquet, who unwittingly partook of the horrid meal" (*Classical Dictionary*). This spectacle is said to have caused the sun to turn aside, and M. suggests that the feasting on the forbidden fruit worked a like effect.

Thyestean; I think that M. intended us to scan 'Thyést(e)an', eliding the *e* of the termination, instead of accentuating it according to the correct rendering 'Thyestéan'. Good critics, e.g. Mr Bridges, recognise a similar scansion in *S. A.* 133, "Chalý|b(e)an tém|per'd steel, and frock of mail"—instead of 'Chalybéan'. Dr Abbot scans 'Epicúrĕan' in *Antony and Cleopatra*, II. 1. 24, and says that "the Elizabethans generally did not accent the *e* in such words" (*Shakespearian Grammar*, p. 395).

689–91. I.e. the sun's course before the Fall must have differed from its present course: otherwise the World would not have escaped extremes of heat and cold then any more than it does now.

693. *sideral*, of the stars (Lat. *sidera*). *blast*, i.e. blasting "influence".

696. *Norumbega*; an obsolete name for a great tract comprehending in modern nomenclature southern Canada and the northern states of America, e.g. New York and Maine. "Norumbega" is marked thus both in Hexham's general map of America and also in that of "New England". In Milton's time the application of names to these distant regions was rather vague.

the Samoed shore, i.e. the shore of north-eastern Siberia, near the Gulf of Obi in the Arctic Ocean. In Milton's *History of Moscovia* is a chapter on "Samoedia, Siberia, and other countries north-east, subject to the Muscovites" (i.e. Russians), *P. W.* v. 403, 404; with references to Purchas's *Pilgrimage*.

697. *their brazen dungeon*; suggested perhaps by the prison of the winds guarded by Æolus; cf. *Æneid* I. 52 *et seq.*

698. *flaw*, a gust of wind; see G. "Gust and flaw" seems to have been a common combination; cf. *Venus and Adonis*, 456.

699, 700. *Boreas*, the north wind, *Cæcias*, the north-east, Gk. καικίας. Cf. Holland's translation (1603) of Plutarch's *Morals*, "like unto the north-east winde *Cæcias*, which evermore gathereth the clouds unto it" (p. 379, quoted in the *Stanford Dictionary*). *Argestes*, the north-west wind; *Thrascias*, the north-north-west; Gk. θρασκίας, also spelt θρᾳκίας, i.e. the wind that blew from *Thrace*.

702. *Notus*, the south wind, *Afer*, the south-west; lit. 'the African' (Lat. *afer*), i.e. wind; cf. *creber procellis Africus* (*Æneid* I. 85, 86).

703. *Serraliona*, i.e. Sierra Leone, off the west coast of Africa; literally the 'Lioness Mountain', from Spanish *sierra*, a saw, hence a jagged mountain ridge or chain of mountains, and *leona*, a lioness. It was evidently proverbial for storms; cf. Hexham's *Mercator*, II. 426: "Sierra Liona is...a very high Mount, the toppe whereof is continually hidde with snowe: from whence there comes fearefull noises, and great tempests."

703–6. To heighten the confusion of the contest between the winds from the north (699, 700) and those from the south (701, 702), there rush forth to the fray winds from either side, viz. Eurus, the east wind, and Sirocco, the south-east: Zephyrus, the west wind, and Libecchio, the south-west.

704. *Levant and Ponent*; the rising and setting winds, i.e. those which come from the quarters where the sun respectively rises and sets. From F. *levant* and *ponent*, used thus. Cf. *levant* = sunrise, e.g. in Holland's *Pliny* (1601), 18, 33, "the Sunne rising or Levant of that day". A later word, with same sense, is *levanter*.

705. *with their lateral noise*; qualifying, I think, "Eurus and Zephyr", as being "lateral" in relation to the north and south winds; but some editors connect the words with "Sirocco, and Libecchio" as describing *their* relation to "Eurus and Zephyr".

706. *Sirocco...Libecchio*; Italian names (whereas all the others in the passage, 699–705, are classical), the two winds being peculiar to the shores of the Mediterranean and the south of Europe. Ital. *sirocco*, from Arabic *sharq*, east.

707. *Outrage*; see G.

710–14. Previously (IV. 340–7) the beasts had known neither strife among themselves nor fear of man.

711. *all*; referring, of course, to the beasts.

714–17. Newton well remarks on the skill with which the transition to Adam again is effected. "We have seen great alterations produced in nature, and it is now time to see how Adam is affected with them, and whether the disorders *within* are not even worse than those *without*."

719. *disburden*, himself; or perhaps 'it' = "worse" in 717.

720. *miserable of happy*; on this idiom see IX. 563; cf. 723.

723. *hide me*, i.e. who hide myself.

the face. Cf. IX. 1080–2.

728, 729. "Meat and drink propagate it ['curse'] by prolonging life, and children by carrying it on to posterity" (Newton).

When William Lauder published in 1750 his *Essay* on Milton, with the object of showing that the poet had 'plagiarised' from a number of minor writers, mostly foreign scholars of the 16th and 17th centuries, he took certain passages of *P. L.*, translated them into Latin verse of various metres, and then pretended that he had found the Latin passages in the works of these foreign scholars: as their writings were obscure and to a great extent inaccessible, he counted on the fraud escaping detection for some time. Thus he translated these lines into *quod comedo, poto, gigno, diris subjacet*, and pretended that the Latin occurred in the tragedy of *Adamus Exul* (1601)—a very rare work—of the jurist Grotius. But his most signal success was won over the great lines in 1. 261–3, which he likewise rendered into Latin iambics and professed to have found in the *Adamus Exul*. One finds the

forged lines sometimes given even in modern editions of Milton, with the remark that he (M.) has evidently "translated" them from Grotius. I may add that two lines earlier in this book (616, 617) were derived by Lauder from an equally fictitious hexameter—*infernique canes populantur cuncta creata*—ascribed to a work published in 1654 by a certain Jacobus Masenius, professor in the Jesuits' College at Cologne.

729. 730. *Genesis* i. 28. See VII. 530, 531.

733. *to succeed*, succeeding.

737. *the execration*, i.e. "Ill fare our ancestor", 735. Cf. 821, 822.

738. *Mine own*; the only noun to which these words can well refer is "curses" (732), but the sense is 'afflictions', 'evils'.

all from me, all the afflictions derived from me, i.e. those of his descendants.

739. *redound*; in the literal sense 'flow back' (Lat. *redundare*). The metaphor is changed in the next line ("light"). Some editions misprint *rebound*.

740, 741. *light Heavy* alight and weigh heavy.

"These curses, though lighting on him their centre, will weigh heavy, though according to the laws of physics they should not weigh anything there, the weight of bodies being only their tendency to the centre" (Keightley).

743. *Isaiah* xlv. 9.

746. *delicious*; several times an epithet of Paradise—IV. 132, 729, VII. 537.

747. *being*, creation.

748. *equal*, fair (Lat. *æquus*). *reduce*; in the literal sense 'to bring back' (Lat. *reducere*), i.e. to the dust of which Adam was made.

756, 757. *then...when*; with M. a favourite (and emphatic) turn of words; cf. IV. 970, "Then, when I am thy captive, talk of chains". So "there...where".

758. *Thou didst*; addressing himself, not his Maker, as in 743—55.

762. *Isaiah* xlv. 10.

766. *of his own*, with the gifts which he had himself bestowed on you.

773. *this day*; more correctly "*that* day"—cf. 49, 210; since the time of the action of this book is the day after Adam's sin. Cf. the time references in 329 ("the sun rose") and 342 ("by night").

777. *Insensible*; emphatic from its position.

778. *As in my mother's lap*; a curious expression from Adam's lips.

783. *all*, entirely; cf. Horace's *non omnis moriar* (*Odes*, III. 30, 6) (said, however, in a different connection, viz. in reference to the immortality conferred by his poetry).

784, 785. *Genesis* ii. 7. *inspired*; in the literal sense 'breathed'.

788. *a living death*; a proverbial phrase; cf. *S. A.* 100, "To live a life half dead, a living death". So in *Richard III*, I. 2. 153; *Lucrece*, 726.

789. *why?* why should it be true?

789–92. The spirit, Adam is made to argue, constitutes life (cf. "pure breath of life") and the spirit alone "sinned": the body is mere "dust", a "clod", and as such "properly hath neither" life nor sin: therefore "death", as the annihilation of life and punishment of sin, must mean the death of the spirit. So the "end" (797) will be not merely the dissolution of the mortal body into its dust but annihilation of the whole being— "*all* of me shall die".

The subject is discussed in the *Christian Doctrine*, I. XIII.

793. *reach*, power of comprehension.

795. *not so*, not "infinite".

798–801. Cf. the *Christian Doctrine*, I. II, where, treating of the "omnipotence" of the Almighty, he says, "It must be remembered that the power of God is not exerted in things which imply a contradiction"; he quotes 2 *Timothy* ii. 13, *Hebrews* vi. 18. See *P. W.* IV. 25, 26. It was a doctrine on which mediæval theologians dwelt.

800. *argument*, proof; cf. "argue" = show, prove, 1014.

805. *beyond dust*, i.e. after death.

806–8. *all causes else...* "All other agents act in proportion to the *reception* or capacity of the subject-matter, and not to the utmost extent of their own power ['sphere']. An allusion to the axiom: *omne efficiens agit secundum vires recipientis, non suas*" (Newton). So, Adam argues, he cannot be punished after death because death is the utmost punishment that he has the capacity to suffer: with death that capacity ends.

810. *Bereaving sense*; cf. "Insensible", 777.

812. *without*, outside; cf. *Macbeth*, III. 1. 47, "They are, my lord, without the palace gate".

816. *Am*; attracted to the nearer and, in Adam's view, more important subject "I".

826, 827. *the same With*, i.e. that which is corrupt like himself.

832. *me, me.* Cf. 936 and Virgil's line *me, me, adsum, qui feci, in me convertite ferrum* (*Æneid* IX. 427).

834. *Fond,* foolish; see G.

840. *past example,* i.e. "of the fallen Angels" (Newton).

841. *like,* i.e. like *in* (or 'as to') crime.

858. *Death comes not at all.* Cf. XI. 491–3, a picture of Death "delaying to strike, though oft invoked". See also Sophocles, *Philoctetes,* 797, 798, and Horace, *Odes,* II. 18. 38–40.

858, 859. Newton compares Horace's *pede Pœna claudo* (*Odes,* III. 2. 32). *Mends,* quickens. *for,* because of.

861, 862. *other...other;* a favourite form of emphasis with M. Cf. *Comus,* 612, 613:

> "Far other arms and other weapons must
> Be those that quell the might of hellish charms";

and *Lycidas,* 174, 175:

> "Where, other groves and other streams along,
> With nectar pure his oozy locks he laves."

song; cf. "their vocal worship", IX. 198 (with note).

866. *regard,* look; cf. F. *regard.*

869. *wants;* cf. "need" used intransitively, 80.

871. *fraud,* deceit.

872, 873. *pretended To;* literally 'stretched before', Lat. *prætentus;* hence 'serving as a screen to', 'masking'.

874. *persisted,* remained.

883. *understood;* the subject "I" is easily supplied from 880.

886. *sinister;* used quibblingly in its literal sense 'left'—a reference to the tradition that the rib out of which Eve was fashioned was taken from Adam's left side (VIII. 465, note)—and also in the figurative sense 'unlucky'.

Scan *siníster,* as in *Henry V,* II. 4. 85, "'Tis no siníster nor no awkward claim". This accentuation survived at least as late as Dryden; cf. *The Hind and the Panther,* III. 492, "In which siníster destinies ordain". In M., as in Shakespeare and Elizabethan writers generally, many words bear the original Latin (and French) accent which later has yielded to the Teutonic tendency to shift the accent on to an earlier syllable; cf. *aspéct,* 454.

887, 888. It was an old belief that Adam as created had thirteen ribs on the left side and that Eve was formed out of the extra one.

888–98. Editors cite similar passages from other poets, in particular a close parallel from Milton's favourite writer Euripides, viz. *Hippolytus,* 616 *et seq.*

898–906. The passage is like a commentary on the proverbial line, "The course of true love never did run smooth", *A Mid-summer-Night's Dream*, I. I. 134. That M. when he wrote the lines was thinking of the circumstances of his own first marriage cannot be doubted.

904–6. A personal allusion appears to be intended. Edward Phillips, the poet's nephew and one of his biographers, states that after Milton's first wife refused to live with him he paid much attention to a Miss Davis (possibly the lady addressed in his 9th *Sonnet*); so that "too late" represented his own experience. Probably "already linked and wedlock-bound" refers to "he", and "fell adversary" to his wife, now a source of "hate or shame" to him; but the sense might be that the man meets "his happiest choice" after *she* is "linked" to his enemy, which state of things occasions him "hate or shame".

921. *forlorn of*, forsaken by; cf. Tennyson's *Œnone*:
"Hither came at noon
        Mournful Œnone, wandering forlorn
        Of Paris."

923. *scarce one short hour*; in her grief she, as did Adam (771–5, 852–9), forgets the words of their Judge (193–205), which clearly showed that "the instant stroke of death" was "removed far off" (210, 211). Adam now sees differently (962, 963).

937–46. Probably Milton's reconciliation with his own wife was present to his thoughts; see p. xvi and cf. *S. A.* 1003–7:
"Yet beauty, though injurious, hath strange power,
        After offence returning, to regain
        Love once possessed, nor can be easily
        Repulsed, without much inward passion felt,
        And secret sting of amorous remorse."

959. *elsewhere*, at "the place" (cf. 932, 953, 1098, 1099), where their Judge appeared to them and pronounced their sentence; or perhaps he means 'in Heaven'.

960. *offices*, kind acts, services (Lat. *officia*).

969. *event*, issue, result.

978. *As in our evils*, considering that we are in such evils; Lat. *ut*. Richardson aptly quotes from Cicero's letters *Ad familiares* XII. 2, *non nihil, ut in tantis malis, est profectum*. Cf. IX. 1091.

979. *descent*; abstract for concrete; 'descendants'.

987. *prevent*, anticipate, forestall; see G.

989. In the early editions the words "so Death" were placed at the beginning of 990—doubtless an error, since there is nŏ

other instance in the poem of a short line (as 989 would be with-out the two words) or of an Alexandrine.

996. *the present object*, the object of your love who is present.

998. *less than none*, equal to any.

1000. *make short*, i.e. 'make short work of it', as we say.

1004–6. *and have.* 'Though we have the power, through choosing the quickest of the many ways of dying, to destroy destruction (i.e. Death's future work of destroying mankind) by destroying ourselves.'

1009. *entertained*, conceived. *pale*; adj. = noun; see IX. 606, note, and cf. IV. 115.

1014. *argue*, show the existence of.

1032–5. Contrast 169–173 (with notes).

1045. *Reluctance*, struggling.

1046–8. Cf. 96, "the mild Judge"; and 1094–6.

1048, 1049. *we expected*... Cf. 852–9, 923.

1053, 1054. He means that the curse in 198–208 applied more to the ground than to himself; so he says quibblingly that it 'glanced' off him and 'fell to the ground', e.g. like an arrow that just grazes the object aimed at.

1065. *this mountain*; see note on IX. 71.

1066. *shattering.* Cf. *Lycidas*, 5, "Shatter your leaves before the mellowing year".

locks. Cf. Lat. *comæ* with its two senses, 'hair' and 'foliage'. See Horace, *Odes* IV. 7. 2 (*arboribusque comæ*).

1067. *which*, i.e. the fact that "the winds blow moist and keen".

1068. *shroud*, shelter; see G.

1069. *this star*, the sun; 'the day-star' (cf. "diurnal"), as it was sometimes called in contrast to the other heavenly bodies. Cf. *Lycidas*, 168, and Sylvester's *Du Bartas*, "While the bright day-star rides his glorious round", Grosart's ed. I. 143. (But commonly 'day-star' meant the morning-star, Lucifer.)

1070. *how*, i.e. *to see* how; understood from "to seek", 1067.

1071. *sere*, dry; see G. *foment*, keep warm. M. uses the word in allusion to its (ultimate) derivation from Lat. *fovere*, 'to warm'; cf. Lat. *fomes*, 'tinder', 'touchwood'.

They are to try to reflect the sun's rays in some mirror-like substance so as to kindle dry leaves and grasses, etc.

1072, 1073. "He seems to suppose that in the collision of two bodies, as two flints or a flint and steel, it is the air that yields the fire" (Keightley). *attrite*, worn by friction; Lat. *attritus*.

1073. *late*, lately; referring to the changes in the elements described in 651 *et seq.*; cf. especially 666, 667, 701–6.

1075. *Tine*, kindle; see G. *thwart*, flashing across the sky. Probably he alludes to one of the theories as to the origin of fire on earth which Lucretius gives, v. 1091–4, viz. that it came through the thunderbolt and lightning.

1078. *supply*, i.e. the place of the sun.

1081. *praying*; conditional. *of grace*, for mercy, pardon.

1085. *native home*; cf. 206–8.

1087. *prostrate fall.* It is curious that the next book begins
  "Thus they in lowliest plight repentant *stood*
  Praying."

1091. *Frequenting*, filling (Lat. *frequentare*). Cf. 'frequent' = crowded (*frequens*), I. 797; 'frequence' = full assembly (*frequentia*), *P. R.* I. 128, II. 130.

1098–104. For a similar instance of repetition (a figure imitated from the classics) cf. IV. 641–56; *Comus*, 221–4.

APPENDIX

A

THE COSMOLOGY OF *PARADISE LOST*

PARTS of *Paradise Lost* are not easily understood without some
knowledge of Milton's conception of the Universe. I shall
attempt therefore to set forth some of the main aspects of his
cosmology: to explain, in fact, what he means by constantly
recurrent terms such as 'Empyrean', 'Chaos', 'Spheres', and
the like.

It is in book V that he carries us back farthest in respect of
time. The events described by Raphael (from line 563, onwards)
precede not only the Creation of the World, but also the expulsion of the rebels from Heaven. And at this era, when the seeds
of discord are being sown, we hear of two divisions of Space
—Heaven and Chaos (V. 577, 578): Heaven lying above Chaos.

In book VI the contest foreshadowed in book V has begun.
Now a third region is mentioned—Hell (VI. 53–5): a gloomy
region carved out of the nethermost depths of Chaos. Its re-
moteness from Heaven may be inferred from I. 73, 74. Milton's
working hypothesis, then—his general conception of space and
its partitionment prior to the Creation—may be expressed
roughly thus: above,[1] Heaven; beneath, Hell; between, a great
gulf, Chaos.

Let us see what he has to say concerning each.

Heaven, or the Empyrean,[2] is the abode of the Deity and His
angelic subjects. It is a vast region, but not infinite. In X. 380
Milton speaks of its "empyreal bounds"; in II. 1049 of its
"battlements";[3] in VI. 860 of its "crystal wall". These fence
Heaven in from Chaos. When Satan voyages through space, in
quest of the new-created World, he kens far off the crystal line
of light that radiates from the empyreal bulwarks, marking where

[1] I.e. from the point of view of this World, the position of which
we shall see.
[2] The terms are synonymous. *Empyrean* = Lat. *empyræus*, from
Gk. ἔμπυρος. The notion was that the Empyrean was formed of the
element of fire (πῦρ).
[3] Cf. Lucretius' *flammantia mœnia mundi* (I. 74) and Gray's "flaming bounds of Space" (*Progress of Poesy*).

runs the severance betwixt Heaven and Chaos (II. 1034 *et seq.*).
In the wall of Heaven are the "everlasting doors" opening on
to Chaos (v. 253–6, VII. 205–9). The shape of Heaven Milton
does not determine (II. 1048); perhaps it is a square (x. 381).
Its internal configuration and appearance he describes in language which reminds us of some lines (574–6) in book v. May
not the Earth, says Raphael, be "but the shadow of Heaven,
and things therein Each to other like, more than on Earth is
thought"? Milton expands this idea, and developing to the
utmost the symbolical, objective presentment of the New
Jerusalem in the *Revelation*, depicts a Heaven scarce distin-
guishable from an ideal Earth.[1] In fact, his Heaven and his
Garden of Eden have much in common; so that Satan exclaims,
"O Earth, how like to Heaven!" (IX. 99). Thus the Heavenly
landscape (if I may describe it in Miltonic language) has its
vales, wood-covered heights and plains (VI. 70, 640–6); it is
watered by living streams (v. 652); and fair with trees and
flowers[2]—immortal amaranth and celestial roses (III. 353–64),
and vines (v. 635). Daylight and twilight are known there (v.
627–9, 645, VI. 2–15). And soft winds fan the angels as they
sleep (v. 654, 655).

These angelic beings, divided, according to tradition (see p.
144), into nine Orders, each with particular duties, perform their
ministries and solemn rites (VII. 149) in the courts of God (v.
650) and at the high temple of Heaven (VII. 148). Their worship
is offered under forms which recall, now the ritual of the Temple
services of Israel, now the inspired visions of St John. They
celebrate the Deity who dwells invisible, throned inaccessible
(III. 377) on the holy mount (VI. 5), howbeit omnipresent, as
omnipotent, throughout Heaven and all space: round whose
throne there rests a radiance of excessive brightness, at which
even Seraphim, highest of Hierarchies, veil their eyes (III. 375–
82).

It has been objected that Milton's picture is too material.
But he himself takes special pains to remind us that the external
imagery under which he represents his concepts is symbolical,
not literal—adopted merely as a means of conveying *some* impression of that which is intrinsically indescribable. The truth,
I believe, is that he has applied to Heaven the descriptions of
'Paradise' in the apocalyptic literature of the first centuries of

[1] The Earth deteriorates after the fall of man (x. 651 *et seq.*).
[2] This is a descriptive detail most conspicuous in early Christian
apocalyptic works; see next page.

Christianity. The *Revelation of Peter* (dating perhaps from early in the second century A.D.) affords an illustration of these descriptions. St Peter is represented as asking our Lord where are the souls of the righteous dead—"of what sort is the world wherein they are and possess glory? And the Lord shewed him [me] a very great space outside this world shining excessively with light, and the air that was there illuminated with the rays of the sun, and the earth itself blooming with unfading flowers, and full of spices and fair-flowering plants, incorruptible and bearing a blessed fruit: and so strong was the perfume that it was borne even to us[1] from thence. And the dwellers in that place were clad in the raiment of angels of light, and their raiment was like their land: and angels encircled them."[2]

The second region, for which Chaos seems the simplest title, is also variously called "the wasteful Deep" (II. 961, VI. 862), "the utter Deep" (VI. 716), and "the Abyss" (I. 21, VII. 211, 234). Here rule the god of Chaos and his consort Night (II. 959–63). According to the long description in book II. 890 *et seq.*, this region is an illimitable ocean, composed of the embryon atoms whereof all substances may be formed—whereof Hell and the World are afterwards formed. It is a vast agglomeration of matter in its primal state, "neither sea, nor shore, nor air, nor fire". Here prevails eternal anarchy of storm and wind and wave and stunning sounds. In VII. 210–14 the Messiah and His host stand at the open gate of Heaven and look forth on to Chaos; and what they behold is an Abyss "Outrageous as a sea, dark, wasteful, wild".

---

[1] I.e. St Peter and the other disciples who are with our Lord on the Mount of Olives. See *The Gospel according to Peter, and the Revelation of Peter* (Cambridge University Press ed., 1892), pp. 48, 49.

[2] Mr James (whose version I have just quoted) gives a similar passage from a rather later work, the *History of Barlaam and Josaphat*, wherein the Paradise of the just is revealed in a vision as "a plain of vast extent, flourishing with fair and very sweet-smelling flowers, where he saw plants of all manner of kinds, loaded with strange and wondrous fruits, most pleasant to the eye and desirable to touch. And the leaves of the trees made clear music to a soft breeze and sent forth a delicate fragrance, whereof none could tire. . . . And through this wondrous and vast plain [he passed] to a city which gleamed with an unspeakable brightness and had its walls of translucent gold, and its battlements of stones the like of which none has ever seen. And a light from above. . . filled all the streets thereof: and certain winged hosts, each to itself a light, abode there singing in melodies never heard by mortal ears."

The creation of Hell, we may perhaps assume, just precedes the fall of the angels.[1] It has been prepared for their punishment when, after the proclamation in v. 600–15, they have revealed their rebellious spirit. To form Hell a part of the abyss has been taken. In II. 1002 Chaos complains that his realm has been encroached upon by Hell—"stretching far and wide beneath". Round it runs a wall of fire (I. 61); overhead spreads a fiery vault or cope (I. 298, 345). At the descent of the angels Hell lies open to receive them (VI. 53–5); then the roof closes (VI. 875), and they are prisoners. Henceforth the only outlet from Hell into Chaos is through certain gates, the charge whereof is assigned to Sin (II. 643 et seq.). At her side, as protector, stands Death, ready with his dart to meet all comers (II. 853–5). To please Satan (her sire), Sin opens the gates. Afterwards she cannot shut them; and all who will may pass to and fro between Hell and Chaos. Later on (when the bridge from Hell has been made) this change becomes terribly significant. For the inside of Hell, we hear of a pool of fire (I. 52, 221); dry land that burns like fire (I. 227–9); and drear regions of excessive cold and heat, intersected by rivers (II. 575 et seq.). Here again the picture is traditional, owing, no doubt, much to Dante, who in turn owed much to the apocalyptic descriptions before mentioned.

Immediately after the expulsion of Satan the World is created (VII. 131 et seq.). By "the World" is meant the whole Universe of Earth, seas, stellar bodies and the framework wherein they are set—in short, all that the eye of man beholds. The Son of God goes forth into the abyss (VII. 218 et seq.), and with golden compass marks out the limits of this World; so that Chaos is again despoiled of part of his realm (as he laments in II. 1001–6). The new World is a globe or hollow sphere, suspended in the abyss, and at its topmost point fastened by a golden chain (see II. 1051, note) to Heaven. In II. 1004–6 Chaos tells Satan of this Universe:

> "Another world,
> Hung o'er my realm, linked in a golden chain
> To that side Heaven from whence your legions fell."

The length of this chain, i.e. the distance of the World from the Empyrean, is not stated, I believe; but the distance was not—comparatively—very great (II. 1051–3, VII. 618).

[1] Cf. the English *Faust-book* (1592) where Faustus asks when Hell was made and Mephostophiles replies—"Faustus, thou shalt know, that before the fall of my lord Lucifer was no hell, but even then was hell ordained" (Thoms' *English Prose Romances*, III. 185).

Also, between the globe (again, on its upper side, i.e. that nearest to the Empyrean) and the gate of Heaven there stretches a golden stair, used by good angels for descent and ascent when they are despatched to Earth on any duty such as that which Raphael discharges in books V–VIII. This stair (suggested by Jacob's dream?) is not always let down (III. 501–18). And hard by the point where the golden stair touches the surface of the globe there is—in later times, after the fall of man—another stair (or rather bridge), which leads, not upward to the Empyrean, but downward to Hell: i.e. it extends over the portion of Chaos that intervenes between Hell and the World (II. 1024–33, X. 282 *et seq.*). This bridge,[1] the work of Sin and Death, is used by evil angels when they would come from Hell (its gates being open) to Earth—"to tempt or punish mortals" (II. 1032).

Hence a good angel and an evil, visiting mankind simultaneously, the one descending the golden stair, the other ascending the bridge, will meet at this point of the surface of the globe. And to enter the globe, i.e. to get through its outer surface to the inside, each must pass through the same aperture in the surface, and descend by the same passage into the interior: as Milton explains in book III. There he describes how Satan journeys through Chaos, till he reaches and walks[2] on the outer surface of the World (III. 418–30). But how to pass to the interior? The surface is impenetrable, and there seems to be no inlet. Then suddenly the reflection of the golden stair which chances to be let down directs his steps to the point where the stair and the bridge come into contact with the globe, and here he finds what he seeks—an aperture in the surface by which he can look down into the interior. Further, there is at this aperture a broad passage plunging right down into the World—being, really, a continuation of the golden stair. Thus Satan, standing on the bottom step of the stair, and looking straight up, sees overhead

---

[1] In the English *Faust-book*, 1592 (Thoms' *English Prose Romances*, III. 194) Mephistophiles says: "We have also with us in hell a ladder, reaching of exceeding highth, as though the top of the same would touch the heaven, to which the damned ascend to seek the blessing of God, but through their infidelity, when they are at very highest degree, they fall down again into their former miseries." With the last part of this extract cf. *P.L.* III. 484 *et seq.* It seems to me highly probable that Milton studied the *Faust-book* (which was immensely popular), as well as Marlowe's dramatic adaptation of it; see II. 596, note.

[2] I.e. like a fly moving up a lamp-globe (Masson).

the gate of Heaven; and, looking straight down, sees the interior of the globe, leagues beneath (III. 526 *et seq*.).

Similarly on the seventh day of the Creation the angels, gazing from Heaven's gate down the stair and down the broad passage which continues the stair, see, as Satan did, into the new-made World (VII. 617–19):

> "not far, founded in view
> On the clear hyaline, the glassy sea."[1]

In short, at the point in the surface of the globe nearest to the Empyrean, there is a choice of ways: the stair leading to Heaven; the bridge to Hell; and the broad passage to the interior of the World:

> "in little space
> The confines met of empyrean Heaven,
> And of this World; and, on the left hand, Hell
> With long reach interposed; three several ways,
> In sight, to each of these three places led."[2]

And descending the broad passage what would an angel find in the interior of the globe? What is this globe as Milton, following the astronomy of his[3] time, has described it?

The globe as then conceived may best be likened (in Plato's comparison)[4] to one of those puzzles or boxes in which are contained a number of boxes of gradually lessening size: remove the first, and you shall find another inside, rather smaller: remove the second, and you shall come on a third, still smaller: and so on, till you reach the centre—the kernel, as it were, round which the different boxes were but successive shells. Now, of the globe of the World the Earth (they said) is the kernel (it is often called 'the centre');[5] and—a stationary body itself—it is encased by numerous shells or Spheres: the number of the Spheres being a subject of dispute and varying in the different astronomical systems. Milton, accepting[6] for the purposes of

---

[1] I.e. the Crystalline Sphere.

[2] X. 320–4.

[3] I do not mean to imply that the Ptolemaic system was still generally believed in at the time when *P.L.* was published, but that it satisfied Elizabethan writers, of whom Milton was the last.

[4] See the Myth of Er in the *Republic* 616, 617; and the note on *Arcades* 64 (Pitt Press ed. p. 59), where the passage is translated.

[5] Cf. perhaps I. 686; and certainly the *Winter's Tale*, II. I. 102, *Troilus*, I. 3. 85.

[6] He was evidently familiar with the Copernican system (cf. IV. 592–7, VIII. 15–178); and the question has been asked why he did not follow it in the poem. The answer surely is obvious. The Copernican

his epic the Ptolemaic system as expanded by the astronomer Alphonsus X of Castille, recognizes ten Spheres. A Sphere, it should be noted, is merely a circular region of space—not necessarily of solid matter. Indeed, of the ten Spheres only one, the Primum Mobile, appears in Milton's description to consist of some material substance. Seven of them are the Spheres of the planets, i.e. the orbits in which the planets severally move.

The order of the Spheres, which fit one within the other,[1] is, if we start from the Earth as the stationary centre[2] of the Universe, as follows: first, the Spheres of the planets successively—the Moon, Mercury, Venus, the Sun, Mars, Jupiter and Saturn; then, outside the last of these (i.e. Saturn), the Firmament or Cælum Stellatum, in which are set the 'fixed stars'; then, outside the Firmament, the Crystalline Sphere; and last, the Primum Mobile enclosing all the others. Compare the famous lines (481–3) in book III describing the passage of the souls of the departed from Earth to Heaven:

"They pass the planets seven, and pass the fixed,
    And that Crystalline Sphere whose balance weighs
    The trepidation talked, and that First Moved."

It remains to note three or four points in these lines. Milton treats the Sun and Moon as planets (v. 177, x. 651–8). Compare Shakespeare, *Troilus*, I. 3. 89, "the glorious planet Sol", and *Antony*, v. 2. 241, "the fleeting Moon no planet is of mine". The 'fixed stars' are referred to four times in the poem—but only once (v. 176) with the word 'star' added: in the other places (III. 481, v. 621, x. 661) they are called simply "the fixed". Though they are unmoved, their Sphere revolves round the Earth, moving from East to West, completing a revolution in twenty-four hours, and carrying with it the seven inner Spheres.[3]

theory was new, without a scrap of literary association and with no poetic terminology: whereas the Ptolemaic view and its delightful fictions as to the Spheres, their harmonies, and the like, had become a tradition of literature, expressed in terms that recalled Marlowe and Shakespeare and Jonson and the *sacri vates* of English verse. To have surrendered this poetic heritage merely out of deference to science had been impossible pedantry—a perverse concession to the cold philosophy that "empties the haunted air and unweaves the rainbow" (*Lamia*).

[1] Cf. Marlowe's *Faustus* VI. 38, 39:
    "As are the elements, such are the spheres,
        Mutually folded in each other's orb."
[2] Cf. VIII. 32, "the sedentary Earth"; and see IX. 107–9.
[3] These have separate motions of their own.

The rapid motion of this Sphere is glanced at in v. 176 ("their orb[1] that flies"). The Crystalline Sphere and the Primum Mobile were not included in the original Ptolemaic system. They were added later, to explain certain phenomena which the earlier astronomers had not observed, and for which their theories offered no explanation. Thus the supposed swaying or "trepidation" of the Crystalline Sphere was held to be the cause of the precession of the equinoxes. This Sphere is described as a vast expanse of waters (see note on VII. 261). It encircles the eight inner Spheres. The original notion may perhaps be traced to the waters "above the firmament" in *Genesis* i. 7. Compare the picture in VII. 270–1 of the World

> "Built on circumfluous waters calm, in wide
> Crystalline ocean."

The main purpose that this "ocean" serves is to protect the Earth from the evil "influences" of Chaos; those "fierce extremes" of temperature which might penetrate through the outside shell (the Primum Mobile) and "distemper" the whole fabric of the Universe, did not this wall of waters interpose (VII. 271–3).

Last comes the Primum Mobile,[2] "the first[3] convex" of the World, i.e. the outside case of our box or puzzle. It is made, as we saw, of hard matter; but for its crust of substance, Chaos would break in on the World, and Darkness make inroads (III. 419–21). The first moved itself, it communicates motion to the nine inner Spheres. In Elizabethan literature allusions to it are not infrequent: we will conclude by giving three. Compare Spenser, *Hymne of Heavenly Beautie*:

> "these heavens still by degrees arize,
> Until they come to their first Movers bound,
> That in his mightie compasse doth comprize,
> And carry all the rest with him around;"

and Marlowe, *Faustus*:[4]

> "He views the clouds, and planets, and the stars,
> The tropic zones, and quarters of the sky,
> From the bright circle of the hornèd moon
> Even to the height of Primum Mobile;"

---

[1] 'Orb' and 'Sphere' are interchangeable terms—when it suits Milton.   [2] Dante's *primo giro* (*Purgatorio*, I. 15).

[3] III. 419. To Satan coming from Chaos it is the first; in our calculation, as we started from the Earth, it is the last.

[4] Scene VI. *chorus*, ll. 5–18, in the third Quarto, 1616; the passage is not in the two earlier editions of 1604 and 1609 (Ward, p. 178).

and Bacon, *Of Seditions and Troubles*: "for the motions of the greatest persons in a government ought to be as the motions of the planets under Primum Mobile".

B

ON THE CHARACTER OF MILTON'S SATAN

I have reserved for this *Appendix* notice of some points in Milton's delineation of the character of Satan. First, as to the rank which Milton assigns to him before his revolt, and the cause of that revolt. Milton speaks of Satan as an archangel[1]—"if not the first archangel" (v. 660): that is, he is inclined to give Satan pre-eminence over all angelic beings. But this pre-eminence is not emphasised so much as we might have expected.

The immediate cause of the rebellion in Heaven is the pro-clamation that all should worship the Messiah as their Head (v. 600–15). Satan resents the command, conceiving himself "impaired" (v. 665) thereby; and he makes its pretended in-justice a means of drawing away a third part of the angels from their allegiance. They are equal, he says, to the Messiah: self-begotten, not created: not liable to pay worship; and so, playing on their pride, he wins them to his side (v. 772–802, 853–66). Meantime, in his own heart an even stronger motive is at work; to wit, ambition to be himself equal to the Deity—nay, superior. He not only disclaims submission to the Son: he strives "against the throne and monarchy" (1. 42) of the Almighty Himself; and it is as the foe rather of the Father than of the Son that the great archangel is set before us in *Paradise Lost*.

Touching both matters there was much tradition, whereof it may be interesting to cite two or three illustrations from popular works[2] with which Milton is likely to have been familiar. To take, for example, the English *Faust-book*: Faustus asks: "But how came lord and master Lucifer[3] to have so great a fall from

---

[1] Contrast the first extract from the *Faust-book*, later on.

[2] I choose three works each of which may, I think, be regarded as a *résumé* of many of the current traditions of demonology. Two of the books—the *Faust-book*, 1592, and Scot's *Discourse*, 1584—were ex-tremely popular, and personally I believe that Milton had studied both. Scot devotes several chapters to "Lucifer and his fall". The third work—Heywood's *Hierarchie*, 1635—is very serviceable to an editor of *Paradise Lost*.

[3] A common name of Satan.

Heaven? Mephistophiles answered, My lord Lucifer was a fair angel, created of God as immortal, and being placed in the Seraphims,[1] which are above the Cherubims, he would have presumed upon the Throne of God...upon this presumption the Lord cast him down headlong, and where [i.e. whereas] before he was an angel of light, now dwells in darkness."[2] Later on Faustus returns to the subject, enquiring "in what estimation his lord Lucifer was, when he was in favour with God": also touching his form and shape: to which Mephistophiles replies, "My lord Lucifer...was at the first an angel of God, yea he was so of God ordained for shape, pomp, authority, worthiness, and dwelling, that he far exceeded all the other creatures of God, and so illuminated that he far surpassed the brightness of the sun, and all the stars...but when he began to be high minded, proud and so presumptuous, that he would usurp the seat of God's Majesty, then was he banished."[3]

The *Faust-book*, it will be seen, agrees with Milton on both points; while, as regards one of them—Satan's rank—it is more explicit than *Paradise Lost*. Equally explicit is Heywood's *Hierarchie of the Blessed Angels* (1635). There (p. 336) we read that of the angels Lucifer was first-created and chief:

> "As he might challenge a prioritie
>   In his Creation, so aboue the rest
>   A supereminence, as first and best."

Heywood mentions Michael, Raphael, and Gabriel, and adds (p. 337) that great as they were,

> "Yet aboue these was Lucifer instated,
>   Honor'd, exalted, and much celebrated."

Reginald Scot goes even further, remarking[4] that according to the teaching of some divines Satan even after his fall exceeded in power any of the angelic host. It seems to me therefore something strange that Milton did not unequivocally invest Satan with superiority over all the angels.

As to Satan's motive Heywood[5] differs from Milton, making jealousy of mankind the cause; while Scot writes:[6] "Our schoolemen differ much in the cause of *Lucifer's* fall [some alleging one thing, some another, while] others saie, that his condemnation

---

[1] The highest of the Hierarchies; see v. 587. We may note the forms 'Seraphims', 'Cherubims'; see G. under 'Cherubim'.

[2] Thoms' *English Prose Romances*, 2nd ed., III. 184.

[3] Thoms, III. 187.

[4] Nicholson's ed., p. 425.

[5] p. 339.   [6] p. 423.

grew hereupon, for that he challenged the place of the Messias."
This accords more with *Paradise Lost* v. 661–5.

For Milton Satan is the type of pride. The type was already
fixed. As an epithet of Lucifer 'proud' had passed into a pro-
verb. Thus Gower said:[1]

> "For Lucifer with him that felle
> Bar pride with him into helle.
> There was pride of to grete cost
> Whan he for pride hath heven lost;"

and Marlowe:[2]

> "*Faust.* How comes it, then, that he is prince of devils?
> *Meph.* O, by aspiring pride and insolence;
>   For which God threw him from the face of heaven;"

and Greene:[3]

> "proud Lucifer fell from the heavens,
>
> . . . .
>
>   Lucifer and his proud-hearted friends
> Were thrown into the centre of the earth."

Milton therefore did not wholly conceive or create the character of the arch-rebel. Tradition, literary no less than theological, prescribed the dominant idea in that nature: enough if
Milton developed the idea in harmony with the design of his
poem. This he did. He depicts Satan as an embodiment of the
spirit of pride and ambition:[4] not the ambition which is an
honourable desire of praise—that last infirmity of noble minds
—but the fevered lust for power which springs from overmaster-
ing self-esteem. In Satan this spirit of egotism is the poison that
permeates his whole being, vanquishing and vitiating all that is
good in him.

For at the outset of the action of *Paradise Lost* Satan has much
that is noble and attractive in his nature. To have made him
wholly evil had repelled, and lessened the interest of the poem,
which turns, in no slight degree, on the struggle between the
good and evil elements in him. Indeed, this very pride is not
without its good aspect. Herein lies the motive power that
nerves him at every crisis to face insuperable difficulties; to
cherish immortal hope—though hope of revenge; and to adventure "high attempts".

On the other hand, it is this same spirit that drives him onward to his final fall. If at any moment he is minded to repent

---

[1] *Confessio Amantis*, book I.   [2] *Faustus* III. 67–9.
[3] *Friar Bacon* IX. 59, 65, 66.
[4] Cf. Satan's own words in IV. 40.

and submit—through pity for the friends whom he has ruined, or mankind whom he schemes to ruin, or himself—through sense of his ingratitude (IV. 42–5) towards the Almighty—whatever the motive—relentless, resistless egotism sweeps aside compunction, and denies him retreat. To sue for grace were to humble himself in the eyes of his followers and in his own: which must not be (IV. 79–83).

Steadily does Milton keep this idea before us. There is no possibility of missing or mistaking his intention. The very word 'pride' recurs[1] like some persistent refrain, ringing clearest at the great crises, the fateful moments when the action of the epic enters on a fresh stage: as when in the fourth book (ll. 27 *et seq.*) Satan looks down upon Eden from his resting-place on mount Niphates, and a brief while is inclined to give up his attempt and seek re-admission into Heaven; or as when in the ninth book (ll. 455–72) he sees Eve in the Garden and is touched by her beauty and innocence, and disarmed of his ill thoughts. Always, however, the end is the same: "the hot hell" of pride in his heart breaks anew into flame; and he goes forward to his work.[2] Had not pride led him to undertake it?

Satan's resolve to compass the fall of man is prompted by several feelings—each a phase of self-esteem. There is jealousy. Man has usurped his place—dispossessed him and his followers. At sight of Adam and Eve he exclaims (IV. 359–60):

> "Into our room of bliss thus high advanced
> Creatures of other mould, earth-born perhaps!"

The same feeling finds expression in almost the same words later on (IX. 148, 149). That others should receive favour from the Almighty—and, as he thinks, at his expense—wounds his pride.

Again, there is desire to assert his supremacy by undertaking an office from which the mightiest of his followers recoil in fear. Nowhere does Satan stand forth so eminent and sublime "with monarchal pride" as in the scene in the second book where he proffers himself for the great enterprise. The counsel of Beelzebub has been applauded by all (ll. 386–9): but who will carry it out? None dare: and then Satan, proclaiming his readiness, once more confirms his sovereignty. Here too pride has ruled.

But the strongest motive remains: desire

> "To wreak on innocent frail man his loss
> Of that first battle, and his flight to Hell."[3]

---

[1] Cf. I. 36, 58, 527, 572, 603—with many other examples.
[2] Cf. Mr Stopford Brooke's admirable *Study* of Milton, p. 148.
[3] IV. 11, 12.

"To spite the great Creator" (II. 385) he will bring ruin on the earth and its inhabitants: which, if not victory, were revenge. The notion flatters his self-conceit. It is born of the old pride. And Milton dwells on it with fitting insistence.[1]

Is Satan the 'hero' of *Paradise Lost*? We might think so did we not read beyond the first books. But to trace his history in the poem to its inglorious close is to dispel the impression. Milton can scarcely intend that we should regard as 'hero'—as worthy of sustained admiration—one who passes from the splendour of archangelic being to the state of a loathsome reptile.[2] The hideous metamorphosis in X. 504–32 is the necessary contrast to those scenes at the beginning of the epic in which the great rebel does appear in heroic grandeur: and we must look on both pictures. If *Paradise Lost* narrates the fall of man, it narrates too—and no less clearly—the fall of man's tempter. The self-degradation of Satan is complete: outward and inward: of the form and of the spirit: a change—ever for the worse—of shape and mind and emotion.

There is the outward sign. Before his expulsion he is pre-eminently a lustrous being, clothed with ethereal radiance and glory—so much does his name "Lucifer" argue.[3] And afterwards he retains something of this "original brightness" (I. 592): howbeit much has passed from him (I. 97, 591–4). But gradually what was left decreases in proportion as the evil in him prevails: so that Uriel perceives the foul passions that dim his face (IV. 124–30); while Gabriel marks his "faded splendour wan" (IV. 870), and the Cherub Zephon taunts him therewith (IV. 835–40). Equal is his loss of physical force. On the fields of Heaven he does not fear to meet Michael in combat (VI. 246 *et seq.*): in the Garden of Eden he doubts himself a match for Adam:

"Foe not informidable! exempt from wound,
    I not; so much hath Hell debased, and pain[4]
    Enfeebled me, to what I was in Heaven."

In fact, he is glad that he has to deal with the woman—not the man (IX. 480–8).

Nor this because of lost strength alone. He shuns the "higher intellectual" of Adam (IX. 483), who would be better able than

---

[1] Cf. VI. 905, 906.
[2] Cf. his words in IX. 163–71.
[3] Cf. VII. 131–3, and the second extract from the *Faust-book*, and Marlowe, "beautiful As was bright Lucifer before his fall" (*Faustus*, v. 155).
[4] See I. 55, VI. 327, notes.

Eve to see through his arguments and so resist temptation. He is conscious of his own decline in intellect. The strong intelligence which inspires his speeches in the first two books has degenerated, by perverse use, into mere sophistical slyness, a base cunning—even as wine may lose its savour and turn to vinegar. He is no more the mighty-minded archangel: he is naught but the serpent—"subtlest beast of all the field". Lastly, every impulse in him towards good has died out. The element of nobility that redeemed his character at the outset from absolute baseness has been killed. In evil he moves and has his being, so that himself confesses "all good to me becomes bane"; and in destroying lies his sole delight (IX. 118 et seq.).

Hardly therefore shall we believe that Milton meant us to see in the fallen and everfalling archangel the hero of *Paradise Lost*. That position surely belongs to Adam.

C

THE SUBJECT OF THE POEM

That Milton was convinced as to the "heroic" character of his subject is clear from the introduction[1] to book IX; nevertheless it has been disputed whether the Fall of Man was a suitable theme for an heroic poem and whether the title "heroic" should be applied to *Paradise Lost*. Thus Dryden writes in the "Discourse" on satire prefixed to his translation (1693) of Juvenal: "As for Mr Milton, whom we all admire with so much justice, his subject[2] is not that of an heroic poem, properly so called. His design is the losing of our happiness; his event[3] is not prosperous, like that of all other epic works."

Addison refers to this objection at the commencement of his papers on Milton. "I shall waive", he says, "the discussion of that point, which was started some years since [i.e. by Dryden], whether Milton's 'Paradise Lost' may be called an heroic poem. Those who will not give it that title may call it (if they please) a divine poem" (*Spectator*, 267).

In his sixth paper (*Spectator*, 297) Addison considers the kinds of subject or "fable" appropriate to "heroic song", admits that a "fable", like the Fall of Man, "wherein the event is unhappy ...is not so proper for an heroic poem" as for a tragedy, but

---

[1] IX. 13–44.   [2] I.e. in *Paradise Lost*.
[3] That is, the end of the action, the issue (Lat. *eventus*).

shows briefly that Milton was conscious of the disadvantage inherent in his subject and combated it. How Milton did so,
Addison explains in the following well-known passage of the
last of his papers on *Paradise Lost*:

"I have hinted in my sixth paper that an heroic poem, according to the opinion of the best critics, ought to end happily, and
leave the mind of the reader, after having conducted it through
many doubts and fears, sorrows and disquietudes, in a state of
tranquillity and satisfaction. Milton's fable, which had so many
other qualifications to recommend it, was deficient in this particular. It is here therefore that the poet has shewn a most exquisite judgment, as well as the finest invention, by finding out
a method to supply this natural defect in his subject. Accordingly
he leaves the adversary of mankind, in the last view which he
gives us of him, under the lowest state of mortification and dis-
appointment. We see him chewing ashes, grovelling in the dust,
and loaden with supernumerary pains and torments. On the
contrary, our first two parents are comforted by dreams and
visions, cheered with promises of salvation, and in a manner
raised to a greater happiness than that which they had forfeited.
In short, Satan is represented miserable in the height of his
triumph, and Adam triumphant in the height of his misery"
(*Spectator*, 369).

Johnson's view is to somewhat similar effect: "Milton, though
he entitled 'Paradise Lost' only a 'poem', yet calls it himself
'heroic song'. Dryden...denies the heroism of Adam, because
he was overcome; but there is no reason why the hero should
not be unfortunate, except established practice, since success
and virtue do not go necessarily together.... However, if success
be necessary, Adam's deceiver was at last crushed; Adam was
restored to his Maker's favour, and therefore may securely
resume his human rank" (*Life* of Milton).

D

THE ORDERS OF THE HEAVENLY BEINGS

According to a mediæval belief the Heavenly beings were divided
into three Hierarchies, and each Hierarchy was subdivided into
three Orders or Choirs. These Orders comprised the Seraphim,
Cherubim and Thrones (θρόνοι), forming the first Hierarchy;
Dominations (κυριότητες), Virtues (δυνάμεις), and Powers (ἐξουσίαι),

forming the second; Principalities (ἀρχαί), Archangels and Angels, forming the third. This system was deduced, in the main, from St Paul's words in *Ephesians* i. 21 and *Colossians* i. 16. First formulated in the treatise περὶ τῆς οὐρανίας ἱεραρχίας, which was long attributed, though falsely, to Dionysius, the Areopagite, the notion had great influence in the Middle Ages; cf. Dante, *Paradiso*, XXVIII. 98–126. Allusions to it are frequent in Elizabethan writers. Works from which many illustrations of the system might be quoted are: *Batman vppon Bartholome* (1582), Reginald Scot's *Discovery of Witchcraft* (1584), Thomas Watson's *Eglogue* (1590), the *Faust-book* (1592), Spenser's *Hymne of Heavenly Beautie* (1596), Bacon, *Advancement of Learning*, i. 28, and Heywood's *Hierarchie of the Blessed Angels* (1635), which deals with the subject at great length.

Milton accepted[1] the tradition and made it the basis of the whole angelical system of *Paradise Lost*.

Each of the Orders possessed some special quality. The Seraphim were the "burning" lustrous beings; cf. Spenser, *Heavenly Beautie*:

> "those eternall burning Seraphins,
> Which from their faces dart out fierie light."

This conception, due probably to the false derivation of *Seraphim* from a root signifying 'to burn', determines Milton's choice of epithets (e.g. 'bright', 'fiery') for this order of the Hierarchies.

The Cherubim had a wondrous power of vision: hence their main duty in *Paradise Lost* is to keep watch. See IV. 778, note. And through this power of vision they enjoyed in a peculiar degree the *Visio Beatifica* or faculty of "contemplating" the Deity. In the words of the treatise περὶ τῆς ἱεραρχίας they were distinguished διὰ τὸ θεοπτικὸν αὐτῶν καὶ θεωρητικόν. And this notion is the key to that line (54) in *Il Penseroso*, the point of which has been so much misunderstood—"The Cherub Contemplation".

The archangels were, as their name implied, the "chief messengers" of the Almighty and the intermediaries between him and Man. Cf. Reginald Scot, "As for archangels, they are sent onlie about great and secret matters"; and Heywood, "The

---

[1] Thus in *Church Government* he says, "the angels themselves... are distinguished into their celestial princedoms and satrapies", *P.W.* II. 442. He several times uses the special terms "Orders" and "Hierarchies"—cf. *P.L.* I. 737, V. 587, 591, VII. 192; while the titles "Seraphim", "Thrones", "Dominations", "Virtues", etc., occur constantly.

Archangels are Embassadors, great matters to declare". Hence Milton makes Raphael in book V and Michael in books XI, XII —each one of the seven archangels referred to in III. 648–53— the bearers of messages and charges from the Almighty to Adam.

One other point in which Milton follows mediæval tradition with regard to the Heavenly beings may be noticed. Descriptions like those in book III, ll. 625–8 and 636–42, are purely traditional. We must compare them with the presentment of angels in works of early Christian art. Poets and painters alike drew upon religious tradition and expressed it by certain conventional details. And this presentment of angelic beings contained a considerable element of symbolism. In *Batman vppon Bartholome*, II. iii, iv, there is a long discourse on the attributes which painters assign to angels and on their symbolical significance. The following brief extracts from it illustrate Milton's pictures of Uriel (III. 625–8) and the "stripling Cherub" (III. 636–42): "When Angells are paynted with long lockes and crispe haire, thereby is understoode their cleane affections and ordinate thoughts. For the hayre of the head betokeneth thoughts and affections that doe spring out of the roote of thought and minde. ...And they be painted beardles: for to take consideration and heede, that they passe never the state of youth, neyther waxe feeble in vertues, neither faile for age.... Truely they be paynted feathered and winged...[as a sign that] they be lifted up in effect and knowledge, and rauished to the innermost contemplation of the loue of God."

E

PARADISE LOST, x. 658–62

Dr Masson illustrates the astrological terms in these lines by a passage translated from "an old Latin catechism or text-book of Astronomy (Blebelius, *De Sphæra*, 1582)"; it runs as follows:

"What are the *aspects* of planets? They are such arrangements and distances of the planets as allow them to intercommunicate their influence. How many species of aspects are there? Five— Conjunction, Sextile, Square, Trine, and Diametral or Opposition. What is the first? The first kind of aspects, called Conjunction, is when two stars or planets are conjoined and as it were connected in one line; by the Greeks it is called *Synod*. What is the Sextile aspect? When two planets or stars are distant from each other a sixth part of the Zodiac, viz. two signs or 60°. What

is the Square aspect (*quadratus aspectus*)? When two stars look at each other at an interval of three signs, making a quadrant or 90°. What is Trine (*Trigonus*) aspect? When the distance of the stars measures a third of the circle,—that is, 120° or four signs. What is the Diametral aspect? It is the opposite configuration of two luminaries, which are distant from each other 180° or half a circle....

"How are the aspects divided? Into happy and unhappy. Which are the happy and prosperous aspects? The prosperous and benign are the Trine and Sextile. Why are they called happy? Because the rays of the planets, falling obliquely and mutually yielding, infuse and communicate to inferior bodies gentler and less violent influences. What are the unhappy aspects? The unhappy or malignant are Conjunction, Square, and Opposition.[1] Why are they called malignant? Because the planets, meeting each other with their rays, mutually collide, and neither can yield to the other on account of the directness of their onset. Therefore they exercise greater force in stimulating and varying seasons, and in mixing the temperaments of animals and the qualities of the air. Whence is this variety of effects known? The effect and variety of configuration were first observed in the case of the Moon, and afterwards transferred to the other planets by artists (*artifices*) who, by great sharpness of intelligence, and more attentive observation, endeavoured to find out and display the causes of events from the very nature of the heavenly motions and the species of the aspects." Dr Masson adds, "Milton, it will be noted, names all the aspects, giving Conjunction its Greek name of *Synod*."

[1] Cf. *Richard III*, IV. 4. 215, "Lo, at their births good stars were opposite", and 402, "Be opposite all planets of good luck".

GLOSSARY

MILTON's diction is essentially Elizabethan: the diction of the Authorised Version (1611) of the Bible and of Shakespeare. Hence, though *Paradise Lost* was not published till 1667, its language is best illustrated by quotations from the works of Elizabethan writers.

A marked feature of Milton's diction, as of his style, is his classical bias. He employs in a classical sense, or with reference to their classical origin, many words derived from Greek or Latin, just as he employs classical constructions (cf. IX. 130, 563, 792, 795, 818; X. 332, 687), and figures of speech (cf. IX. 648). This classicism of diction is still more conspicuous in his prose, in which he introduces numbers of long, sonorous words derived from the Latin. Sometimes he invents such words. These books of *Paradise Lost* contain numerous examples of his classical diction.

Book IX. Cf. *argument, involve, sentence, officious, obnoxious, entire, front, event, secure, voluble, spire, fraud, fluctuate, science, divine, devote, sacred, fact, certain, oblige, elegant.*
See 13, 75, 88, 104, 170, 292, 330, 334, 371, 436, 502, 643, 668, 680, 845, 901, 924, 928, 953, 980, 1018.

Book X. Cf. *moment, derive, person, sagacious, mole, inoffensive, pontifical, virtue, detriment, reduce, supplant, reluctant, complicated, station, just, sublime, redound, equal, pretend, office, reluctance, foment, attrite, frequent.*
See 45, 77, 156, 281, 300, 305, 313, 372, 409, 438, 513, 515, 523, 535, 536, 739, 748, 872, 960, 1045, 1071, 1073, 1091.

Abbreviations:

A.S. = Anglo-Saxon, i.e. English down to about the Conquest.

Middle E. = Middle English, i.e. English from about the Conquest to about 1500.

Elizabethan E. = the English of Shakespeare and his contemporaries (down to about 1650).

O.F. = Old French, i.e. till about 1600. F. = modern French.

Germ. = modern German.   Gk. = Greek.
Ital. = modern Italian.   Lat. = Latin.

The dates, of course, are only approximate: such divisions must be more or less arbitrary and open to criticism.

adamant, x. 318; Gk. ἀδάμας, 'unconquerable' (from ἀ-, the negative prefix, + δαμάειν, 'to tame'), which was used substantively for a 'very hard metal or stone'. *Diamond* comes from the same source. Cf. F. *diamant*.

addressed, IX. 672, 'prepared, ready'; cf. 2 *Henry IV,* IV. 4. 5, "Our navy is address'd, our power [i.e. army] collected". M. uses the noun *address* = 'preparation' in *S. A.* 731, "she makes address to speak", i.e. prepares.

ambrosial, used by M. of that which delights the sense of smell (IX. 852) or taste. Strictly, ἀμβροσία, from ἀμβρόσιος (a lengthened form of ἄμβροτος, 'immortal'), meant the food of the gods.

amiable, IX. 899, 'lovely'; its sense in the two other passages, IV. 250, VIII. 484, of *P. L.* in which it occurs. Cf. *Psalm* lxxxiv. 1, "How amiable are thy dwellings" (*Prayer-Book*). From Lat. *amicabilis*, 'friendly'; not from Lat. *amabilis*, 'lovable'.

amphisbæna, x. 524; Gk. ἀμφίσβαινα, 'a kind of serpent that can go either forwards or backwards' (Gk. ἀμφι, 'on both sides', + βαίνειν, 'to go'). See the *Agamemnon,* 1206. It was supposed to have a head at either end of its body: hence the allusion in Tennyson's *Queen Mary,* III. 4:

> "For heretic and traitor are all one;
> Two vipers of one breed—an amphisbæna,
> Each end a sting."

animate, IX. 112. In Elizabethan E. the form of the past participle of a verb of Latin origin is often clipped so that it resembles the Latin form. Cf. **frustrate** for 'frustrate*d*', IX. 944; **satiate,** IX. 792, where *-ate* (modern E. *-ated*) = Lat. *-atus,* e.g. in *satiatus.* So **devote** (*devotus*) for 'devote*d*', IX. 901; **convict** (*convictus*) for 'convic*t*ed', x. 83.

annoy, IX. 446; derived through O.F. *anoi,* 'vexation', from Lat. *in odio,* used in the phrase *in odio est mihi,* 'it is *odious* to me'. Cognate with '*noi*some' = unpleasant, especially of smell, which practically is short for '*anoi*some'.

apparent, x. 112 = 'visible, manifest' (Lat. *apparens*); as in the two other places where M. uses it, viz. IV. 608, *P. R.* II. 397. Cf. *Richard III,* III. 5. 30, "apparent open guilt", and *King John,* IV. 2. 93, "It is apparent foul play".

approve, IX. 367, 1140, 'to show' by bringing a thing to the test (Lat. *ad*, 'to', +*proba*, 'a test'). Cf. 2 *Corinthians* vii. 11, "In all things ye have approved yourselves to be clear in this matter".

argument, IX. 13, 42 = Lat. *argumentum*, in the sense 'subject, theme'. Cf. I. 24, where he describes the Fall of Man, the subject of *P. L.*, as "this great argument".

asphodel, IX. 1040, Gk. ἀσφόδελος, a kind of lily, supposed to flourish especially in the Elysian fields. *Daffodil* is a curious corruption of ἀσφόδελος through Low Lat. *affodillus*.

assay, X. 567, 865, 'to *try*, attempt'; M. always uses this form, from O.F. *assai*, a variant of O.F. *essai*, whence comes our commoner form *essay*. Lat. *exagium*, Gk. ἐξάγιον, 'a weighing, *trial* of weight'. Now *assay* is commonly used of the testing of metals.

astonied, IX. 890; the p.p. of the old verb *astony*, whence *astonish* and *astound* have been formed; O.F. *estonner*, F. *étonner*, Lat. *extonare*, 'to thunder'. So the original notion in *astonied*, *astonished* and *astounded* is 'struck senseless, stupefied, as with a thunderbolt'.

bases, IX. 36. Cf. the *Faerie Queene*, V. 5. 20:

> "She made him to be dight
> In womans weedes, that is to manhood shame,
> And put before his lap a napron white,
> Instead of Curiets [i.e. cuirasses] and bases fit for fight."

Peele in his *Polyhymnia*, 1590 (a description of a tournament), speaks of a knight clad "In armour gilt and bases full of cost".

blanc, X. 656, 'pale', from the literal sense 'white', F. *blanc*. For the form *blanc* (i.e. *blank*), obsolete as an adjective, cf. the noun *blanc*, 'white paint'.

blow, IX. 629, 'to flower, bloom'; cf. *Lycidas*, 48, "When first the white-thorn blows". Cognate with *bloom*, *blossom*, Germ. *blühen*.

brown, IX. 1088, 'dark'; in poetry a constant epithet of shade and twilight. Cf. *Il Penseroso*, 134, "shadows brown"; *P. R.* II. 293, "alleys brown", i.e. shady paths. Imitated from the similar use of *bruno* and *imbrunire* by Italian poets. Thus in his 2nd Ital. *Sonnet* M. has "al *imbrunir* di sera", with which editors compare Petrarch, *Canzoni* 4. 3, and Tasso, *Gerusalemme Liberata* 5. 76.

causey, X. 415, 'a raised way'; now obsolete. Cf., however, *Proverbs* XV. 19, "the way of the righteous is *made plain*", where the margin has "raised up as a causey". In 1 *Chronicles* XXVI. 16 the Bible of 1611 had "by the *causey* of the going up", afterwards changed to *causeway*; the latter is a compound of the old

word *causey+way*. From Late Lat. *calciata* (i.e. *calciata via*), literally 'a way made firm by treading with the heel' (*calx*). Not connected with *calx*, 'lime'.

Cherubim; the correct form = Hebrew *Kherūbhīm*, the plural of *Kherūbh*. The oldest forms in English, as still in French, were *Cherubin*, singular, and *Cherubins*, plural. Cf. Coverdale, "Thou God of Israel, which dwellest upon Cherubin", *Isaiah* xxxvii. 16; and Wyclif, "Two Goldun Cherubyns", *Exodus* xxv. 18. Later, as in the Bible of 1611, *Cherub*, singular, and *Cherubims*, plural, were used, as being closer to Hebrew. For the singular M. wrote '**Cherube**' (a still nearer approach in sound than 'Cheru*b*' to the *ū* of the Heb. *Kherūbh*), and the true plural **Cherubim**, adopted in the Revised Version of the Bible. *Kherūbh* is said to come from the Babylonian word for the figure of the winged bull which stood at the door of a house to keep off evil spirits. The Jews probably owed it to the Phœnicians.

coast, x. 89, 'region'; commonly used so in the plural; cf. VIII. 245, "Glad we returned up to the coasts of light". Literally 'side', 'border' (IX. 67); F. *côte*, Lat. *costa*, 'a rib'.

connive, x. 624; Lat. *connivere*, 'to close the eyes', 'wink', hence figuratively 'to shut one's eyes to a fault'. Now 'connive' always has the bad sense of 'winking at something wrong'; but in Elizabethan E. it also had the good sense 'to tolerate, be long-suffering'. Cf. *S. A.* 465–7:

> "He [the Almighty]
> Will not connive, or linger, thus provoked,
> But will arise and his great name assert."

In *Of Reformation* M. praises "the constancy of our nobility and commons of England, whose calm and temperate connivance could sit still and smile out the stormy bluster of men", *P. W.* II. 406.

damp, IX. 45, 'to depress', literally 'to suffocate'. Cf. the *Areopagitica*, "this...had damped the glory of Italian wits", *P.W.* II. 82. So the adjective = 'depressed' in I. 523, "downcast and damp". See XI. 293, 544.

demur, IX. 558; Lat. *demorari*, 'to linger, delay': hence the radical notion is 'to hesitate'. Now only used in 'demur *to*' a thing, i.e. hesitate about agreeing to it.

devote, IX. 901 = 'devoted'; used by M. in the sense of Lat. *devotus*, 'set apart by a vow' (*votum*), especially 'set apart for destruction', and so 'doomed'. Cf. XI. 821, "A world devote to universal wrack" (i.e. wreck, ruin).

divan, x. 457, 'a council', properly the council of the Sultan

or some Oriental sovereign or governor; Arabic *diwán*, 'a council, tribunal'. F. *douane*, 'a custom-house', comes from *diwán*, which also meant 'a register of accounts'.

draff, x. 630, 'refuse food', especially food given to swine. Cf. Cotgrave's *French Dictionary* (1611), "Mangeaille pour les porceaux: Swillings, washings, draffe". Samson was given "the draff of servile food", *S. A.* 574. Used figuratively; cf. Milton's *Doctrine of Divorce*, "the brood of Belial, the draff of men", *P. W.* III. 173. Cognate with *drab*, 'an untidy woman'; cf. *drafty* = 'dirty', as in Hall's *Satires* v. 3, "all within is drafty sluttish geere" (i.e. gear).

explode, x. 546; used = Lat. *explodere*, 'to drive off the stage', i.e. by clapping (*ex*, 'off, away', + *plaudere*, 'to clap'). So in xi. 669 and in the *Animadversions upon the Remonstrant's Defence*, "ceremonies and tyrannies, which God and man are now ready to *explode and hiss* out of the land", *P. W.* III. 43.

flaw, x. 698, 'a gust of wind'; a poetic word. Cf. *Hamlet*, v. 1. 239, "the winter's flaw"; and Tennyson, *Marriage of Geraint*, "Like flaws in summer laying lusty corn". The same as *flaw*, 'a crack' = Swedish *flaga*, 'a crack', also 'blast of wind'. Perhaps 'sudden burst' is the radical notion.

foil, x. 375, 'a defeat'; cf. the *Paraphrase on Psalm cxiv* made by M. in his boyhood, "As a faint host that hath received the foil". O.F. *fouler*, 'to trample under foot'; cf. *foule*, 'a crowd'. The original notion is seen in the *Faerie Queene*, v. 11. 33:

"Whom he did all to peeces breake, and foyle
In filthy durt, and left so in the loathely soyle."

fond, x. 834, 'foolish'; its old sense. Cf. *King Lear*, IV. 7. 60, "I am a very foolish fond old man". Hence **fondly** = 'foolishly' (IX. 999, X. 564). Originally *fond* was the p.p. of a Middle E. verb *fonnen*, 'to act like a fool', from the noun *fon*, 'a fool'. The root is Scandinavian.

forfeit, x. 304; originally 'to do wrong', then 'to lose by wrongdoing'. Low Lat. *forisfactum*, 'a trespass, fine'; the p.p. of *forisfacere*, 'to act beyond', i.e. beyond what is right.

gloze, IX. 549, 'to speak falsely, flatter'. Middle E. *glosen* meant 'to make glosses, explain', from Late Lat. *glossa*, Gk. γλῶσσα, which signified (1) the tongue, (2) a language, (3) a word, (4) an explanation of a word. The verb *glosen* got the idea 'to explain falsely', whence 'to deceive'. So *glozing* = 'deceptive'; cf. George Herbert, *The Dotage*, "False glozing pleasures". Especially used of flattering, false speech; cf. *Comus*, 161, "words of glozing courtesy"; *P. L.* III. 93, "glozing lies".

harbinger, IX. 13, 'forerunner'; in *P. R.* I. 71, 277, John the Baptist is called the "harbinger" of Christ. Originally it meant an officer who went in advance of an army or prince to make provision for the night's shelter. Cf. Florio's *Dictionary*, 1598, "Foriere, a harbinger for a camp or a prince". From Icelandic *herbergi*, 'an army shelter'; cf. the cognate German words *heer*, 'army' + *bergen*, 'to shelter'.

heinous, IX. 929, X. 1; spelt *hainous* in the original edition, as often in old writers. F. *haineux*, 'hateful'.

impress, IX. 35, 'a device, generally with motto, on a coat of arms, scutcheon, shield'. Also spelt *imprese* = Ital. *impresa*, 'a device, emblem'; literally 'something impressed', i.e. stamped. Cf. *Richard II*, III. 1. 24, 25.

> "From my own windows torn my household coat,
>   Razed out my imprese, leaving me no sign";

i.e. the family coat of arms blazoned on the stained glass.

influence, IX. 107, X. 662; Late Lat. *influentia*, literally 'a flowing in upon'. It was an astrological term applied to the power over the earth, men's characters, fortunes, etc., which was supposed to descend from the celestial bodies. Cf. "planetary influence", *King Lear*, I. 2. 136; "the skyey influences", *Measure for Measure*, III. 1. 9. M. generally uses *influence* with reference to this astrological notion; cf. the *Nativity Ode*, 71, "The *stars*...Bending one way their *precious influence*".

malignant, X. 662, 'injurious, hostile'; often used by Elizabethans with reference to astrology, as here. Cf. 1 *Henry VI*, IV. 5. 6, "O malignant and ill-boding stars".

maw, X. 601, 991, 'stomach'; cf. Germ. *magen*. A vulgar word applied rather to animals than men. Cf. Milton's *Sonnet* to Cromwell:

> "Help us to save free conscience from the paw,
>   Of hireling wolves, whose Gospel is their maw."

obvious; always used by M. in one of the senses of Lat. *obvius* —e.g. 'coming to meet' (X. 106), or 'lying in the way' (VI. 69).

offal, X. 633; properly 'bits that *fall off*'; cf. the cognate Germ. *abfall*, 'rubbish'. Commonly used of meat unfit for human food.

officious, IX. 104; used = Lat. *officiosus*, 'obliging, serving'. Cf. *P. R.* II. 302, where Satan, coming back after his first repulse, says, "officious I return", i.e. eager to serve Christ. Now *officious* implies 'meddlesome, too eager to help'.

outrage, X. 707. F. *outrage*, in which *-age* is a termination. The radical idea is 'a going beyond bounds'; cf. F. *outre*,

'beyond', Lat. *ultra*. Hence the notion 'excessive violence', 'fury', helped perhaps by wrong association with the noun *rage*, the word being pronounced somewhat as if it were a compound of *rage*.

owe, IX. 1141; in its original sense 'to have, possess'. Cf. *Macbeth*, I. 4. 10, "the dearest thing he owed", and *The Tempest*, III. 1. 45, "the noblest grace she owed". Closely akin to *own*.

plat, IX. 456; another form of *plot*, 'a small piece of ground'. Cf. 2 *Kings* ix. 26, "and I will requite thee in this plat...Now therefore take and cast him into the plat of ground". So in *Il Penseroso*, 73, "Oft, on a plat of rising ground".

purchase, X. 579, 'acquisition'. The verb *purchase* meant first to hunt after (O.F. *purchacer* = F. *pour* + *chasser*); "then to take in hunting; then to acquire; and then, as the commonest way of acquiring is by giving money in exchange, to buy" (Trench). To 'acquire, gain' was a common Elizabethan sense; cf. 1 *Timothy* iii. 13, "they that have used the office of a deacon well purchase to themselves a good degree" (Revised Version 'gain').

quarry, X. 281, 'prey'; a hunting term. O.F. *cuiree*, the intestines of a slain animal, the part given to the hounds; so called because wrapped in the skin—F. *cuir*, 'a skin, hide', from Lat. *corium*, 'hide' (Skeat).

quire, IX. 198; the older form of *choir*, Lat. *chorus*: cf. O.F. *quer* and F. *chœur*. "In Quires and Places where they sing", *Prayer-Book*.

ravin, X. 599, 'prey'; cf. the *Faerie Queene*, I. 11. 12 (the description of the 'Old Dragon'):

> "his deepe devouring jawes
> Wyde gaped, like the griesly mouth of hell,
> Through which into his darke abysse all ravin fell."

Through O.F. *ravine* from Lat. *rapina*, 'plunder'; so that *ravin* and *rapine* are 'doublets'.

sciential, IX. 837, 'yielding knowledge'. Ben Jonson in a compliment to James I says (*Masque of Blackness*):

> "His light sciential is, and, past mere nature,
> Can salve the rude defects of every creature."

secure, IX. 371, X. 779. Elizabethan writers often use *secure* in the sense of Lat. *securus*, 'free from anxiety, unconcerned'; i.e. to indicate a false feeling rather than actual state of safety. Cf. Fletcher's quibbling lines:

> "To secure yourselves from these,
> Be not too secure in ease";

and M. in *Eikonoklastes*, XVIII, "With a bloody *surprise* [he] falls on our *secure* forces", *P. W.* I. 442. So *security* = 'over-confidence, carelessness', in *Macbeth*, III. 5. 32.

seneshal, IX. 38, 'steward'; literally 'old servant', whence the idea 'senior in standing, chief'. Through O.F. from Gothic *sins*, 'old' + *skalks*, 'servant'; cf. '*marshal*', literally 'horse-servant'.

sere, X. 1071, 'dry'; also spelt *sear*, A.S. *seár*, 'dry'. Commonly said of flowers or leaves, with the sense 'faded', 'withered', as in *Lycidas*, 2, "ivy never sere".

sewer, IX. 38; a servant who set the dishes on the table at a feast and removed them. In *Eikonoklastes*, XXIV, M. refers contemptuously to the chaplains of Charles I as "the sewers or the yeomen-ushers of devotion", *P. W.* I. 459. Connected with A.S. *seaw*, pottage; not with any French word.

shroud, X. 1068. Properly *shroud*, A.S. *scrúd*, meant 'a garment': hence any 'shelter, covering', as often in Elizabethan writers. Cf. *Comus*, 147, "Run to your shrouds within these brakes and trees". Outside Old St Paul's Cathedral in London there was a covered place called "the Shrouds", where sermons were preached in wet weather, instead of at St Paul's Cross, which was in the open.

Sophi, X. 433: a corruption of Arabic *safī*, 'elect, chosen', which was a title, like the 'Cæsar' of the Roman emperors, borne by each Shah or sovereign of the dynasty that ruled Persia from 1505 to 1725. In Elizabethan writers the expression 'the Sophy' (or 'Soph*i*') is exactly equivalent to 'the Shah' in modern English. Cf. *The Merchant of Venice*, II. 1. 25, "That slew the Sophy and a Persian prince"; and Ben Jonson's *Volpone*, III. 5, "the Persian Sophi's wife". Persia is called "the Sophian Empire" in Hexham's English edition (1636) of *Mercator's Atlas*, II. 411. The derivation (often given) of *Sophy* from *sufī*, 'wise', is wrong.

sovran, IX. 532, 612, X. 144; spelt thus always in *P. L.*; cf. Ital. *sovrano*. M. has a partiality for Italianised forms: cf. 'harald' (I. 752), Ital. *araldo*; *sdein* (IV. 50), Ital. *sdegnare*. The common form *sovereign* comes through O.F. *soverain*, later *souverain*. Lat. *superanus*, 'chief'.

state, X. 445, 'canopy'; more often 'chair of state, canopied throne', as in *Macbeth*, III. 4. 5, "Our hostess keeps her state". Cotgrave, *French Dictionary*, 1611, explains *dais* by: "A cloth of Estate, Canopie or Heauen, that stands ouer the heads of Princes thrones, also, the whole State or seat of Estate".

suggestion, IX. 90, 'temptation'; cf. *Macbeth*, I. 3. 134, "why do I yield to that suggestion?" So the verb; cf. *Richard II*, III. 4. 75, 76.

> "What Eve, what *serpent*, hath *suggested* thee
>   To make a second fall of cursed man?"

sung, X. 642, 643. In Elizabethan E. this incorrect form for the past tense is much used. Shakespeare has *sang* only once (*Sonnet* 73), and then for the rhyme. In M. *sang* occurs only three times, III. 383, VII. 192, *Lycidas*, 186, and in each case he probably used the form for a special consideration of sound (e.g. in III. 383, VII. 192 to avoid the jingle *sung...son*). Similarly he has **rung** (IX. 737) as the past tense of *ring*, except in the *Nativity Ode*, 158, where the rhyme (with *clang*) requires *rang*. Cf. too *sprung* (VII. 58, VIII. 46).

targe, IX. 1111, 'a shield'; cf. *Antony and Cleopatra*, II. 6. 39, "targes undinted", i.e. not battered by blows. Of course, *target* is a diminutive of *targe* and formerly was used = 'shield'; cf. *Coriolanus*, IV. 5. 126; *Hamlet*, II. 2. 334. A mark to fire at is called 'a target' from its resemblance to a round shield.

thrall, X. 402; a Scandinavian word; cf. Icelandic, *þræll*, 'a serf'. From a root meaning 'to run', hence literally 'a runner on messages', i.e. a servant. The attempt to derive 'thrall' from 'thrill' because the ears of serfs were 'thrilled' or 'drilled', i.e. pierced, involves a vowel-change—*i* to *a*—which cannot be admitted.

tine, X. 1075, 'to kindle'; cf. the *Faerie Queene*, III. 10. 13, "To quench the flames which she had tyn'd before", and Fletcher's *Apollyonists*:

> "Oh! why should earthly lights then scorn to tine
>   Their lamps alone at that first sunne divine."

An obsolete verb, also spelt *tind*; cf. *tinder*.

tinsel, IX. 36; a shining, silver-like cloth. M. renders the Homeric epithet for the goddess Thetis, ἀργυρόπεζα, 'silver-footed', by 'tinsel-slippered', *Comus*, 877. F. *étincelle*, Lat. *scintilla*, 'a spark'.

uncouth; A.S. *uncuð*—from *un*, 'not', + *cuð*, the past participle of *cunnen*, 'to know' (whence come *can* and *could*). In *P. L.* *uncouth* always means 'unknown, strange, unfamiliar', with an implied notion 'alarming' or 'unpleasant'. Thus the word is thrice (II. 407, 827, X. 475) applied to Satan's perilous journey through the unknown Chaos. The wounded Moloch experiences "uncouth pain", VI. 362.

unweeting, X. 335, 916. M. always uses this form, never

unwitting; the *ee* represents the sound of the long *i* in A.S. *witan*, 'to know'. *Wit* and *wise* are cognates from the same root as Gk. οἶδα and ἰδεῖν and Lat. *videre*.

usher, x. 94, 'introduce'. Cf. IV. 355, "the stars that usher evening"; which recalls Shakespeare's 132nd *Sonnet*, "Nor that full star that ushers in the even". *Usher* (F. *huissier*, Lat. *ostiarius*) meant properly a doorkeeper, then someone who went in front of any great person in a procession: hence the notion 'introduce'.

virtue; often (IX. 110, 145, 616, 649) used by M. in the sense 'efficacy, might'; cf. *Luke* viii. 46, "virtue is gone out of me": hence **virtuous** = 'full of efficacy', IX. 795, 1033. Also = 'courage', x. 372. Lat. *virtus*, 'worth, *manly* excellence, valour' (Lat. *vir*, 'man').

wanton, IX. 211. The word means literally 'unrestrained': hence 'luxuriant' as used of growth. Cf. *A Midsummer Night's Dream*, II. 1. 99, "the quaint mazes in the wanton green". Of motion it implies 'tossing about', e.g. like the 'undulating' coils of a serpent (IX. 517).

INDEX OF WORDS AND PHRASES

*This list applies to the **Notes** only; words of which longer explanations are given will be found in the **Glossary**. The references are to the pages.*

Abbreviations:

adj. = adjective.   n. = noun.   trans. = transitive.   vb. = verb.

INDEX OF NAMES

9/6

KU-111-115